5/99

Closet Stages

Closet Stages

Joanna Baillie and the Theater Theory
of British Romantic Women Writers

CATHERINE B. BURROUGHS

PENN

University of Pennsylvania Press

Philadelphia

10 9 8 7 6 5 4 3 2 1

Published by
University of Pennsylvania Press
Philadelphia, Pennsylvania 19104-6097

Library of Congress Cataloging-in-Publication Data

Burroughs, Catherine B., 1958–
    Closet stages : Joanna Baillie and the theater theory of British
romantic women writers / Catherine B. Burroughs.
        p.   cm.
    Includes bibliographical references (p.   ) and index.
    ISBN 0-8122-3393-X (alk. paper)
    1. Baillie, Joanna, 1762–1851—Knowledge—Performing arts.
2. English drama—Women authors—History and criticism—Theory, etc.
3. English drama—19th century—History and criticism—Theory, etc.
4. Women in the theater—Great Britain—History—19th century.
5. Romanticism—Great Britain.   I. Title.
PR4056.B87   1997
792'.01—dc21   97-3949
                                                                   CIP

Frontispiece: Joanna Baillie. Engraving by H. Robinson from a miniature portrait
by Sir William John Newton, in the possession of the British Museum.

To Rick, body and soul

Contents

Preface

Fittingly for a literary critic who, by virtue of also being an actor, views the acting process as "the recovery of a 'lost' physical of reading" (Cole 1), this study in its current form began with a physical sensation—my first experience of stage fright—that dry-mouthed, face-flushing, stomach-tightening feeling in which, because of an imagined or actual experience on stage, one becomes so paralyzed by fear of performing that even the thought of being onstage generates a physiological response. In the early 1830s, actress Frances Anne Kemble (1809–93), niece of Sarah Siddons (1751–1831), described her stage fright as follows: "a violent headache and side-ache . . . had made me so nervous that the whole of the day was spent in fits of crying. . . . [T]he last act of [*The Gamester*] gives me such pains in my arms and legs, with sheer nervous distress, that I am ready to drop down with exhaustion at the end of it" (*Records of a Girlhood* 246).

Although I have acted in many plays and am a member of Actors' Equity Association, my first stage fright took place *off* the stage during a time when I had not done a show for several months. That is, I never experienced these feelings of tortured fear until the year I began to see some of my articles and reviews on Romantic theater and dramatic literature published in academic journals. As several pieces that I had written shortly after graduate school began to appear in print, I suddenly wished that I could revise my work even as it was irrevocably appearing on the printed page. Accustomed to working in a medium that makes revision its hallmark—the theater's liveness allows for at least the *illusion* of remaking and unmaking work during each night a play is performed—I had difficulty confronting the idea that the criticism I was publishing could not also be tinkered with and eventually dismantled like the sets torn down at a theater strike.

Though in retrospect I realize that this revulsion at one's own work is far more common than I then thought, I can still recall the physical sensations that seemed, at different intervals, to be trying to take over my body. I wanted alternatively to move in and out of the sanctuary of an imagined closet space: I wanted to write without showing my work to anyone, just as a "closet actor" might wish to perform a play without an audience.

This idea of being a closet actor took hold as I began to realize, shortly after taking my first job in the academy, that I was fast becoming an actor in theory rather than practice, a person who performs in his or her closet or private study in possible perpetual deferment of a presentation before actual others. Because it has continued to be difficult to find the right context for "doing theater," I, like a number of those theater theorists who are the subject of this book, have been strongly motivated to ask where the most fulfilling performances of plays could be found. In the classroom? In rehearsals that resist public performances as their goal? In the closet spaces of domestic life?

The search for these answers, coupled with a desire to have a go at the ideas I had formulated at an earlier age, has challenged me to try to revise, or at least clarify, some of the ideas I have expressed elsewhere in print. As a result, this book was written in homage to revision (which Hannah More and Peter Brook celebrate in the passages cited at the start of Chapter 1), that process which changes past perceptions and engages in a dialogue with a multiplicity of voices, in an effort both to secure the strength of its own voice and to allow that voice to recede in favor of the strengths of others.

Certainly one of the spurs to this approach has come from the women writers whose texts are the focus of this study, especially Joanna Baillie (1762–1851), whose concept of "sympathetic curiosity" informs much of the theory and practice comprising this book—that is, an approach to producing plays that teaches spectators compassion for others by piquing their interest in what at first may seem foreign and strange. The emphasis that Baillie and other women writers of the Romantic period placed on revising one's critical perspective through using the imagination and seeking new experiences—as well as their sensitivity to the efforts often required for women of their era to move from the closet study into public forums and back again—has served to remind me how relevant their work is for our age.

Acknowledgments

This book owes its final shape to the interest, generosity, and intellectual support of many. It began and ended with grants from the National Endowment for the Humanities, for two seminars: one in 1989 called "English Romanticism and Gender," directed by Anne K. Mellor, and another in 1995 called "Feminism and Enlightenment: Women Writers and the

1790s," directed by Mary Jacobus. Between those years, I was assisted by grants from the University of Chicago, the William Andrews Clark Memorial Library, The Huntington Library, and Cornell College, and I have also benefited from the assistance of the staffs at the British Library, The Newberry Library, Olin Library at Cornell University, the University of California at Los Angeles, and the University of Iowa Library. In addition, I want to thank Winthrop Wetherbee, chair of the English department at Cornell University, for appointing me a visiting scholar during my sabbatical year and providing me with access to the materials and resources necessary for the completion of this project.

Readers of my manuscript in its different permutations have given generously of their time and advice. I gratefully acknowledge the comments and responses of Fredric V. Bogel, Elizabeth Bolton, Toni Bowers, Steven Bruhm, Jeffrey Cox, Mary Jacobus, Anna Lott, Marie McAllister, Anne Mellor, Bonnie Newman, Judith Page, and Judith Pascoe. For helpful conversations about Romantic drama and theater and other related issues, I would like to thank Julie Carlson, Thomas Crochunis, Paula Feldman, J. Ellen Gainor, Greg Kucich, Caroline McAllister, James McGavran, Jeanne Moskal, Reeve Parker, Marjean Purinton, William Snyder, and Kathleen Wilson.

A number of conferences and colloquia have enabled me to refine this material, and I would like to acknowledge the sponsors of these forums here: American Conference on Romanticism, Association for Theatre in Higher Education, American Society of Eighteenth-Century Studies, Carolina Philological Association, Eighteenth- and Nineteenth-Century British Women Writers Conference, The Huntington Library, Midwest Modern Language Association, Modern Language Association, The Newberry Library, North American Society for the Study of Romanticism, Western Society for Eighteenth-Century Studies, and the Women in Theatre Conference at Hofstra University.

I am grateful to the publishers of the following journals and edited volumes for allowing me to reprint portions of this manuscript, which first appeared in *Nineteenth-Century Contexts*; *Re-Visioning Romanticism: British Women Writers, 1776–1837* (University of Pennsylvania Press); *Romantic Women Writers: Voices and Countervoices* (University Press of New England); and *Texas Studies in Literature and Language*.

At my home institution, Cornell College, I would particularly like to acknowledge Dennis Damon Moore, for underwriting some of my research with several grants; Tom Shaw, for ordering books indispensable to my project; and Sue Lifson, for her tireless and swift procurement of many interlibrary materials. Other individuals at Cornell College who, in a variety of ways, gave their support to this project are Carol Brokel, Diane Crowder, Helen Damon Moore, Tony DeLaubenfels, Alison Ames Galstad, Diane Harrington, Jan Lehr, Roberta Ringold, and Karen See-man. Student assistants Paige Davis, Sarah Gatson, Gretchen Niemiec, Sarah Peel, and Kristi Robinson were extremely helpful in ways too numerous to mention. My colleagues in the Cornell College English Department—Robert Dana, David Evans, Leslie Hankins, Scott Klein, Stephen Lacey, Tim Liu, Richard Martin, and Ann Reckling—nurtured the development of this work by helping to create a congenial climate for teaching. I especially appreciate the contributions to this book of Steve Lacey—that "orchestrator of private gaiety, curator of richly encrusted happiness," to borrow a phrase from F. Scott Fitzgerald. Large-souled and unfailingly generous, Steve has been an inspiration to me as a colleague and friend.

I also extend thanks to family members who have been interested in the progress of this work: Alexander, Liz, and Fay Bogel; Lee, Scott, Parker, and Brooks Bradway; and Jean and Julian Burroughs.

And lastly, I thank Rick Bogel—to whom this book is inscribed—for a journey of remarkable turns. To this extraordinarily perceptive and passionate person, I dedicate these pages—and much more.

1. "The Value of Our Criticism": Constructing Women's Theater Theory

> The critic, even of his own works, grows honest, if not acute, at the end of twenty years. The image, which he fancied glowed so brightly when it came forth fresh from the furnace, time has quenched; the spirits which he thought fixed and essential, have evaporated. . . . We not only discover that what we thought we had invented we have only remembered; but we find also that what we believe to be perfect is full of defects; in what we had conceived to be pure gold, we discover much tinsel. For the revision . . . is made at a period when the eye is brought by a due remoteness . . . which disperses "the illusions of vision," scatters the mists of vanity, reduces objects to their natural size, restores them to their exact shape, makes them appear to the sight, such as they are in themselves, and such as perhaps they have long appeared to all except the author.
>
> —Hannah More, "General Preface" to *The Works of Hannah More* (1835)

> *I have never* believed in a single truth. Neither my own, nor those of others. I believe all schools, all theories can be useful in some place, at some time. But I have discovered that one can only live by a passionate, and absolute, identification with a point of view.
>
> However, as time goes by, as we change, as the world changes, targets alter and the viewpoint shifts. Looking back over many years of essays written, ideas spoken in many places on so many varied occasions, one thing strikes me as being consistent. For a point of view to be of any use at all, one must commit oneself totally to it, one must defend it to the very death. Yet, at the same time, there is an inner voice that murmurs: "Don't take it too seriously. Hold on tightly, let go lightly."
>
> —Peter Brook, *The Shifting Point, 1946–1987* (1987)

For those who would expand the picture of pre–twentieth-century Western theater history to include a range of women's writings about the stage, these passages written by Hannah More, a late-eighteenth-century playwright (1745–1833), and Peter Brook, a late-twentieth-century director, remind us that revision is a constant of the critical enterprise. Yet to expect that More and Brook would today be spoken of together as theorists of theater requires a revision of theater history as traditionally formulated. Not only has the gendering of criticism until very recently ensured that early modern women's generalizations and speculations about the theater arts would either be ignored or devalued, but it has also often caused us to neglect a variety of "theoretical moments" that occur in a wide range of texts and performance situations.

The problem of women's erasure as critical thinkers and theorists—this book's main focus—was addressed by Anna Jameson (1794–1860) midway through the nineteenth century. Looking back to the era traditionally called the British Romantic period, Jameson wrote that Goethe once said of some woman: "She knew something of devotion and love, but of the pure admiration for a glorious piece of man's handiwork—of a mere sympathetic veneration for the creation of the human intellect—she could form no idea" (*Commonplace Book* v–vi). Jameson challenged this commentary by retorting that this might have been true of the individual woman referred to "but that female critics look for something in the production of art beyond the mere handiwork, and that 'our sympathetic veneration for a creation of human intellect,' is often dependent upon our moral associations is not a reproach to us. Nor, if I may presume to say so, does it lessen *the value of our criticism*, where it can be referred to principles. Women have a sort of unconscious logic in these matters" (309; my emphasis).

Although Jameson suggests that women's critical judgments are largely intuitive, her phrase "the value of our criticism" points to an obvious fact that nevertheless must be underscored when the subject of women as theorists arises: not only have women thought critically about the theater arts throughout history and in many cases put these thoughts into writing, but some of these writers, like Jameson, have looked critically at the problems women theorists encounter when moving from "the closet" to engage critics in public space.

By focusing on Joanna Baillie, the most important female British playwright between Aphra Behn (1640?–1689) and the twentieth century, my book explores Baillie's theory of the stage in the context of the writing produced by middle- to upper-class women who wrote for and about the London theater between 1790 and 1840.[1] (Texts by women writers whom we more commonly associate with the Victorian period are also included here when these works concern subjects related to British Romantic theater.) In this study, I look closely at some of the strategies British Romantic women writers used to represent their gendered positions in those places traditionally (but problematically) called public and private spheres.[2] My aim is to explore a number of the ways in which these writers' conceptions of femininity influenced their speculations and generalizations about theatrical practices, as well as those social performances for which theatrical analogies were sometimes used.

Because I believe that the commentary of the writers featured here will interest scholars of British Romanticism, theater history, and gender studies, in addition to theater practitioners, I have chosen to discuss these women theorists within a framework that views many as forerunners of some of the theoretical trends and stage practices introduced by women in late-twentieth-century Western theater. I want, of course, to avoid "making historical criticism a transhistorical echo of the politics of the present" (Klancher, "English Romanticism" 77), a problem recently addressed by Margaret Ezell, who criticized scholars of women's literary history for constructing a narrative based on "a nineteenth-century model of narrative historiography" (21), one in which a coherent and continuous "tradition" of women's writing "evolves" into texts with a "higher" degree of feminist consciousness. A feminist new historicist approach, in Ezell's words, is designed to "[strip] away layers of assumptions between us and these past texts without seeking to impose immediately a preconceived hierarchy of literary values and the progress of feminist thought on what we find" (133). Yet this approach can also cause us to overlook how particulars of women's material condition may persist across historical periods. Like Linda Kintz, in her recent analysis of feminism and Greek tragedy, I am equally concerned with the fact that "as historical differences show up, broad, long-term similarities among periods seem to fade from view" (2).

To address this problem, this study prominently features some of the current theoretical issues brought into play when one looks back at British Romantic women's theoretical writing. Although late-eighteenth- and early-nineteenth-century British women writers rarely complain directly about the workings of sexual politics in theater, they do reveal an understanding that at some level—in the words of contemporary playwright and critic Michelene Wandor—the "theatre industry, like other cultural industries, operates through a hierarchical structure, in which artistic and administrative decisions are largely in the hands of men" (xix). To varying degrees, the discourse of these writers also shows their awareness that "culture viewed as speech, gesture, and action is performance" and that we can never "shed our status as cultural beings"; "we remain actors" (Tuan 236). Thus, by demonstrating some of the ways in which attitudes toward theater practices—as well as the practices themselves—arose from a specific cultural context and, in turn, produced and reinforced standards of behavior structuring social intercourse,[3] Romantic women's theater theory reminds us of the persistence of certain standards in the professional lives of women theater artists today.

The Process of Recovering Women Theater Theorists

One of the striking barriers to appreciating similarities between the situation of early-nineteenth-century London theater artists and that of women who work in contemporary Western theater is the term "theater theory" itself. Because the term has been used historically to connote a masculine tradition, centered on the "ostensibly objective observer whose authority rests upon his ability to keep his eyes focused on the object of his observations" (Straub, "Women, Gender, and Criticism" 855), women's contributions have been consistently absent from anthologies of theory and criticism, and thus the vital field of contemporary feminist theater theory, which began to emerge in the late 1970s, appears to have sprung from a void.

Approximately a decade ago, in the impassioned prefaces to her several books on women intellectuals—*Women of Ideas and What Men Have Done to Them* (1982) and *Feminist Theorists: Three Centuries of Key Women Thinkers* (1983)—Dale Spender argued for accommodating women's attempts before the current era to "describe and explain the experience of women in a male-dominated society" (*Women of Ideas* 23–24) by looking more closely at the terms "theory," "theorist," and "criticism." Appalled that "one would be hard-pressed to stock even a small shelf with books containing the theories of women," Spender sought to revise attitudes toward "[t]heorising [as] something men do" by offering "glimpses" of a female intellectual tradition in vital need of recognition (*Feminist Theorists* 1). To revise "the categories and the terminology of critical discourse" was also the aim of Susan Sniader Lanser and Evelyn Torton Beck, who, in 1979, posed the following question in the title of their essay "[Why] Are There No Great Women Critics?" (89). Stating that "not only the conception of criticism, but the critical theories themselves, have been seriously distorted by the omission of women's thought" (87), Lanser and Beck anticipated the 1995 anthology edited by the Folger Collective on Early Women Critics, which includes excerpts from women's theoretical discourse written between 1660 and 1820.[4] As Lanser noted at the first Modern Language Association session to concentrate on early women writers and their criticism (December 1991), however, "there is more at stake in reading early women writers than a revised understanding of women's place in the critical projects of the eighteenth century" ("Women Critics—and the Difference They Make" 5). The feminist reader will want to raise a number of questions that focus on the more general issue of how "to go about telling the history of women critics and their work" (ibid. 8).[5]

Some of these questions can be derived from looking closely at ways in which women in the past have written critically about the theater arts. Although Romantic women theorists produced texts for traditional forums—the usually anonymous play reviews and theater commentaries published in periodicals,[6] as well as prefaces, advertisements, prologues, and epilogues attached to single and collected editions of plays—a good deal of their commentary does not conform to what has traditionally been called "theater theory": that is, "statements of general principles regarding the methods, aims, functions, and characteristics of this particular art form," a term Marvin Carlson distinguishes from "aesthetics, dealing with art in general, and . . . from the criticism of particular works and reviews of particular productions" (*Theories of the Theatre* 9). Rather, most of this discourse survives in a "crude" and "imperfect" state—the words William Godwin used to describe a comedy sketch by Mary Wollstonecraft (before he "judged it most respectful to her memory to commit it to the flames")[7] —an indication that many women writers overcame impediments to their theorizing by using modes and genres not readily associated with theoretical writing.

Romantic women's theater theory offers especially dramatic examples of how the very process of locating this discourse can help us reconsider some of the ways in which the narratives of theater history have been constructed and, more specifically, how the term "theater theory" has traditionally been used to mean an intellectual pursuit practiced primarily by men. In Anna Jameson's *A Commonplace Book of Thoughts, Memories, and Fancies, Original and Selected* (1854), which juxtaposes Jameson's early-nineteenth-century entries about the stage with other reflections on a variety of topics unrelated to the theater arts—the author confesses that she debated at some length about whether even to preserve this writing.[8] "For many years," Jameson wrote in the book's preface,

> I have been accustomed to make a memorandum of any thought which might come across me—(if pen and paper were at hand), and to mark (and *remark*) any passage in a book which excited either a sympathetic or an antagonistic feeling. This collection of notes accumulated insensibly from day to day. The volumes on Shakespeare's Women, on Sacred and Legendary Art, and various other productions, sprung from seed thus lightly and casually sown, which, I hardly know how, grew up and expanded into a regular, readable form, with a beginning, a middle, and an end. But what was to be done with the fragments which remained—without beginning, and without end—links of a hidden or a broken chain? Whether to preserve them or destroy them became a question, and one I could not answer for myself. In allowing a portion of them to go forth to the world in their original form, as unconnected fragments, I have

been guided by the wishes of others, who deemed it not wholly uninteresting or profitless to trace the path, sometimes devious enough, of an "inquiring spirit." (v–vi)

Evoking the problem of anxious authorship that Sandra Gilbert and Susan Gubar have discussed at length in their analyses of nineteenth-century women writers,[9] Jameson's preface raises two of the central issues with which this and the next chapter are concerned: when do "unconnected fragments"—what Jameson calls "links of a hidden or a broken chain"— "become" theory, and who decides what kinds of texts will bear this label? Does this "metamorphosis" occur when the hypothetical, philosophical, or speculative modes are employed, and must these modes dominate a passage for it to be termed "theoretical"? If one isolates as the central marker of theoretical discourse a tendency to move from particular observations to generalizations and vice versa, then how much generalizing must there be to consider a text theoretical in kind: a page, a paragraph, a couple of sentences, one sentence only? Or is theory more commonly the name of one discursive thread in a text rather than of its exclusive, or even dominant, mode?

We can begin to address this problem, discussed at greater length in Chapter 2, by turning briefly to several passages by Romantic women that focus on translating and adapting plays for London theaters.[10] In a letter written in December 1798, biographer Mary Berry (1763–1852) described playwright Elizabeth Inchbald's (1753–1821) adaptation of August von Kotzebue's *Lovers' Vows* (1798) as follows:

"Lover's Vows" disappointed me. The necessary curtailments which have been made from the German "Natural Son," to avoid *des longueurs*, and to suit it in some degree to our manners upon the stage, destroy the effect of many situations and sentiments, by having in a great degree taken away their efficient, or at least *sufficient* cause, and consequently making them appear awkward or misplaced, or more or less than enough to the minds of the spectators: in short, a good play must ever be a *whole* form which it is quite impossible to take out a bit here and put in a bit there without disfiguring and degrading the original, even when the original would not succeed in representation, as is certainly the case with the "Natural Son," as I read it, closely translated from the original. (Berry, *Extracts* 2:77–78)

Using the occasion of a letter to formulate her opinions about the complex process of stage translation, Berry suggests that it is important for the translator to respect the integrity of the original play script rather than adapting it to "suit . . . our manners," the conventions of English stage practice. Emphasizing the superior pleasure of reading in a closet study over theatrical representation, Berry implies that translations and adaptations are a precise science with the potential to "disfigure" and "degrade" the original text (it "must ever be a *whole* form") and, therefore, that alterations must be carefully done or not at all, since often they "destroy the effect" of a play's "situations and sentiments."

This was a view with which playwright Sophia Burrell (1750?–1802) disagreed. In Burrell's dedication to her translation of a Corneille play called *Maximian* (1800), she remarked that she "ventured to deviate, in some parts of the play, from the original, as I thought a literal translation would be too formal, and that more bustle and variety were necessary to render it interesting, particularly at this era, when splendid effect is the peculiar fashion of the day" ("Dedication"). In contrast to Berry's concern that dramatic translations are too greatly focused on suiting the play to "our manners upon the stage," it is precisely the conventions of the English stage—primarily the emphasis on "splendid effect"—which evidently guided Burrell's practice.

As if responding directly to Berry and Burrell, Elizabeth Inchbald's preface to *Lovers' Vows* in *The British Theatre* (1806–9) offers a rationale for the choices to which Berry objected and seems to echo Burrell's criteria for executing an effective translation (it should, to repeat Burrell's words cited above, "deviate . . . from the original" in the interest of eschewing "formality"; it adds more "bustle" and "variety" to make the play "interesting"; it tries to use "effects" that meet audience expectations). Inchbald justifies her choices, first by telling her readers that she was given a "literal translation" by a German writer, which she thought "tedious and vapid," and then by employing a strategy common to women theorists of this period: she calls attention to the dubious position of female artists even as she asserts the significance of her literary contributions. "It was no slight misfortune, to have an example of bad grammar, false metaphors and similes, with all the usual errors of imperfect diction, placed before *a female writer*" ("Preface on the First Publication of *Lovers' Vows*" 4; my emphasis),[11] Inchbald writes, just before stating with apparent confidence how she believes a successful translation should be rendered:

> if, disdaining the construction of sentences,—the precise decorum of the cold grammarian,—she [the female translator] has caught the spirit of her author,—if, in every altered scene,—still adhering to the nice propriety of his meaning, and still keeping in view his great catastrophe,—she has agitated her audience with all the passions he depicted, *the rigid criticism of the closet* will

be but a slender abatement of the pleasure resulting from the sanction of an
applauding theatre. (4; my emphasis)

Here Inchbald provides a rebuttal to Berry's admonition against tamper-
ing with a play in its original form by drawing on the era's familiar opposition between the closet and the stage. Unlike Berry, however, she equates
"closet criticism" with "rigidity" and underscores "the pleasure" that can
result from "the sanction of an applauding theatre" in order to support her
assertion that the ideal translator respects "the spirit of her author." As long
as one adheres "to the nice propriety of meaning" and follows the play's
dramaturgical contours—that is, its "major catastrophes"—the translator
is otherwise liberated to "disdain" the "construction of sentences" and "the
precise decorum of the cold grammarian." In short, Inchbald suggests that
a successful translator is someone who, by challenging "the rigid criticism
of the closet," can entertain one culture while preserving "the spirit" of
another.[12]

The Closet Versus Stage Controversy

The opposition between closet and stage[13] as it appears in the theoretical
discourse of the British Romantic period points us to a second obstacle
that has prevented us from recovering women's theater theory written before 1900. This is the tendency to associate the closet with reading only, to
oppose it to theatricality, and to forget that, during the early nineteenth
century, not only did the phrase serve as a metaphor for privacy and intense intellectual engagement, but it also identified a literal space in which
a variety of theatrical activities—many particular to women—took place.

Influential twentieth-century accounts of the theater criticism written
by Romantic men (i.e., Charles Lamb, Samuel Taylor Coleridge, William
Hazlitt, Leigh Hunt, and Lord Byron) have traditionally portrayed these
critics as exchanging a theater of the body for a theater of the mind in
the process of calling for a retreat to that inner sanctum of private life,
the closet, an architectural feature of the floor plans of eighteenth-century
British great houses. The following passage by Charles Lamb is often used
to represent this position:

So to see Lear acted,—to see an old man tottering about the stage with a
walking-stick, turned out of doors by his daughters in a rainy night, has nothing in it but what is painful and disgusting. We want to take him into shelter

and relieve him. That is all the feeling which the acting of Lear ever produced in me. But the Lear of Shakespeare cannot be acted. . . . The greatness of Lear is not in corporal dimension, but in intellectual. . . . On the stage we see nothing but corporal infirmities and weakness, the impotence of rage; while we read it, we see not Lear, but we are Lear,—we are in his mind. (107)

This seeming preference for submergence in closet space, where one can read rather than be forced to watch a play performed in all its excruciating bodiliness, has been alternately reviled and defended since the Romantic period.[14]

Before the 1980s, scholars generally explained the antitheatricality of the "closet critics" by focusing on the Stage Licensing Act of 1737, which created a theatrical monopoly in London for over a hundred years. Vincent J. Liesenfeld writes that the importance of the Licensing Act cannot be overstated: "Next to the laws protecting copyright, the 1737 act has probably had the most profound influence on English literature of any official measure in the last three centuries, and has been in many respects the model censorship device in modern Western society" (3). By authorizing only two theaters, Covent Garden and Drury Lane, to perform the "legitimate" British drama, this legislation ensured that any other theater wishing to produce a play in the established English repertory had to convert it into a melodrama by adding songs or inventing a new theatrical genre altogether that combined elements from mime, farce, burlesque, operetta, and spectacle. The Licensing Act also established—under the auspices of the Lord Chamberlain, formerly the Master of the Revels—the position of the Licenser of the Stage (later, Examiner of Plays), who was charged with approving a play's political, sexual, and religious content.[15] Lasting in part until 1843, when the monopoly was repealed, and, in another form, until 1968, when the position of the Examiner of Plays was abolished, during the Romantic period the Licensing Act officially limited the production of canonical drama to two huge auditoria that could seat over three thousand people and were better suited for opera than for theater speech. In perhaps its most positive form, it forced the minor or illegitimate theaters to become fruitful outlets for experimentation in acting and playwrighting.

There is no doubt that the "arrogant and despotic edicts of a Theatrical Oligarchy . . . roused the honest and indignant feelings of the English heart" (Macarthy 10). Even those less upset about the strict division between "major" and "minor" theaters had good reasons to be disenchanted with Romantic theater, because it was often difficult to hear, see, and attend the plays shown. Yet, more recently, Romantic scholars have offered alternative explanations for the closet critics' antitheatricality. Mary Jacobus locates the male Romantic poets' bias against the stage in their distrust of "the inherent theatricality of the imagination itself" (" 'That Great Stage' " 387), an imagination often associated in this literature with traditional conceptions of feminine behavior as excessively emotional, overly expressive, embarrassingly histrionic, and physically infirm.[16] William H. Galperin, Julie Carlson, and Steven Bruhm have each focused on "the body" in Romantic criticism and dramaturgy to show how male Romantic writers chafed against the theater's elevation of the corporeal.[17] The passage from which the above Lamb quotation was taken indicates that he was not so much opposed to representation per se, since earlier in this text he wrote: "I am not arguing that *Hamlet* should not be acted, but how much *Hamlet* is made another thing by being acted" (101). Rather, Lamb argued against what he regarded as the stage's prioritizing of body over mind: "What we see upon a stage is body and bodily action; what we are conscious of in reading is almost exclusively the mind, and its movements" (108).

In the search for theater theory by Romantic women, revisiting the phenomenon of closet criticism reminds us, in Jeffrey Cox's words, that if "we have neglected romantic drama, we have [also] clearly failed to pay enough detailed attention to *the theories of the drama* during the cultural shift from what we call the Enlightenment to what we view as the romantic period" ("Review" 92; my emphasis). Greg Kucich has attempted to redress this problem by arguing for a more complex analysis of the male critics' enterprise. In an important essay, Kucich warns that "the problem of accounting for the apparent contradiction between the era's passionate dramatic aspirations . . . and its seeming abandonment of theatrical activity . . . arises from a concentration on a relatively small and sensational body of Romantic theoretical statements about the non-representational nature of dramatic writing, many of which have been read out of context and seriously distorted" (65).[18] Though the closet critics revered the dramatic legacy of Shakespeare and therefore celebrated reading his plays in the privacy of closet space, Kucich argues that they also felt uneasy about the canonical drama's promotion of an elitist and conservative politics (73). Their retreat to the closet, then, rather than conservatively motivated, can be viewed as a form of protest against an increasingly conservative public stage. Martyn Corbett describes this unease in the following way: "[a]s children of the divorce between literary drama and the stage which took place during the closing years of the eighteenth century," their "feelings about the theater were ambivalent and confused" ("Lugging Byron" 361).

The point I want to emphasize here is that traditional representations of closet criticism have steered students of theater history away from appreciating the complexity of Romantic discussions about the London stage, discussions that often focused on the closet's *theatrical* potential and that were often engaged in by women.[19] Because the "closet" trope has been discussed primarily in reference to male writers of the period, and used to argue the era's antitheatricality, we may be apt to forget that closet space[20] also has strong associations with women's intellectual and artistic expression. G. J. Barker-Benfield notes that the physical presence of the closet in the British great house encouraged a cult of female letter writing in the eighteenth century, and "while letter writing was associated with intimacy, privacy, and domesticity, it is also true that writing letters, reading novels, and the incorporation of purchased objects into domestic space very significantly elevated women's 'horizons'" (162). In addition to enjoying the closet's feminine paraphernalia—curiosities and valuables, female-authored novels and letters, writing desks, recipes for candy, "banquet stuffs," medicinal remedies, conduct books, a teapot or two[21]—middle- to upper-class women could, for instance, draw upon these props and others to propel their own dramatic writing, to rehearse roles and cultivate identities that conformed to and diverged from cultural expectation, to reflect upon their experiences of performing gender in public and private theaters, and to theorize about a variety of theatrical stages. In brief, the female closet of the Romantic period may be viewed as a small experimental theater in which dramas and gendered identities were conceived and rehearsed, sometimes in preparation for public viewings, at other times for private or semiprivate readings and dramatizations. To reinforce this view, it is helpful to remember that some closet spaces during the Regency period were larger than we might think, and that their entrances were even hung with curtains, a feature suggesting a little stage.[22]

Rather than comparing the closet unfavorably with the formal theaters, a number of women who wrote about London playhouses theorized an approach to theater practice that allows, indeed encourages, an appreciation of the theatricality of both kinds of arenas. This seeming unwillingness to discriminate against performance spaces bespeaks a flexibility and imagination that may in part be tied to women's experience of performing femininity on social "stages" and to their understanding of how a cleavage between public and private realms obtruded upon their lives. Analyzing spectatorship in eighteenth-century England, Kristina Straub has written that "actresses' inherent challenge to the gendered, opposing spheres of public and private becomes increasingly the object of rhetorical containment and erasure" (*Sexual Suspects* 89) as the century experienced an ideological evolution "that constructed feminine sexuality as domestic and private" (97). But certain theoretical moments in women's texts of the Romantic era—some authored by actresses—reveal their awareness that the private sphere is inherently theatrical, a move that forecasts twentieth-century experiments in women's performance art, which often seek to uncover the experiences of actual women whose lives have been closeted away. At the same time that Romantic women theorists expressed their interest in the private sphere where a closeted kind of theater was generated, they did not often disdain the forum of the public stage, even in their most moralistic moments, but instead sought to determine how their own fraught relationships with public space could be used to formulate responses to the issue of theatrical reform.

Resituating "Closet Drama": The Theater Theory of Joanna Baillie

Joanna Baillie's body of theoretical writing, published as early as 1798 and keenly concerned with the problems the Licensing Act had created, provides us with ways of looking critically at the trope and concept of "the closet" in Romantic theatrical criticism. Rather than reinforcing the idea that closet spaces are incompatible with theatricality, Baillie's theory suggests that they are sources of passionate, valuable, and instructive drama—the literal site where one can trace the progress of "the soul" as it etches its passions on the countenances of men and women during their most private moments. Baillie's theory brings into stronger focus the fact that British Romantic closet spaces contained self-conscious, sometimes ritualized, stagings of events traditionally associated with women's solitary pleasures, a point that will be developed throughout this book, and most pointedly in Chapter 5 when I discuss the British private theatrical in connection to Baillie's first comedy, *The Tryal* (1798).

Drawing upon the trope of the closet, Baillie's theory of theater argues for seeing the theatrical potential of those experiences that often go unperformed due to their private associations: "For who," she asked in the preface to her first volume of plays, "hath followed the great man into his *secret closet*, or stood by the side of his nightly couch, and heard those exclamations of the soul which heaven alone may hear" (8; my emphasis).[23] When referring to the closet in her theory, Baillie suggests its seventeenth-

and eighteenth-century associations with private devotion and prayer.[24] But throughout her prefatory remarks Baillie makes it clear that her closet dramas are to be performed publicly, to be dramatized before live audiences who hold the power to approve or reject what they see. By advocating that "closet dramas" be brought into public view, Baillie validates both the drama and the theater of domestic life. In this sense, her plays belong to that tradition Nancy A. Gutierrez identifies with early-seventeenth-century closet dramas, which emerge not as marginalized genres but as "mainstream" vehicles of "cultural engagement" (238).[25]

Baillie's theory and dramaturgy are important signposts in theater history. Yet when scholars have turned their attention to the drama and theater of the British Romantic era, they have tended to privilege the "experimental dramas" composed by major male poets (Otten 4) as the era's most significant theatrical contributions.[26] This tendency has, until very recently, caused both literary critics and theater historians to ignore what was actually happening theatrically on and off the Romantic stage. It has also reinforced perceptions of the period as an age without viable theater or dramatic variety. Jane Moody (1996) writes provocatively that the "enduring critical division between romanticism (a discourse which has appropriated poetic drama as a canonical form) and theatre, should be recognised as an ideological classification which has attempted strategically to distinguish between the aesthetically clean and the unclean, the sacred and the taboo" (239). In studies of Romantic theater, the "clean" has been equated with the lyrical dramas of Romantic men, while the messy and chaotic have been associated with every other feature of the theatrical culture. For example, in one of the earliest revisionist studies of the period written in 1966, Richard Fletcher narrowly defined Romantic drama as "drama in blank verse" (19), meaning the approximately twenty plays composed by William Wordsworth, Samuel Taylor Coleridge, John Keats, Percy Shelley, and Lord Byron. Arguing that the "true father of Romantic drama" is Coleridge, because the latter wrote the "first contemporary drama to be performed on a nineteenth-century London stage composed wholly in blank verse" (20), Fletcher is representative of those closet drama scholars who have distorted the picture of Romantic theater history, first by neglecting to contextualize the Romantic poets' dramatic production in reference to the theatrical entertainments that abounded in Georgian England, and second, by failing to recognize the centrality of Joanna Baillie, whom Fletcher finds "less successful than Coleridge" (65).

As the author of twenty-six plays (one of which, *De Monfort* [1798], was a blank-verse tragedy professionally performed for the first time in 1800), Joanna Baillie must take a pivotal place in any study of Romantic drama, especially when the term is defined as Fletcher does. Certainly Baillie is Romantic drama's "mother": by a number of criteria that could be used to argue for the emergence of a "new" kind of play in the late eighteenth century, she is both originator and innovator. Donald Reiman has stated that "the blank verse in Baillie's early plays is, perhaps, the best dramatic verse of the age—simple and natural, supple and original. It lacks the Renaissance echoes and overtones of Coleridge's *Remorse* and Shelley's *Cenci* and the intellectual vitality of Byron's dramas—but it seems closer to the natural speech—not of real people—but of real actors, given their roles and situations" (*Series of Plays* 1.vii).

When a writer like Joanna Baillie is dropped from anthologies of British Romantic literature and collections of plays, we should suspect the canonizers' motives rather than automatically doubt the author's historical, intellectual, or cultural worth. Terry Eagleton (1990) has intensively analyzed the ways in which aesthetic judgments mask ideology, and, more relevant to my discussion here, Jeffrey Cox has suggested that critics have tended to look askance at Romantic closet drama because of being under the sway of what he calls, after Jerome McGann (1983) a "dramatic ideology." By constructing the canon of Western plays through an ahistorical " 'great man' account of the drama," which selects a few plays from different periods for the features they have in common (Cox, *Seven Gothic Dramas* 3), traditional approaches to theater history have ensured that rich theatrical offerings from a variety of periods would be ignored. Marilyn Gaull has written that "the apparent necessity of theatrical experience" (255) during the Romantic period resulted in an exciting range of entertainment that appeared on the London patent stages, in unlicensed theaters, on street corners, and within private homes, a situation noted by Romantic playwright Elizabeth Inchbald, who observed that "the English theatres never flourished as they do at present" ("Remarks on *Every One Has His Fault*"). Yet, despite this historical reality, the act of recovering Romantic women writers as significant theater theorists and dramatists has been impeded by the disproportional attentions of scholars to Romantic closet plays written by men and the failure to contextualize these plays in relation to other Romantic dramas and performance venues.

This situation is changing as theater historians and literary critics turn yet again to closet plays by male Romantic playwrights, but this time for the purpose of considering the historical and metatheatrical issues that the genre of the closet play inevitably raises.[27] What does it mean, closet drama revisionists are asking, to describe a work of dramatic literature as "unperformable"? Might a play labeled "literary" rather than "theatrical" teach us about shifting concepts of the dramatic, as we ask in whose terms, in what settings, and for what kinds of audiences certain plays have been removed to the library? Like Shakespearian critics, who have been debating for a number of years how to navigate between what Harry Berger, Jr., identifies as the "conventional armchair readers" and "New Histrionicists," closet drama revisionists are trying to propose alternative methods for reading closet plays as well as considering practical ways of performing them in late-twentieth-century theaters. With this trend, opportunities arise for highlighting Romantic women's contributions to the reconceptualization of closet drama.

Michael Evenden, for instance, has employed the perspective of feminist deconstructionists in order to examine the performance potential of closet dramas by Seneca, Roswitha, Byron, Stein, and Brecht. Evenden argues for "the stageability" of Byron's plays—particularly the fragment *The Deformed Transformed* (1822)—by showing how these closet dramas "make distinctions problematic between not only the actor's body and the role with which s/he is identified but also between 'drama and poetry, the I and the Other,' and ultimately between 'the closet' and the stage" (Burroughs and Ehrenreich 11). Like Evenden, Thomas Crochunis and Steven Bruhm foreground the body in Romantic plays to argue for the genre's theatrical potential; its vacillation between written text and embodiment puts the focus of potential productions on questions of how historical events have shaped cultural attitudes toward performance, spectacle, theatricality— even acting. Crochunis demonstrates that Byron chooses to "hover on the edge of embodiment and disembodiment, to explore the paradox of 'mental theatre'" by opting for "an unstageable theatricality in order to use the enactment of other historical periods to comment on his own" (59–60). Bruhm puts this paradox in different terms: although Byron, Coleridge, and Shelley "preferred the sentiments of Burke's disembodied, aesthetic drama, their political allegiance to Paine's representational government continually drew them toward the presentation of the aesthetic in its physical, empirical sense" (69). To study the closet play, then, is to focus on what Thomas Whitaker calls "the problematic relations between 'text' and 'performance'" ("Some Reflections" 148) and to locate a source of dramatic action in the genre's ability to force on its audience a dialectical movement between acting and reading.

Before its associations with gay dramaturgy,[28] the term "closet drama" was used to refer to plays that were never intended to be performed on stage or to plays that, for whatever reason, were never acted.[29] Om Prakash Mathur, for instance, defines a closet play as dominated by "the 'literary' element" and which "'reads' much better than it acts" (1). Yet as some scholars recognize, not only does this dichotomy between reading and performance fail to describe a number of closet plays written and produced during the Romantic period, but it is precisely this opposition between "literariness" and "theatricality" that the genre itself deconstructs: written to resemble a play script and therefore implying a potential theatrical performance, the closet play makes dramaturgically explicit the bifurcated character of all dramatic literature, tensed between script and live performance. Whereas Mathur labels the closet play as "the strangest case ever known to the science of dramaturgy" and uses analogy to describe his puzzlement over the form—"it is like a bird which flies with difficulty, if at all, but walks immeasurably better" (1)—this strangeness is precisely what has attracted readers in the 1980s and 1990s who are interested in the problematics of terms such as "theatricality," "the dramatic," and "the performable."

A study of Baillie's early plays suggests the extent to which closet dramas show characters struggling with what are today considered subjects central to gay dramaturgy—that is, the ways in which particular characters comply with or rebel against prescribed gendered and sexual identities in both private and public settings. As Chapter 4 will argue, Baillie's dramas are ripe for analysis by those feminist theorists who have helped us to see more clearly some of the ways in which the category of gender is a cultural rather than a natural phenomenon; that masculine and feminine behaviors are learned rather than innate; and that the performance of socially sanctioned gender roles resembles an "act" in the theatrical sense of that word (see Butler 1988). By stating that "a whole cluster of the most crucial sites for the contestation of meaning in twentieth-century Western culture are consequentially and quite indelibly marked with the historical specificity of homosocial/homosexual definition" (*Epistemology of the Closet* 72), Eve Sedgwick offers a framework for appreciating why a late-twentieth-century reader of Baillie's theory and drama may find it difficult to keep at bay contemporary associations with the word "closet," especially because the kinds of issues Baillie raises resemble some of those with which queer theorists currently engage. Because Baillie's early dramaturgy shows a number of characters moving in and out of "closets" in the effort to create alternative "selves" that may either become integrated into or rejected by the plays' fictional worlds, her work is historically important for women looking for a tradition of (women) theater artists who have theorized the performance of gender on both social and theatrical stages.

Social Stages, Performance, and "Performativity"

When British Romantic women writers use theatrical analogies or metaphors in their nonfictional writing, one is reminded that a good deal of the theorizing about stage practices produced before the twentieth century occurred in response not just to the theater proper. Some of this theory emerges from women's experiences of performing gender on the public stages of "social theaters," forums in which consciously constructed improvisational performances were created for the pleasure of those who were alternately spectators and performers. It would be confusing to categorize women's generalizations about acting in social venues as theories of the stage because, as Bruce Wilshire argues, there are necessary limits to the theatrical metaphor that links life and art (social acting is not exactly like performance before a paying audience, for example). However, as Chapter 5 discusses in reference to the private theatrical, an exploration of the discourse that concerns acting in social theaters provides an important context for understanding why much of women's theater theory is often structured by the opposition between the public stage and the private closet.

Because women's remarks about their activities in social and domestic settings constitute a fruitful perspective for analyzing how the closet/stage dichotomy influenced their theory, and how the theatricality of private spaces provided certain writers with models for alternative approaches to public performance, I have had to consider carefully to what degree passages that link social with theatrical stages should be included in this study. Discussions about "performativity"—"ways that identities are constructed iteratively through complex citational processes" (Parker and Sedgwick 2) [30]—have been especially useful, as they direct us to look more closely at how linguistic utterances bring into sharper view the dynamics of particular cultural contexts surrounding Romantic women's writings about theater. The concept of performativity also helps us discern how these writers drew on actual theater practices to theorize social performances of gender, and how this social theory influenced women's writings about formal theaters.

Some scholars in theater studies have rightly complained that a focus on performativity does not currently draw us back often enough to questions concerning the practice of theater itself. Jill Dolan reminds us that it is precisely this appropriation of the performativity metaphor by critics working in disciplines *other* than theater studies that requires theater scholars both to "borrow back the use-value other fields have found in ours" ("Geographies" 418) and to reclaim the theater's potential to visualize some of the practical questions that a focus on this metaphor of performativity raises: "Where does gender begin in a gesture? Can there be a gesture not already marked by a gender performance? . . . How can audiences be encouraged to read and critique performances of gender?" (434). Dolan's desire that "theatre studies [be] acknowledged and visited, rather than raided and discarded, as part of the proliferation of the performative" (420) stands counter to Judith Butler's recent attempts to distance performativity from "the theatrical" and calls for a renewed engagement with bringing performativity to bear on the issues of concern to theater theorists.

Concerned that theatrical associations with the word "performance" might lead readers to believe that an individual—like the actor performing a character in a play—possesses more agency to transform her identity than she or he actually does, Butler warns that performativity is enacted within the context of constraint: it is not "a singular 'act,' for it is always a reiteration of a norm or a set of norms." Nor should this act be regarded as *"primarily theatrical*; indeed, its apparent theatricality is produced to the extent that its historicity remains dissimulated (and, conversely, its theatricality gains a certain inevitability given the impossibility of a full disclosure of its historicity)" (*Bodies* 12–13; my emphasis).

Butler's use of performance metaphors to discuss the process of closeting and uncloseting identities has strongly inflected my reading of British Romantic theater, but I am also attracted to Dolan's directive, which urges scholars to employ the concept of performativity *as a means* by which to actively reconceptualize theater practices and terminology. For this reason, then, at different points in this study, I explore some of the social contexts that produced Romantic women's theater theory, with the aim of returning to questions concerning the theater proper.

A brief discussion of a passage by Mary Wollstonecraft seeks to clarify this aim. This late-eighteenth-century feminist theorist is not obviously associated with British Romantic theater, even though tantalizing information in her biography suggests that had she not died in childbirth she might have contributed dramatic literature to the formal stage. In his memoirs of Wollstonecraft's life, William Godwin tells us that she penned "the sketch of a comedy, which turns, in the serious scenes, upon the incidents of her own story" (255), perhaps including, as Richard Holmes has suggested, her tortured love affair with American painter Gilbert Imlay. It is certainly "intriguing" (305), in Holmes's words, to speculate how this tragicomedy might have dramatized Wollstonecraft's attitude toward the way she performed femininity in this affair, especially as most plays from the Romantic period mask their topical or biographical contexts through references to exotic locations and historically distant periods. Though this comedy sketch does not endure, its existence at one point in time suggests that Wollstonecraft might have been interested in the formal stage as this medium could provide her with a forum for dramatizing, as she did in her novels, scenes from her own life.

This information is worth noting because, although Wollstonecraft did not leave behind a text readily categorized as "theater theory," she nevertheless drew upon theater history and her knowledge of the late-eighteenth-century stage for metaphors with which she could formulate her critical readings of women's cultural position. In the well-known passage from her twenty-second letter of [*Letters Written During*] *A Short Residence in Sweden, Norway, and Denmark* (1796), Wollstonecraft mused: "All the world is a stage, thought I; and few are there in it who do not play the part they have learnt by rote; and those who do not, seem marks to be pelted at by fortune; or rather as sign-posts, which point out the road to others, whilst forced to stand still themselves amidst the mud and dust" (186). Underscoring the spectacle of men's and women's participation in what Sue-Ellen Case and Janelle Reinelt call "the performance of power"—moments when there is a "'playing out' of power relations, a 'masking' of authority, a 'scenario' of events" (x)—Wollstonecraft reveals her awareness of the problems and strengths associated with the mode of theater performance that we might today call improvisatory. She draws upon Shakespeare's famous phrase from *As You Like It* to highlight, not only the performative character of power relations, but also the idea that social actors are generally undeviating drudges, wedded to a script "they have learnt by rote." By contrast, improvisational actors—those who do not follow a prescripted role—can be viewed as laudable trailblazers of social change: they "point out the road to others"; they serve as "sign-posts" for instructing spectators in alternative ways of enacting cultural identities. At the same time, however, Wollstonecraft's language expresses an ambivalence toward improvisation by evoking the ignominious position of those masters of

spontaneous acting—the strolling players (coated in "mud and dust")—
who, though their impromptu performances frequently brought pleasure
to rural audiences, were often also feared because of their liminal relationship to community, law, and religion. As numerous testimonies from the
period show, these kinds of actors risked actual physical abuse for representing the possibility of straying from prescribed identities; there was
always the chance that a strolling player might be "pelted."

The point to emphasize here is that, when we read Wollstonecraft's
nonfictional writing through the lens of performativity, we are not only
alerted to the fact that she performed cultural critique by attending to the
theatricality of social acting, which Butler's theory helps us to see. But such
an approach also reveals, as Dolan would remind us, some of the ways in
which Wollstonecraft drew directly from her knowledge of theatrical culture in order to dramatize her political ideas. In this way, Wollstonecraft
may be said to have participated, in a limited way, in helping to shape
that culture. In addition, looking at the passage above from the perspective of Romantic women's theater theory highlights the fact that certain
theoretical concepts formulated by contemporary feminist theorists—"the
performance of power," for one—have a history deeply rooted in theatrical practice, a history that emerges more forcefully when we start to piece
together what women theorists from other eras wrote about their relationship to performances on a variety of social stages. As this example from
Wollstonecraft indicates, because many of the theorists in this study are
not writers whom we typically associate with London Romantic theater,
to neglect one kind of performance arena from the Romantic period is
inevitably to misread the contours of another. It is also to forget that late-
twentieth-century theater theory arises from a history of women writing
about the problematics of moving as gendered performers between closeted and uncloseted space.

Women in British Romantic Theater:
An Interdisciplinary Project

The scholarship produced by feminists in Romanticism and theater studies
during the past decade has become indispensable to the interdisciplinary
project of recovering women's contributions to British Romantic theater.[31]
Anne K. Mellor has been instrumental in demonstrating how conceptions
of "romanticism" and the British Romantic period change once we shift

our attention from the major male Romantic poets—Blake, Wordsworth, Coleridge, Byron, Keats, and Shelley—to "the numerous women writers who produced at least half of the literature published in England between 1780 and 1830" (*Romanticism and Gender* 1). Offering the categories of "masculine" and "feminine" romanticism to describe how an author's experience of gender affects the content and form of his or her writing, Mellor observes that many women writers "promoted a politics of gradual rather than violent social change that extends the values of domesticity into the public realm" (ibid. 3).[32] Indeed, one of Joanna Baillie's most important innovations was the development of a theory that advocated looking for theater in the closeted, or private, spaces of domestic life while consistently urging that her dramas of the closet be performed on formal stages.

The same year that Mellor published the landmark volume of essays, *Romanticism and Feminism* (1988), Sue-Ellen Case brought out *Feminism and Theatre*, which has been influential in its attempts to reevaluate terms such as "theater," "drama," and "playwright." To talk about a legacy of women playwrights, Case argues, requires that one rethink what s/he means by "play," since women did not always use the forms acknowledged by men (29).[33] Because throughout history there is evidence of women having "made" drama that was not necessarily written down, the first women playwrights "created in the medium their cultures allowed them— the language of the body," and they focused on issues rooted in women's experience of domestic life (ibid.). When women have told stories in nurseries, for example, or brought together a group of women for formal or informal discussions in the garden or salon in the manner of English bluestocking circles, or orchestrated holiday celebrations from the recesses of a kitchen, they may be regarded as having produced and/or participated in what Case calls "personal theatre."[34]

This is a concept that helps us appreciate, not only how social rituals managed by women constitute artistic production, but also how the tradition of women writing closet plays is connected to the tradition of women directing and managing the production of private theatricals. As my fifth chapter argues, the late-eighteenth-century British private theatrical provides us with a glimpse of how sexual politics and cultural codes were enacted in the ostensibly apolitical venue of home-produced entertainment. In addition, the gendering of this genre that flourished between 1770 and 1810 points to the connections that existed between "domestic dramas," which took place in the home and on the stage, and the genre of closet play, reintroduced by Baillie at the turn of the eighteenth century. Moreover, a study of this genre (as it yields information about the way in which women used closet space to stage their experiences of domestic life and drew upon its contours for their own more formalized dramaturgical experiments) helps to establish connections between—for instance—Elizabeth Craven's (1750–1828) authorship and management of private play productions in the late eighteenth century and Frances Maria Kelly's (1790–1882) acquisition in the 1830s of a theater of her own that would showcase the talents of the young actors she had trained in her private house at No. 73 Dean Street.

These connections not only enrich the narrative of (women's) theater history but also require us to reexamine our approach to constructing historical narratives in the first place.[35] The extension of the label "theater" to women's consciously constructed performances in closet or domestic space widens the net for catching neglected or undiscovered women theater artists and raises the issue of what constitutes "the theatrical" and "the performable." By suggesting that throughout history women have consistently created dramatically viable performances that occur behind closed doors—sometimes literally in the closet—Case and other feminists provide a context for reconsidering why some experiences, and not others, have been performed on the stage.

My project has benefited even more directly from several recent publications on late-eighteenth- and early-nineteenth-century British theater: Mary Anne Schofield and Cecilia Macheski's edited volume, *Curtain Calls: British and American Women and the Theatre, 1660–1820* (1991), Julie Carlson's *In the Theatre of Romanticism: Coleridge, Nationalism, Women* (1994), and Ellen Donkin's *Getting into the Act: Women Playwrights in London* (1995).[36] Although Schofield's and Macheski's essays are weighted away from Romantic theater and focus mainly on women who worked on the stage prior to 1780, their collection of essays helps "revive lost reputations, reconstruct theater history, and . . . kindle interest in these women whose careers, whose plays, and whose work, deserve a critical encore" (xxiii).

Carlson's study opens up a space for considering women in Romantic drama and theater by discussing the closet critics' anxieties about female theater artists. Demonstrating that "the 'too close-pressing reality' of women in the theatre" (29) preserves the "homosociality of romantic men by effacing the power of women" (20), a power embodied in the acting performances of Sarah Siddons, Carlson argues that "underneath all the variety of these writings on theatre lies a persistent effort to impose masculinist visions of vision and love on everyone" (156). These visions were threatened by the "power of [Siddons'] acting," which "disrupts gender identifications that her roles are meant to solidify" and "feminizes audiences, particularly powerful men" (171–72).

The threat to male-dominated arenas posed by the rise of women playwrights in the late eighteenth century is Donkin's focus in her study of seven women who overcame "the mechanics of a system that worked with remarkable efficiency to keep women voiceless, propertyless, and acquiescent" (2). In her early-nineteenth-century memoir and analysis of the state of the theater, Romantic actress Ann Catherine Holbrook (1780–1837) complained bitterly about the tyranny of the theater managers for whom she had worked.[37] But Donkin's study distinguishes between the supportive (if patronizing) administration of David Garrick, which would have "crucial implications for [women playwrights'] work and their sense of professional acceptance, much more so than for men" (21), and the post-1800 era, when the situation for women playwrights changed to the point where "women playwrights in London once again were perceived to be a rarity, isolated, and exposed" (186). Extending the feminist components of these studies, my analysis of Romantic women theater theorists examines what happens to our perceptions of Romantic theater and drama when we consider how women of the era discussed theatrical space, playgoing, acting, and playwrighting in relation to the pervasive critical tropes of the period, the stage and the closet.

As recently as 1989 Tracy C. Davis worried that the "fear of 'segregating' women" was so "acute" among theater historians ("Questions" 60) that this might negatively affect the recovery of women's particular contributions to theater history. Her concerns were not unwarranted. Scholars have been influenced by literary historians such as Gillian Beer (1989), who has warned against "re-presenting" the past by reading women's texts in isolation from men's, since this approach contradicts one of the basic assertions of feminist theory, "that men have dominated discourse" (65). Segregating female from male writers in Beer's opinion, "leads to theoretical confusion because it expunges economic, epistemic, shared historical conditions of writing and makes it impossible to *measure* difference" (65).

I want to urge patience, however, for an archaeological study focused primarily on bringing to light undiscovered or long-forgotten texts of women writers, since many feminist theater historians are currently engaged in what we might regard as "first-phase scholarship," identifying women playwrights, actor-managers, critics, reviewers, and theorists of the stage from a variety of historical eras. At the time of this book's writing, the category "theater theorist" has yet to be applied to women from the British Romantic period or (to my knowledge) to women who wrote about theater prior to the 1900s, and discussions of women critics in general are still uncommon enough to warrant segregating the theoretical discourse of British Romantic women from that of men in order to show more clearly what these women have actually produced.

I also want to urge patience for a project that uses gender as its operative mode of analysis, especially given the tendency in the American academy to describe as outdated those very approaches that attract a significant number of practitioners. It is certainly important not to ignore feminist theorists who worry that "privileging the oppression of gender over and above other oppressions effectively erases the complex and often contradictory positionings of the subject" (Smith and Watson xiv). Nor would I want to put aside poststructuralist arguments that "the critique of the subject means more than a rehabilitation of a multiple subject whose various 'parts' are interrelated within an overriding unity, a coalitional subject, or an internal polity of pluralistically related points of view" (Butler, "Gender Trouble" 327).

Yet to rebut those who would argue that "gender feminists"[38] have had their day, we need only point to "that deep imprinting of cultural beliefs, values, and expectations on one's biological sex" that form "a fundamental component in a person's sense of identity"; that "system of difference between men and women" (Bell and Yalom 5) whose workings on female bodies and minds are all too powerfully discernible in the theater arts. The fact that we may feel we know all we want to about how gender operates as a category (in conjunction with the categories of class, race, and sexuality) does not entail that we ignore how the concept of gender (specifically) affects the material conditions of women throughout theater history or apologize for privileging it as one's analytical framework. On the contrary, even though academics are by now more than familiar with many features of "the plot" that is produced by a focus on the sex/gender system in literary analysis, we cannot afford to ignore how women's concerns with the performance of gender structured their theories of theater during the British Romantic age, or how such a focus caused them to confront some of the same issues with which women in Western theater are wrestling today. To do so would be to misrepresent the fact that gender ideologies have dominated the reception of British women on the stage from the time female performers made their debut in the middle seventeenth century to the current age. Although there is no need to posit "woman" or "gender" as a coherent category, the historical manifestations of this sex-gender system on the lives of women (and men) in the theater arts during the British Romantic period merit serious consideration.

The following chapters are designed with several aims in mind: to feature women writers from the British Romantic era *as theater theorists*; to discuss the process of constructing a female-authored theater theory before 1850; to present a picture of Romantic theater and drama from the perspective of women who performed on (and off) the London stage; and to provide a historical context for my analysis of Joanna Baillie's theory and dramaturgy. This context is the main focus of Chapter 2, which considers how British Romantic women—in a certain sense female actors all—conformed to social strictures for the "correct" performance of feminine behavior while also finding ways to experiment with alternative approaches for enacting feminine roles in the closeted and public spaces of formal and social theaters. Concentrating on the theater theory produced by important but neglected writers—Anne Mathews, Mary Berry, Anna Jameson—and better-known figures—Sarah Siddons, Dorothy Jordan, and Helen Maria Williams—I discuss the concept of the female actor from several angles: her representation in celebrity memoirs; her discussions of acting and performance style; and her performances in social arenas. This analysis is designed to show how the tension between public and private spaces could be creatively negotiated when women turned their attention to the act of theorizing, especially styles of acting.

To further the process of reclaiming Baillie's theory and to argue her importance as one of the most significant theater theorists of her generation, in Chapter 3 I analyze Baillie's prefatory discourse—primarily those prefaces attached to the volumes of dramas she published between 1798 and 1812—in the context of other prefaces produced by Romantic women playwrights. Chapter 4 performs a reading of Baillie's first two tragedies, *De Monfort* and *Basil*, to describe some of the ways in which her plays enact cultural criticism, another mode of theorizing in which women of the period productively confronted their precarious position as theater artists. Chapter 5 reads Baillie's first comedy, *The Tryal*, in the context of the British private theatrical movement (1780–1810) in order to connect her work with a tradition of women performing (and theorizing about) theater in domestic, private, and "closeted" spaces. It is the very marginalization of closet stages, and the opportunities such private spaces afforded nonprofessional female theater artists to analyze the performance of gendered behavior in public and private theaters, that Joanna Baillie's theory of closet theater brings to our attention. Along with that of her female contemporaries, Baillie's theory directs us to investigate more fully the tradition of "closet drama" that still flourishes today, in a variety of guises, among experimental theater artists.

2. Representing the Female Actor: Celebrity Narratives, Women's Theories of Acting, and Social Theaters

According to celebrity memoirist Anne Mathews (1782–1869), in a book of anecdotes about early-nineteenth-century theater artists, one evening a quadruplegic spectator named "Miss Biffin" was deposited "at some minor theater in the neighbourhood of the Strand" by a magician friend who was later to perform there.[1] Wrapping her in a cloak and placing her in a seat before the audience comes in, Emperor Ingleby (the magician) initially seems solicitous of his charge. Yet, after the performance, Ingleby does a disappearing act, even though he had earlier promised to "come and carry [Miss Biffin] out as soon as the better endowed visitors had taken away their respective legs and arms, conjuring her to sit very quiet until the theatre was quite empty" (*Anecdotes of Actors* 239). This situation forces the young woman to have to explain her condition to a boxkeeper cleaning up after the show, who challenges her remaining presence in the auditorium. When she tells him she is unable to move, the boxkeeper runs away in fright, believing "that nobody but the devil could have placed her there" (240), and Miss Biffin is left to wait for Ingleby, who returns at last without an explanation.

Mathews does not provide her readers with any further commentary on this odd little tale, but she does include a description of one of the ways in which Miss Biffin attempted to deal positively with her physical condition. Though "curtailed by Nature's fair proportions," Mathews tells us, Miss Biffin "outran the generality of her sex in works and ingenuity, and handled a pair of scissors with as much dexterity as a Parisienne *couturiere*, 'cutting out watch-papers and painting pro-*files* with *nothing* but her *mouth*'" (238).

Mathews's anecdote provides us with a vivid if melodramatic image for beginning a discussion about theater theory written by Romantic women. For just as Miss Biffin uses her mouth to compensate for her inability to use her hands, so Romantic women theorists often overcame restrictions upon one form of expression by ingeniously working to develop another. Their resistance to disabling cultural imperatives and the approaches they used to describe their dexterous oscillation between different kinds of stages are the focus of this and the following chapters.

Often embedded in a variety of genres—including reminiscences, autobiographies, celebrity memoirs, interviews, play prefaces, advertisements, letters, journals, diaries, and dedicatory remarks—the theater theory of British Romantic women writers is frequently structured by an act of mediation between private and public spaces as this movement encapsulates the following dilemma: How can women conform to social strictures upon the correct performance of feminine behavior and still experiment with new ways to enact feminine roles in a wide range of forums?

Restrictions against theatrical representations that might reveal more overtly the actual experiences of middle- and upper-class women forced women writers to consider (perhaps more carefully and urgently than their male counterparts) the particular contours dividing private from public arenas, to learn where the boundary lay between the closet and the stage, and to contemplate how to traverse this boundary without losing "reputation." This concern with moving effectively between spaces—and women's heightened awareness of the differences between venues—makes Romantic women's theater theory especially fruitful for highlighting some of the ways in which Romantic theatrical discourse in general was produced by anxieties about gender dislocation in the wake of political and cultural revolution. Indeed, the power of London theaters to assist in blurring boundaries between public and private spheres—in which male theorists imagine closets without women, and women bring their experience of the closet to the stage—elicited a cultural distress about the position of women that permeates the discourse of the early nineteenth century.

Linda Colley reminds us that "those who argue that the period witnessed an actual contraction in women's public role in Britain as elsewhere and an unprecedented confinement of women to the private sphere confuse . . . angry polemic and symbolic gestures with what was happening in fact": in Great Britain the "boundaries supposedly separating men and women were, in fact, unstable *and becoming more so*" (250). Yet when looking at what women wrote about the stage, it is important to realize that many of these texts portray their authors as either unable or unwilling to view positively what Joan Landes describes as "a turning point for women in the construction of modern gender identity" (22). Although there was exhilaration in late-eighteenth-century England about the events taking place across the Channel, there was also widespread fear, most powerfully

and hysterically articulated by Edmund Burke, that the bloody horror un-
leashed during Robespierre's reign and culminating in the beheading of
Louis XVI and Marie Antoinette might infect the English political system. Mary Wollstonecraft became a symbol for this fear and was pitted
against the ideal woman, "the proper lady" whom Mary Poovey has so
carefully described. In 1816 Charles Inigo Jones summarized the popular
early-nineteenth-century view of Wollstonecraft and the feminism of the
late eighteenth century by distinguishing actress Eliza O'Neill (1791–1872),
generally regarded as Sarah Siddons's successor during her brief acting
career (1814–19), from the taint of "the sophistry of the new philosophy":
"A Mrs. Haller [a wayward character in Kotzebue's *The Stranger*] and a
Mary Wolstancroft [*sic*] are the same; and if their morality is to be the
guide and standard of female excellence, virtue will be but an empty name,
and guilt lose all its turpitude" (Jones 49).

The conservative backlash that arose at the turn of the century in response to the writings of Wollstonecraft, Catharine Macaulay, Mary Hays,
Elizabeth Inchbald, Maria Edgeworth, and Amelia Opie inevitably placed
early-nineteenth-century women writers who would theorize theater in a
precarious relationship to a culture that was still smarting from the rise of
liberal feminist thought and the French Revolution. As David Simpson
writes in *Romanticism, Nationalism, and the Revolt against Theory* (1993),
"[w]hile the merest hint of an interest in theory and system was enough
to cast any writer as a Jacobin, the threat was all the greater if the writer
or heroine happened to be a woman" (121). The reason Joanna Baillie published her theoretical remarks on the stage in 1798 anonymously, Ellen
Donkin has suggested, was in order to ensure a serious hearing, for "the
discovery that the author of *Plays on the Passions* was a woman apparently
damaged both the sale of her book and the box-office receipts" (*Getting
into the Act* 165).

Generally not encouraged to inhabit the critical position that Wollstonecraft described with the phrase "the philosophical eye,"[2] when Romantic women did create theory, they were considered to be inappropri-
ately grasping after intellectual ("masculine") authority.[3] For this reason,
fictional and nonfictional portraits of female theorists condemn as "fatal
and unproductive" the woman who "delight[s] over abtruse systems of
morals and metaphysics, or new theories in politics" (Opie, *Adeline Mowbray* 2). In *Mansfield Park* (1814), for example, Fanny Price is "invested,
indeed, with the office of judge and critic, and earnestly desired to exercise it . . . but from doing so every feeling within her shrank, she could

not, would not, dared not attempt it; had she been otherwise qualified for criticism, her conscience must have restrained her from venturing at disapprobation" (189). In Joanna Baillie's play *Enthusiasm* (1836), Lady Worrymore protests that she is "an ardent admirer of the Muses, but no critic—" (594).[4] And in the novel *Adeline Mowbray* (1802) Amelia Opie's narrator finds Editha Woodville problematic because "while wrapt in philosophical abstraction, . . . she suffered day after day to pass in the culpable neglect of positive duties"; and while "professing her unbounded love for the great family of the world, she suffered her own family to pine under the consciousness of her neglect; and viciously devoted those hours to the vanity of abstruse and solitary study, which might have been better spent in amusing the declining age of her venerable parents, whom affection had led to take up their abode with her" (2–3). Historian Catharine Macaulay, when citing in her preface the reasons she had decided to reprint her *Letters on Education, with Observations on Religious and Metaphysical Subjects* (1790), chose not to omit a letter with the following misogynist statement about women theorists. Calling Mr. Badcock a "sufficient authority" (vii), she offers his words as testimony to the worth of her work: " 'I have at last seen Mrs. Macaulay Graham's metaphysical performance. Her work is really wonderful considering her sex; and in this I pay no ill compliment I hope to the ladies; *for surely they themselves will generally acknowledge that their talents are not adapted to abstract speculations*' " (cited in "Preface," *Letters on Education* vii; my emphasis).

A number of forums existed in which women could raise inquiries and offer strongly articulated opinions about theater—perhaps most readily in salon-like gatherings at the homes of other women. But to generalize or speculate about the theater arts with the intent of asserting one's opinions in mixed company—or of eventually publishing them—was an activity in which few women could involve themselves without the knowledge that they were venturing into forbidden territory and leaving behind their femininity and good citizenship. Kristina Straub has written that female writers throughout history have "seen criticism's potential for empowering [their] point of view and for challenging dominant social and literary conventions." Yet, at the same time, their willingness to draw upon a masculine tradition of objectification and authoritative discourse has often "been qualified by strong reservations about participating in an activity that has so constantly been one of the means of their own oppression" ("Women, Gender, and Criticism" 857). For a woman to theorize during the Romantic period—even for herself, in private—meant that she was adopting an aggressively solipsistic posture as well as flying in the face of a culture that equated "the demonization of theory" (Simpson 123) with French excess and the destruction of a recognizable gendered social order (ibid. 82). Although many women from the Romantic period theorized about the stage and published their remarks, this and the chapters to follow demonstrate that they did so with an intense awareness of the psychic and social costs involved.

The fragmentary condition of British Romantic women's theater theory would seem to suggest that much of it was produced incidentally, often within private spaces—the antechambers and closet spaces of genres not immediately associated with theater—and was composed in the middle of lives devoted to pursuits other than the formal stage and sandwiched in between discussions of nontheatrical subjects. Indeed, like Keats's letters, which we are accustomed to regarding as theoretical writing, Romantic women's theories of performance and dramaturgy are frequently found on textual stages traditionally marginalized in canons of theoretical discourse. This seemingly casual placement does not, however, imply that women writers regarded their theory as inconsequential. Rather, it points to their need to seem not to obtrude *as theorists* into public consciousness.

When Lawrence E. Klein reminds us that, during the eighteenth century, the terms "public" and "private" were "aligned with the difference between openness and secrecy, between transparency and opaqueness" (104), he directs us to look more carefully at how Romantic women's theoretical documents reflect these distinctions. Their journals, letters, and diaries written for private circulation often functioned historically as closet spaces did, providing the writer a comparatively safe haven for self-expression. Because considered "private" or "secret," the offstage texts generally contain relatively candid generalizations about the realities that informed women's performances of gender. By contrast, "onstage" documents—that is, the celebrity memoir, play preface, advertisement, dedication letter, prologue, and epilogue attached to play scripts—are usually less explicit about gender issues because of being structured as public performance. They permit the author to approach her reading audience as if in the greenroom or in front of a stage curtain and to talk about the process of composing texts as a female writer. Because these documents are concerned with a relatively large audience, the writer attends more to the issue of how her work will be received than to the act of divulging her personal concerns. These onstage documents required specific rhetorical gestures—apology, self-abnegation, circumlocution, indirectness, feigned or sincere humility—in order to indicate that the writer was sufficiently intimidated by the opportunity to speak authoritatively. But this is not to suggest that a number of women did not escape the cultural demand that they deny the importance of their writings. Rather, it is to underscore the fact that spatial politics dominates their discourse.

One of the reasons Joanna Baillie's theoretical writing is so crucial to understanding the thematic concerns of Romantic women's theater theory is that she draws specifically on the image of "the closet" to advocate a particular kind of play in which the traditionally marginalized is not only written about but publicly performed. A number of her female contemporaries also theorized the stage in language that argues the importance of the private sphere for giving life to stage-worthy theatricality, highlighting closet space as the site where alternative approaches to London theater could be realized and then used to influence the popular theatrical fare. Because of this intense concern with negotiating closet and public space, women theorists called attention to the fact that the private sphere is productive of political theater, one governed largely by women and with the potential to reform and transform formal public stages. In reference to Helen Maria Williams's description of a private performance of "a charming little piece" called "La Federation, ou La Famille Patriotique," Mary Favret has suggested that when Williams chose to portray the statue of Liberté in the drawing room of a French chateau, she placed "the spectacle of domestic pleasure and feminine 'sensibilité' at the center of revolutionary France" ("Spectatrice as Spectacle" 286). The same may be said for women theater theorists in Great Britain who, in addition to encouraging recognition of the theatricality of domestic space, developed a public discourse in which this theatricalization figured prominently.

As we turn to look at this theory, it is helpful to keep in mind its broad outlines, its attentiveness to the major theoretical arguments articulated by British writers whom women would have read in the libraries available to them, such as Dryden, Steele, Addison, Goldsmith, Garrick, Sheridan, Boswell, Hume, Burke, and Johnson; and Continental writers ranging from Diderot, Voltaire, and Rousseau to Lessing, Goethe, Schiller, and Herder.[5] Like their male contemporaries, Romantic women writers wrestled with the degree to which dramaturgy should adhere to Aristotelian principles; the extent to which theater as an institution could or should instruct its audiences in moral behavior; and the degree to which actors must balance artificiality with "naturalism." They also drew upon a legacy of British women writing about the stage during the Restoration and eighteenth-century periods—among them Aphra Behn (1640–89), Catharine Trotter (1679–1749), Elizabeth Griffith (1720–93), and Elizabeth Montagu (1720–1800). One can trace Montagu's and Griffith's influence, for example, on Elizabeth Craven's *Modern Characters from Shakespeare* (1778), Mary Lamb's preface to *Tales from Shakespear* (1807),[6] Anna Jameson's *Characteristics of Women* (1832), Frances Anne Kemble's *Notes upon Some of Shakespeare's Plays* (1892), and Mary Cowden Clarke's *The Girlhood of Shakespeare's Heroines in a Series of Tales* (1891). Responding to both a male and female tradition, then, Romantic women created a varied and significant theoretical discourse that investigated the rich theatricality of the period, from closet stages to social theaters to public performances in the patented London playhouses.

Women, Romantic Theater, and Gender Ideology

When Elizabeth Inchbald observed that a "good play, like a female beauty, may go out of fashion before it becomes old" ("Remarks on *The West Indian*"),[7] with her analogy she suggested the degree to which the London theater was becoming "womanized" during the Romantic period. By the time David Garrick retired from the stage in 1776, the number of women involved in London play production (discounting actresses) had substantially increased from the previous era. Judith Phillips Stanton's "statistical profile" of English women writing from 1660 to 1800 shows that by 1779 there were eleven more female playwrights than in the previous decade, a number that peaked in the 1790s when women's writing in nearly all genres multiplied in England as well as in France and Germany. Between 1798 and 1832, the dates that traditionally bound the British Romantic period, over forty women saw their work produced on public and/or private stages.[8]

These numbers can be put in some perspective, however, when one realizes that during the whole of the eighteenth century "*The London Stage* lists fifty women who had at least one play produced in London during the 1700s" (Katharine Rogers viii). Although more than forty women writing for some kind of theatrical venue during the Romantic period sounds like a relatively high figure—especially in comparison to the century before— during the first half of the nineteenth century, as John Russell Stephens points out, Allardyce Nicoll records more than seven hundred playwrights and opera librettists in his *Handlist*, of which only a fraction are female translators, adaptors, and playwrights (2–3).[9] According to Stephens, in the Romantic era, Inchbald "is the only" female playwright "who could properly be considered a full-time professional writer for the stage" (3), and her career was over by 1805. There is no doubt, as Sandra Richards writes, that Sarah Siddons's phenomenal onstage success in the late eighteenth and early nineteenth centuries (coupled with her dignified offstage persona), garnered increasing respectability for the position of the actress (73), a profession in which women could make quite a bit of money.[10] But the professional situation of women playwrights during the British Romantic period was rather bleak, and the necessity for them constantly to brave a gender ideology that discouraged achievement in theater's public world worked to demoralize and intimidate.

Familiar as this ideology may be to us, it bears thinking about again briefly. When we recognize that the ability to perform femininity "correctly" was essential to women's comfortable survival in both private and public settings, it becomes more understandable why many female theorists seem to be preoccupied with the issue of how to act their gender "properly."

To acknowledge even obliquely that gender is performative does not necessarily result in efforts to minimize the work of performing one's gender well. On the contrary, exhortations to enact femininity "with correctness"—coupled with rationalizations for doing so—argue the necessity, the difficult labor, of learning how to act with relative ease. Time and again in late-eighteenth-century discourse, one finds this necessity encouraged by texts that, through the equation of female bodies and minds with breakable art objects, rationalize restricting women's achievement. Because women were considered emotionally and physically frail and easily shatterable, they were portrayed as being in need of protection from a world bent on assaulting them physically and, with a word, capable of undermining their reputations. We may recall the language of Evelina's guardian, Mr. Villars, who admonishes her as follows in the 1778 novel of playwright and novelist Frances Burney (1752–1840): "Remember, my dear Evelina, nothing is so delicate as the reputation of a woman; it is, at once, the most beautiful and brittle of all human things" (*Evelina* 164).

Frequently compared to porcelain, middle- to upper-class British women were taught to maneuver carefully through courtship rituals in order to arrive at marriage with their fragile hymens—and the cultural virginity they symbolized—intact. In her conduct book, *Letters to Young Ladies* (1786), Hannah More, a successful late-eighteenth-century playwright, asked rhetorically, in reference to adolescent girls: "do [we] not put the finest vases, and the costliest images, in places of the greatest security, and most remote from any probability of accident or destruction? By being so situated, [young women] find their protection in their weakness, and their safety in their delicacy" (11). This comparison of young women to precious merchandise, More hastened to add, "is far from being used with a design of placing young ladies in a trivial, unimportant light; it is only introduced to insinuate that where there is more beauty, and more weakness, there should be greater circumspection, and superior prudence" (11).

But precisely because the female vessel teetered on the shelf of social intercourse, More thought it necessary to urge "young females" to become "accustomed very early in life to a degree of restraint." More's much remarked pragmatism can be seen perhaps most clearly in her belief that young girls' relative ease on social stages depended upon their skillful execution of gendered behavior:

> The natural cast of character, and the moral distinction of the sexes, should not be disregarded, even in childhood. That bold, independent, enterprising spirit, which is so much admired in boys, should not, when it happens to discover itself in the other sex, be encouraged, but suppressed. Girls should be taught to give up their opinions betimes, and not pertinaciously to carry on a dispute, even if they should know themselves to be in the right. . . . It is of the greatest importance to their future happiness that they should acquire a submissive temper, and a forbearing spirit, for it is a lesson which the world will not fail to make them frequently *practise*, when they come abroad into it. . . . (91; my emphasis)

Christine L. Krueger has argued that More's evangelicalism, her rhetorical strategies forged in a tradition of female preachers, enabled her "to encourage the intellectual and verbal empowerment of women without being ostracized" (122). This is certainly true: More worked carefully within accepted systems of belief in order to help women navigate their culture with a relative degree of ease. But though More herself maneuvered successfully, if precariously, among competing ideologies, the passage quoted above recalls the fact that, during the Romantic period, mainstream documents portrayed the sexes as strongly differentiated from birth in ways that were deeply damaging to women's ability to achieve success in the theater. As Ellen Donkin has written of women playwrights in the late eighteenth century, "the province of art and imagination, and the province of being female in a culture constituted on the notion of male authority and female obedience, were in profound and irreconcilable conflict" (*Getting into the Act* 157).

This belief that the sexes were radically different from birth was insidiously reinforced by the assumption that masculinity and femininity were biologically determined rather than socially constructed. Yet the degree to which gender roles were "natural" is refuted by More's language as seen above, which emphasizes lengthy and arduous "practise" as the key to a woman's social success and personal fulfillment. Indeed, although More conveys her awareness that "the very components of perceived gender—gait, stance, gesture, deportment, vocal pitch and intonation, costume, accessories, coiffure—indicate the performative nature of the construct" (Senelick ix), she does not question the degree to which a young woman's mastery of this performance will ultimately do her harm. Even the most successful woman playwright of the late eighteenth century, Elizabeth Inchbald, indicated how tenaciously gender ideology held sway over her professional life—she who had managed to confound cultural expectations for feminine performance by becoming a financially successful theater artist. "The fatigue of being a fine lady . . . is too much for any common strength," James Boaden quoted her as saying, surpassing "hard bodily labour" (cited in Boaden, *Memoirs of Mrs. Inchbald* 2:55).

The British Romantic Celebrity Memoir and the Actress as Public Woman

Toward the end of the Romantic era, in *Winter Studies and Summer Rambles in Canada* (1838), Anna Jameson theorized the paradoxical position of the Romantic actress, who existed in a kind of indentured servitude to audiences and male managers and yet was considered morally flawed for participating in a profession that encouraged women's "availability."[11] She also drew parallels between the actress's difficult situation and that of women in general, especially those whose performance arenas were on social stages. Jameson states that

> there is nothing in the profession of an actress which is incompatible with the respect due to us as women—the cultivation of every feminine virtue—the practice of every private duty. . . . That the position of an actress should sometimes be a false one,—a dangerous one even for a female, is not the fault of the profession, but the effect of the public opinion of the profession. When fashion, or conventional law, or public opinion, denounce as inexpedient what they cannot prove to be wrong—stigmatise what they allow—encourage and take delight in what they effect to contemn—what wonder that from such barbarous, such senseless inconsistency, should spring a whole heap of abuses

and mistakes? As to the idea that acting, as a profession, is incompatible with female virtue and modesty, it is not merely an insult to the estimable women who have adorned and still adorn the stage, but to all womankind; it makes me blush with indignation. (1:50–51)

Further working her way up to a powerful anger, Jameson describes the experience of "a young and admired actress [who] was hurried before the public in an agony of reluctance" and had to play a part that evoked difficult circumstances from her own life. From this example Jameson generalizes that "woman, as a legal property, is subjected to [such exhibitions of power over her person] in her conventional position; a woman may be brought into a church against her will, libelled and pilloried in an audacious newspaper; an English matron may be dragged from private life into a court of justice, exposed, guiltless and helpless, to the public obloquy or the public sympathy, in shame and in despair." In suggesting that all women, even those who do not act, experience the same kinds of injustices, Jameson uses language that ties together public and private spaces, social and theatrical stages, and compels us to look more closely at how late-twentieth-century theorists have theorized the situation of the British actress on the early modern London stage: "If such a scene *can* by possibility take place," Jameson concludes, "one stage is not worse than another" (1:60–61).

As Jameson reminds us, although the similarities between the woman who acts professionally and the one who performs the role of "woman" outside the theater are striking, nonetheless actresses move between public and private spaces perhaps more radically than any other group of female performers. Tracy C. Davis has recently described "the lives of actresses as a category unique among performers and possibly among the categories of people typically excluded from full and uncontested public participation":

> They cannot be fully members of the public (in the sense that men can), they cannot be in the public without implicating their private and/or intimate status, they rarely form an effective counter-public resisting hegemonic ideology, they cannot retreat to a fully private existence, and their intimate lives become fair game (whether on the basis of speculation or fact) for public exposure. ("Introduction: Private Women" 71)

Such an anomalous position meant that actresses in the British Romantic period who wished to perform femininity correctly in formal theaters and offstage in social settings learned to traverse from closet to stage and back again with a dexterity that reveals their astonishing attentiveness to the dilemmas and advantages created by this liminality. Anthropologist Juliet Blair urges us to view this traversal as a positive defiance of the "normal distinctions between 'private' and 'public,'" which are "neither incumbent upon nor possible for the actress" because she "may be structurally located in a 'private' relationship to society at large." The "unique" position of the actress "permits her . . . to bring the naturally secluded private interpersonal sphere of women in the home into the light of public scrutiny" (200). Though her "role as a public woman has traditionally denied the actress her social status within polite society," Blair views as liberating the fact that the actress can sometimes "invent her own standards, and live by her own directives," acquiring "a certain moral and economic independence" (209–10).

By "'domesticating' public space" (216) and existing in a different kind of relationship to public and private spheres from the average woman, the actress is an important source for understanding where and how the boundaries delimiting these spheres operate in specific cultural moments. As Leigh Hunt observed, it is the figure of the actor that provides people with "a link between the domesticities which they represent, and the public life to which they become allied by the representation. . . . [T]he business they deal in brings us into their society as if into their own houses, humours, and daily life," and, in "reading accounts of [actors], we naturally incline . . . *more to the women than the men*" (2:137; my emphasis).

British Romantic celebrity memoirs were indeed fascinated with female performers. Proliferating in what Leo Braudy calls the "fame-choked world" of late-eighteenth-century England (425), celebrity narratives investigated the boundary dividing closet from public space by using the female body as a stage for enacting morality plays designed to encourage virtuous behavior in female readers even while sexually arousing male "spectators." Because celebrity memoirs often resemble a conduct book that attempts to uphold an ideology of domestic tranquillity dependent on female chastity and an ignorance of all things carnal, in these narratives one finds early-nineteenth-century cultural attitudes toward "Woman" writ large—attitudes that help to explain not only the notes of anxiety that women writers sounded in their theories of the stage but some of the approaches they performed in texts that theorize the representation of female theater artists.

A few examples from these narratives provide an important context for appreciating the tone and emphasis of women writers' discussions of celebrity, acting, and social performance. In the histrionic biography of

Eliza O'Neill (1791–1872) mentioned above, Charles Inigo Jones makes it clear that he is less interested in O'Neill's acting than in using the events of her life off the stage both to moralize about proper female behavior and to fantasize about O'Neill's sexuality. Contemplating her sexual appeal as an unmarried woman, he writes: "while she continues Miss O'Neill, and an interesting unprotected female, she will find that patronage which generosity and every better bias of public regard will continue undiminished to extend her." However, once O'Neill marries and "places herself under the protection of a husband . . . the charm is over": she inevitably *"sinks into a wife"* (97)—an allusion to the famous scene between Millamant and Mirabel in William Congreve's *The Way of the World* (1700), an allusion, moreover, which misreads Millamant's feminism by refusing to note her irony. Jones urges O'Neill to remain "in a state of *single blessedness*" (98). Because the actress's private life informs the audience's reception of her performances onstage, her potential to titillate will be extended the longer she resists marriage. Jones pontificates:

> Mrs. Siddons began as a wife, and in that character was only known to the public; but even she had long to climb the boards. Mrs. Crawford began as Mrs. Barry, the wife of a favourite and first-rate actor, and under his wing, and with the aid of his reputation, came forward. Miss Duncan appeared at first with every advantage, but she sunk into Mrs. Davidson. The same may be said of many others. . . . [T]ill she [O'Neill] has amply fixed her reputation, and got hold of public opinion, which cannot be shaken, it is the advice of friendship, not to hazard the change of her name. (97–98)

Jones's conclusion—that if "this is the opinion of this country towards *frail fair* ones in a single state, how much stronger does it fall to be, where the unfortunate female is a mother and a wife" (61)—suggests how brief a period was granted the actress for exploring the effects of her sexual attractiveness on the public. And during the time she was allowed to test the degree of her allure, she was constantly being reminded by biographers like Jones to watch her step. This moralizing was one of the most disingenuous features of the celebrity memoir, for audiences not only thrilled to an actress's potential fall, they expected it.

In a biography similar to Jones's, the anonymous author of the *Secret Memoirs of* [actress] *Harriot Pumpkin* (Harriot Mellon, 1778?–1837) [12] exposes "the frailties of a woman in the last century" in order to "caution the females of the present against crimes of ingratitude and malice," as well as "to impress upon their minds the necessity of avoiding dissimulation, and if chance or misfortune should lead them into error, that they may be enabled to avoid the courses I have set forth; and that in whatever station of life they may be placed, kindness and good nature are as easily practised as the hypocritical and vindictive conduct and errors of the Heroine of these Memoirs" (48).[13] During her heyday, Mellon inflamed many of her fans by making a "green-room marriage"—the term for a wedding between an actor and a member of the aristocracy.[14] Greenroom marriages often agitated the public because they represented the actress's violation of boundaries of both female ambition and class distinction. In order to make the point that Mellon was inordinately ambitious socially—and therefore to be damned by (especially) female readers, who ought to cultivate contentment with their station in life—Mellon's memoirist recounts an anecdote concerning a wealthy woman called "Lady C." and her black servant:

> Lady C——— had a favorite Negro boy, to whom she was much attached; but from some antics he had performed, she considered a portion of *gentle* correction necessary for his health and happiness; and having no twig near her, she made free with the *poker*, and lent *Blacky* a *topper* on the upper story, which brought him senseless to the ground. He lay for dead, and Lady C. considered it the denouement of a *Tragedy*. She thought prudent to decamp without beat of drum and sound of trumpet; and having packed up a few necessaries, she departed for the Continent full of sorrow and an humbled state of mind. As to the poor boy's skull, that was nothing to Mother Pumpkin Croesus [Mellon]; but to be disappointed of the glory, that happiness she promised herself by an introduction to Royalty, and to be envied by her own sex, would have been as delicious as her favorite *Lunch* washed down with *Madeira and soda*. What made the disappointment more cruel, she never heard of Lady C.'s topper on poor Blacky's *pericranium*, until she was ready dressed to pop into her new coach. What was the life of a poor black boy to so terrible a disappointment? nothing to be sure; but what cannot be cured must be endured. Her delicate feelings were strongly outraged, not for the consequence of a Lady amusing herself with her Slave, but the misfortune of not being presented at Court was barbarous in the extreme. However, as Blackey's wound was not mortal, the Lady C. returned with a determination not to meddle with edge tools in the future, and to curb those passions which too often enslave both sexes and render them dangerous company; and though the Lady C. was sometimes irregularly afflicted in this kind of way, she was upon the whole *good natured* and *affable*, and a very different person from the Heroine of these memoirs, who felt horribly chagrined at not having it in her power to shew off her Gingerbread and Jewels—her greasy neck and mutton fists, set off with Rings like the wife of a Jew butcher, or a Pawnbroker's Journeyman. (29–30)

Although trying to demonstrate his/her compassion for servants—"What was the life of a poor black boy to so terrible a disappointment?"—the anonymous author is less enraged by Mellon's ostensible indifference to a suffering servant than by her desire to supersede her social station and be introduced at Court. Equated with the Jew and the (allegedly synonymous) pawnbroker, who evidently infuriate the author for having achieved economic success (thus threatening to erode class distinctions), Mellon— or "Mother Pumpkin Croesus"—is chided throughout this narrative for having marketed her public visibility as an actress into economic privilege, especially by marrying into the peerage. Thus, this memoir concludes with a moral aimed at young women typical of the genre:

> However glaring the glitter and shew of nobility, the allurements of riches, the vanity of being exalted from a cart to a coach, and the envy that may inspire young females to be raised above their companions, they should take into account, that in the Lottery of Life there are ten chances to one in favor of a woman marrying a man as nearly as possible to her own rank in life, and that one of those unequal matches seldom brings real happiness. (50)

Leigh Hunt wondered why this envy of the actress who married money was not more often converted to sympathy: "the surprise of the public is, that she [the actress] puts up with a private gentleman" (2:167), he wrote in his essay called "Duchess of St. Albans [Harriot Mellon], and Marriages from the Stage," which, in paying special attention to Mellon's story, discusses the history of public reaction to greenroom relationships from the time of Charles II and Nell Gwynn's liaison. The "staid conduct and previous elegance of a succession of coroneted actresses" and "the spread of education" have "rendered it . . . ridiculous to make this sort of lamentation over a marriage with the green-room" (2:167).

But this absurd response, as Hunt acknowledges it, was tied to the era's need to differentiate between public and private spaces of performance. Just as the theorists of the era were absorbed with investigating the boundaries that gave rise to both closet and public drama—to the differences between one's experience of plays read and that of plays performed— so social narratives that centered on the backstage arena of the theater or greenroom depended for their dramatic tension not only upon class divisions but also on the strict delineation of behavior appropriate to both public and private venues. In what could be called the greenroom's real-life closet dramas, social actors could imagine themselves stage actors and vice versa by mingling with each other behind the curtain, while at some level understanding that barriers to their social intercourse actually sustained the intrigue of these theatricals of private life. (Likewise, as Chapter 5 describes, private theatricals—the term used by theater historians to designate the plays performed primarily in the late eighteenth century by aristocrats and the middle classes in the privacy of their homes or in theaters built to showcase amateur performances—depended for a portion of their appeal on an audience's ability to discern the degree to which the amateur performers both adhered to and departed from performance standards established by the two theaters licensed to perform the "legitimate" drama, Covent Garden and Drury Lane.)

The titillation of bringing the closeted into public view for the purpose of drawing sharper distinctions between one kind of space and another is the focus of James Ridgway in his anonymously published memoir (1792) of singer-actress Elizabeth Billington (1765 or 1768–1818). In this narrative Ridgway uses information about Billington's private life to support the author's defense of "the sacred tie of matrimony, one of the great links in the chain of society" (75). Dedicating his narrative to a man "who has the unexampled happiness of having six daughters, possessing invariably, the most unsullied virtues," Ridgway describes Billington as "immersed in the horrible depths of human depravity" (v) and as "a wretch, who has been the sole cause of alienating the affections of an indulgent husband, from an amiable virtuous wife, and a numerous, beautiful offspring" (xv). Billington is criticized for a whole range of sins: she allegedly gave her child a venereal disease, cuckolded her husband and then laughed about it to her mother, and had sex in front of a number of men backstage. Nothing seems to arouse Ridgway's compassion for his subject. In fact, although he tells readers that Billington may have been abused as a child—"the truth is, her father was detected in attempting an intercourse with his musical offspring, before she could *possibly*, from her tender years, have had any tendency to vice" (3)—he is much more upset about the fact that theatrical spectators seem to court corruption by celebrating Billington's stage performances. Applause, in Ridgway's view, "makes her callous to every tender sentiment; and she begins a new career of vice, every time she is applauded upon the stage, because she is not made sensible that her morals are sunk into the basest depravity" (73).

The tendency of Romantic memoirs to focus on the body of the actress even as they ostensibly prescribed to readers a restrictive mode of feminine behavior that would eradicate female sexuality[15] occurs dramatically in the pseudonymously written memoirs of Madame Vestris (Lucia Elizabeth Bartolozzi, [1800–56]).[16] Here, the writer uses gallantry toward his subject to suggest that—"as a near relative of the lady" (8)—it is appropriate that he challenge "the absurd falsehoods which have . . . issued from the press" (4) concerning Vestris's "ancestry, birth, parentage, and connections" (4). But "Arthur Griffinhoof"[17] defends Vestris's reputation only to underscore the sexual intrigue that surrounded the actor-singer: he seems compelled, for example, to tell readers that she "came to her husband's arms, a spotless virgin," inevitably evoking the rumors of her alleged promiscuity as well as her reputation as a woman around whom men "swarmed . . . like flies round a honey-pot on a day in June" (24). In addition, he displaces onto Vestris's sister, Josephine, the sexual detail that theatrical readers would have expected from his narrative. The following story about how the fifteen-year-old Josephine was deflowered with a dildo serves as a substitute for lurid tales about Vestris's own sex life, and it indicates some of the ways in which a number of celebrity memoirs from the Romantic period resemble "whore biography":[18]

> A little more champagne had its exhilerating [*sic*] effect, and at the close of the repast, Josephine had become so overpowered with the wine and the excitements, that she permitted Best to undress her, and place her in bed. There she became his prey in a very curious manner. Her extreme youth and delicate make opposed much difficulty to the completion of his designs. Whether his over anxiety had weakened his powers, as it will in some cases, or whether his debauched life had so enervated him as to render him incapable, is uncertain, but all his attempts were in vain. The roué, no doubt, would have been more gratified could he personally have broken through all defences, and accomplished his object without assistance. Perhaps when contemplating her sylph-like form, her delicacy had given birth to doubt his own capability: but whatever was the cause, he was prepared even for this emergency. Finding every project futile, he slily drew forth something from beneath the pillow, which in its outward shape bore a strong resemblance to one of nature's primest productions. By stifling her cries, he succeeded to his purpose; and then replaced the natural for the artificial, his triumph was at once complete. (32)

Even though this scene has little to do with a narrative purportedly celebrating the life of a famous cross-dressing actress, the introduction of Josephine's sexual initiation functions to satisfy a readership that would have expected some "dirt" on Vestris. This story also underscores the fact that male biographers of this period often used actresses as objects for the projection of their own sexual attitudes and beliefs about gender identity.

Indeed, Griffinhoof's memoir reveals as much about his cultural biases as it does about his subject. For instance, his language shows him identifying with the position of the unscrupulous Captain Best—"The roué, *no doubt*, would have been more gratified could he personally have broken through all defences," "*Perhaps* when contemplating her . . . her delicacy had given birth to doubt his own capability," and "his *triumph* was . . . complete" (my emphasis). And in other sections of the memoir, when Griffinhoof expresses his dislike of Vestris's ability to impersonate male roles in musical comedies and light operas such as *Giovanni in London, The Beggar's Opera*, and *The Marriage of Figaro*, he reveals that his interest in actresses lies not in their achievement as practitioners of a craft but rather in the alleged sexual content of their private lives and in the physical responses their bodies can incite:

> For our own parts we must candidly confess that we are not partial to witnessing a delicate woman assume a masculine part, and thus strut and fret her hour upon the stage. To my mind, the shape of a fine woman is seen to more advantage—more delightful to the eye and heart, through the wavings of white satin or silk, than the light costume of flesh-coloured pantaloons or slashed doublets of chamois leather. There is something more to be guessed at, and which is the more endearing from being concealed. (63)

The biographer's preference for a costuming that "conceals" and allows one to "guess at" the shape of the woman underneath suggests how an ideology that would seek to deny the sexuality of the female body could actually stimulate the cultural production of a gaze that pinned women into vulnerable sexual postures without allowing them sexual agency. Framed by the theatrical arch, a woman actor could not escape the fact that, in Laurence Senelick's words, "to appear on stage is to display one's body to strangers. . . . The inscription of gender as allure, in a more blatant manner than society condones, becomes one of the theatre's most potent attractions and, to the authorities, one of its most dangerous features" (xii).

Drawing on a long tradition of antitheatrical rhetoric, a number of writers from the period responded to this perceived danger by portraying the stage as an instrument of social corruption. Though writing on behalf of women in *The Female Advocate; or, An Attempt to Recover the Rights of Women from Male Usurpation* (1799), Mary Anne Radcliffe (1745?–1810?) combines misogyny with what Jonas Barish has described as "the antitheatrical prejudice" in the process of worrying about the "numbers of unguarded young men, even with hearts inclined to virtue, [who] have unhappily been drawn on to vice" by women associated with the theaters.[19] And not just to prostitutes, although these were everywhere in evidence. According to Radcliffe, women in theater—whether actresses onstage or sex traders in the audience—are "like Eve in Paradise, [who] is no sooner fallen herself than, by deceitful artifice, she spreads the net of destruction to catch others" (42–43). "[N]eed we go any farther than the theatres," Radcliffe asks rhetorically, "the resort of all, both good and bad, and where abandoned females, of all ages and degrees of profligacy, attend to make their harvest, and gather in their unlawful plunder, to supply the ordinary wants of the ensuing day?" (43).

Whereas in 1813 the anonymous author of an essay on the popular comic actor Dorothy Jordan (1761–1816) asserted that "we cannot admit the privilege of any individual, to convert the theatre, into a scene of public inquisition on the morals and domestic character of the performers" (81–82),[20] in the passage below, written seven years earlier, John Styles targets the theatrical medium as culturally degrading because it features women in attractive roles outside the domestic space. His *Essay on the Character and Influence of the Stage on Morals and Happiness* (1806; rpt. 1807 and 1815) is notable not only for its nostalgia for an ideal of domestic happiness, pre-figuring the Victorian ideology that enshrined women as "angels of the house." With its references to domesticity, it also underscores the era's longing for submergence in closet space, albeit a closet emptied of remind-ers of women's growing literacy and intellectual competence. The fact that in their own theoretical discourse women were describing a movement be-tween closet and stage—moving outward from their homes and embracing the public stage for its ability to showcase their theater of the closet while also calling attention to these "closet theatres" themselves—makes more resonant Styles's diatribe against the London stage as "the principal source from whence have flowed those contaminating streams, which have had so fatal an influence in depraving the female character in the higher classes of society" (36).

Hymning "the importance of woman in society" as the purveyor of "social comfort and domestic joy" (32), Styles targets "the Stage" as the "enemy" that dashes "the cup of domestic enjoyment to the ground." Prob-lems occur when "the love of home and a taste for the sweetly interesting employments of the domestic scene [are] exchanged for the pursuits of theatrical entertainment, and the vagrant disposition of a stylish belle," for then "the female is degraded, and society has lost its most powerful, capti-vating charm; [and] man is comfortless and alone. . . . he must go abroad for pleasure—miserable wanderer! his children clasp the knees of a menial stranger—home has no attractions—he has no kindred heart to partake of his joys and sorrows; the world is before him; it allures and intoxicates, but it does not make him happy" (34). Referring to adaptations and translations of German plays by Kotzebue as a code for the corruption of female virtue,[21] Styles suggests that the female spectator who appreciates these kinds of theatrical events resembles the "polluted" prostitute:

> If a daughter of mine could visit the Theatre, and tell me that she could view with pleasure the scenes in Pizarro, the Stranger, the Virgin of the Sun, John Bull, and twenty other popular dramatic pieces I could name, I should clasp my lost child to my bosom, weep at the thought of innocence for ever fled, and mourn the day that made me a parent:—her soul is polluted, and that is the essence of prostitution; the dignity of virtue is lost—and what remains? If the mother of my children could spend her evenings at the Theatre, and be gratified with what is passing there, she would lose my confidence and forfeit my regard; for I should be sure she had lost the best qualifications of a wife. (34–35)

Pitting "the theatrical stare" and the "imposing, dauntless front of the actress" (36) against the closeted countenance of the ideal wife,[22] Styles advocates the same ideology that the celebrity memoir promoted through its concentration on the actress's body: the good woman cannot possibly enjoy public performance or even the hint of theatrical artifice, since this pleasure would indicate that her seeming obedience to a social project designed to squelch her ambition and her theatrical impulses was suspect, and that the underpinnings of a pre-Victorian culture that increasingly idealized domestic space as the appropriate location of female happiness would be revealed as distressingly shaky.

Women's Responses to Celebrity and the Celebrity Memoir

Thomas Postlewait has rightly cautioned scholars against depending on theater autobiographies for reliable details of an actress's life: "as historical documents, they often fail to describe accurately what happened in the public career and private life of the actress; as narratives, they fail to articulate fully the social significance and personal consciousness of a professional woman in theatre" (268). The problem with autobiographies by actresses, as Mary Jean Corbett has observed in reference to the female Victorian performer, is that how actresses "define themselves on stage and in autobiography . . . becomes contingent less on the 'facts' of their private lives, and more on how well they can publically imitate and reproduce the signs and attitudes that mark individuals as belonging to a certain class and gender" (108). This is why Cecilia Macheski urges us *not* to look to Romantic playwright Elizabeth Inchbald's memoirs to determine how she saw herself, but rather at the portraits that she sat for during her career, since in Macheski's view these images show Inchbald exerting more control over how she was represented.[23]

If we are to understand more readily how a Romantic woman writer's "version of events is controlled by internalized gender conventions" (Relke 120), then it is useful first to attune ourselves to one of the ways in which celebrity memoirs about women—especially those authored by men—provide instances of their subjects' resistance to cultural prescriptions for gendered behavior. Many celebrity memoirs from the Romantic period contain tantalizing pieces of information that hint at, rather than make explicit, the character of a woman's involvement with the professional stage. For instance, we are told by Elizabeth Farren's (1762–1829) less-than-empathetic biographer that, prior to marrying the count of Derby, she was "appointed to preside over the Stage Business" in the private theatricals sponsored by the duke of Richmond, "an employment for which she expressed great fondness, as it afforded her an opportunity of being introduced to many of the first Nobility in the Kingdom, and thereby gave her an importance unknown to any Theatrical Company" (Arbiter 19). That Farren may *not* have been motivated by "vanity gratified to the full extent of her wishes" (ibid.) but was gratified instead by the artistic challenges of stage management does not occur to her biographer. But his description of her "fondness" for this position encourages readers, especially those encountering these texts in the 1990s, to consider Farren's perspective as a means of counterbalancing her biographer's often libelous presentation.

Female-authored celebrity narratives can be important repositories for theater theory, if only because one sometimes finds women writers confronting the problem of how to portray the female actor to a public audience. In this chapter we have already seen how Harriot Mellon was criticized for marrying into the peerage; her marriages made her so wealthy, in fact, that she left approximately 600,000 pounds to a range of relatives at the time of her death in 1837. Biographer Margaret Cornwell Baron-Wilson—in writing to redeem the "character of the late Duchess of St. Albans," who "has been so frequently misrepresented during many years, and was indeed so little understood by those who merely met her in society" (1:1)—decided on an approach that certain readers have called "fiercely and sentimentally partisan" (Highfill, Burnim, and Langhans 10:169), one in which Mellon is portrayed as an embodiment of the virtues of Charity, Truth, Generosity, Cheerfulness, and Wit. But it is important to realize that Baron-Wilson's "main object" was "to give a just impression of [Mellon's] natural qualities, rather than a regular narrative of her life" (1:1), and that she was writing against the tradition of "the regular narrative"—against those theater (auto)biographies in which the character of the woman's public and private life is sacrificed to prurient eyes.

Even very brief passages in celebrity memoirs by women contain instances of how the author attempted to counteract cultural stereotypes. In her 1806 biography of Anna Maria Crouch (1763–1805), Mary Julia Young (?–1821) states that she intends to portray the actress as "not perfect;— she was a *woman*—not an *angel*" (2:320). Situating Crouch in a community of other artistic women with whom she either worked or came in contact—Hannah Cowley, Sophia Lee, Elizabeth Farren, Elizabeth Inchbald, Sarah Siddons, Eglantine Wallace, Mariana Starke, Teresa DeCamp— Young shifts focus from the actor's sexual history to her efforts to become a skilled artist. To this end, Young highlights Crouch's appreciation of the acting technique of Frances Abington, a technique that informed a portion of Crouch's career and may have influenced her teaching of acting after she retired from the stage.[24] "Miss Phillips [Crouch's maiden name] was very sorry when Mrs. Abington quitted Drury-lane theatre," Young writes, "because she could not have so many opportunities of seeing that charming actress."

> One day, speaking on this subject to a friend, Miss Phillips said—"Mrs. Abington does not know how I have looked up to her for improvement! If she *did*, such, as I have heard, is her delight in doing good, that I am sure she would give me an order [to be permitted to watch her from Covent Garden] every night she performed, that I might still pursue my study of her and nature. . . ." (1:156)

This seemingly unremarkable passage deserves note primarily for the fact that the author focuses on one way in which acting techniques were transmitted from one female actor to another.

As the sexual aspects of an actress's private life customarily took center stage in theater autobiographies, the biographer interested in other features of the actor's life had to walk a fine line. Required, on the one hand, to celebrate the famous woman's ability to move between public and private spaces without wavering in her skillful gender performance, the woman author who wanted to protect the reputation of her female subject also had to resist the impulse to give readers information about her domestic life that might impinge upon that reputation. Yet ignoring the private performance meant that the portrait of the woman would inevitably be thinner, if not more distorting. Therefore, women writers made frequent attempts to feature the very negotiations undertaken by a female performer as she struggled to move between public and private arenas without losing any social currency she either already possessed or had acquired.

In relation to the issue of celebrity and Romantic representations of the female actor, the remarks of Anne Mathews, author of the "Miss Biffin anecdote" cited at the start of this chapter, will seem particularly valuable to the feminist theater historian in their anticipation of some of the concerns of contemporary cultural critics.[25] As recently as 1992, Jib Fowles observed that there existed neither a coherent nor an extensive body of literature on celebrity and stardom (x). But in 1844 Mathews wrote about the differences between an actor's offstage and onstage performances in ways that raise a number of questions relevant to this study: What motivates fans to want to follow the actor into his or her greenroom or secret closet? What kinds of satisfactions are these theatrical spectators seeking? What cultural functions does the cult of celebrity serve?

Mathews begins her introduction to *Anecdotes of Actors* by stating emphatically that "[a]ctors are indubitably the legitimate property of the public" (1–2). To underscore the tradition of their dependency from the time when they were household players and members of strolling companies during the Middle Ages Mathews uses feudalistic metaphors: "While upon *the boards*, actors are not only 'her majesty's servants,' but the vassals of all those who, for the time, possess the purchased right not only to taste of their quality, but to pronounce upon its flavor" (2). Nineteenth-century audiences resemble spectators in the great households of early Tudor England by exercising "full impunity of power," purchasing with their tickets the "brief authority of the hour" (2) by which to make the commodity actor perform according to their will. Depicted by Mathews as a tyrannical conglomerate that enslaves the actor, spectators buy access even to a performer's sexual favors:

> John Bull claims—in commercial phrase—the indisputable privilege of using up the "article" for which he has paid "cash," according to his own peculiar fancy and humour, rigorously exacting his money's worth. Nor is he satisfied with fair and full measure of the commodity, but demands a something "*in*," "an overplus," in an *encore* of his favourite song, or a "blessing," in the repro-

duction of a chosen performer upon the stage, . . . whereon he [the actor] is required to appear *au naturel* when his work is done, and bend with due humility to his patrons. . . . (3)

This description of the actor as naked and bent over (taking a bow) highlights the vulnerability of the early-nineteenth-century performer. Yet, despite Mathews's pessimistic metaphors, in the second part of her analysis she proceeds to show how this exposed body ceases to be a "commodity" the minute the actor leaves the theater.

By returning to domestic space, the actor exerts power by frustrating spectators who want to follow him or her into the closet. While members of the audience must "creep back to their dull homes, and dream of lost dominion" (3), actors can exit into the protective mysteries of their private stages, into what the anonymous author of *The Secret History of the Green-Room* (1795) calls the "DRAMA of *real life*" (1:vii). "No money can purchase a key to the blue chamber of an actor's privacy," Mathews writes, "no *order* achieve the *open sesame*!! of his street door. . . . There is no *free admission* for the general patrons of the actor, but within the walls of the theatre, whence they may pursue him to the utmost limits of open space; but once within his own domestic fence, he is invisible to outward ken" (4).

But not necessarily invisible to the celebrity memoirist and theorist. Mathews distinguishes herself from the mere spectator by suggesting that, even when at home, the actor may inevitably become "outed" when faced with the inquiring eye of someone with special insights into actors and acting. As a commentator on celebrity life, Mathews portrays herself as more than competently positioned to fulfill the audience's desire to peer into the actor's private chambers, and thus she suggests that the audience's desire to determine "what [the actor] *really* is when his 'lendings' are 'off,' and he returns unto himself" (5) can be satisfied by reading her writing. Describing herself as moving between the space inhabited by her theatrical reader and that of the pursued performer, she says proudly: "it is no mean boast in the writer of these remarks that she has *crossed the very threshold* which has divided the 'curious' from their insight into the private nature and pursuits of public performers; and . . . plunged into the very heart of their mystery" (6; my emphasis).

On the one hand, Mathews depends as much upon her theatrical readers' whims as do the actors she discusses—that is, she must edge herself into the "presence" of the reader "somewhat in the fashion of a pedlar" who will "open my miscellaneous wares piecemeal . . . trusting . . . that the commodities may so far please as to ensure your future custom" (7). But, also like the actors who run out the stage door, she can elude this reader's dominion by transgressing the boundary that divides public performances on the stage from private performances in domestic settings. This is because, through the act of theorizing, Mathews occupies an important cultural position, one that allows—indeed requires—that she move with fluidity between stage and closet.

In the Closet with Sarah Siddons:
Her System of Acting

No professional actor during the Romantic period moved between so-called private and public spaces more successfully than did Sarah Siddons, in the sense that very few scandals appeared in her life, and none had any real impact on her reputation as a highly respectable actor, mother, and wife. Yet although inarguably more highly praised in Romantic theater than any other male or female artist—both as an actor and as a person—Siddons's self-representation in the slim volume of reminiscences she wrote at the end of her life deflates the kind of rhetoric that still swirls around the facts of her career. Critics today point to Siddons as having played an "innovative cultural role" (Pat Rogers 50) by extending to women the possibility of performing heroism on stage (63) and by creating a "subject, rather than an object, position in representation" for female actors (Donkin, "Mrs. Siddons" 276). Siddons's memoirs (written in 1830, published in 1942) paint a different picture, however, highlighting rather than minimizing the difficulties she encountered as a public woman. She describes her stage debut as "my fierey [sic] trial" (Reminiscences 10) and challenges her readers to imagine what she says "can not be described": the "awful consciousness that one is the sole object of attention to that imense [sic] space, lined as it were with human intellect from top to bottom, and on all sides round" (11). Though confessing that she was "an ambitious candidate for fame" (16), nevertheless Siddons devotes a portion of her memoirs to remembering—in the context of being booed off the Drury Lane stage in 1784 and fainting in her brother's arms—how "wretched is the being who depends on the stability of public favour!" (29).[26] And it is her audience's "persecution" with which Siddons ends her narrative, as she ironically refers to spectators as "the *Generous Public*." For after the debacle of 1784 this "Public" greeted her entrance "each succeeding night with shouts, huzzas and waving of handkerchiefs." But Siddons's narrative makes it clear that these actions "were not sufficiently [gratifying] . . . to obliterate from memory the tortures I had endured from thier [*sic*] cruel injustice, and the degrading humiliations incidental to the profession of the Drama" (32).[27]

Siddons's remarks on acting underscore the fact that we need to pay serious attention to how actors have theorized their craft, especially in the case of female performers, since such comments often contradict both the actor's self-representation and the titillating portrait of scandalous behavior so cherished in the annals of celebrity narratives. When looking more closely at how Siddons describes the process by which she created her characters, suddenly one encounters, not the melancholy person she presents in her *Reminiscences*, but someone highly energized by the acting profession, whose passionate commitment to textual analysis reveals an excitement about the emotional and intellectual challenges that acting for a public audience can generate. Not surprisingly, Siddons's remarks on acting reveal her to have been a serious student of performance who relished the closet as a space for theorizing her craft.

In the eighteenth century James Boswell confessed that "we would read an Essay by Mr. Garrick on the art of acting, as we do Xenophon and Caesar, or the King of Prussia, on the art of war" (469). More recently, Karen Malpede urges us to view the actor as the locus of a uniquely valuable critical perspective. Because "no one but the actor devotes herself so thoroughly to the study of what it means to be an individual" and because her theory "comes so directly out of personal experience,"[28] what the actor says about her craft is inevitably "direct, precise, and full of feeling for the mysteries of theatre and life" (17).[29] Phillip B. Zarrilli states that every time "an actor performs, he or she implicitly enacts a 'theory' of acting—a set of assumptions about the conventions and style which guide his or her performance, the structure of actions which he or she performs, the shape that those actions take . . . and the relationship to the audience" (4). But though it would seem logical to ask the performer what she or he believes about the art of acting, and to view these opinions as offering important philosophical insights into the experience of performance, it is still fairly unusual to find actors described as theorists and vice versa. Especially in the American academy, the lines between those who perform and those who talk about performance are clearly drawn.

Frances Anne Kemble, a popular actor during the Romantic period, used the example of her aunt Siddons to distinguish the theorist from the stage performer. In her essay "On the Stage" (1863), Kemble separates the instinctual ("the dramatic") from the self-conscious ("the theatrical") as the former faculty is aligned with the childlike actor and the latter describes the theorist. Drawing on the dichotomous vocabulary that underlies debates about acting throughout the Romantic era, in which "the theatrical" or artificial (French) style of performance is pitted against a more naturalistic (or English) approach, Kemble generalizes: that "which is dramatic in human nature is the passionate, emotional, humourous element, the simplest portion of our composition, after our mere instincts, to which it is closely allied; and this has no relation whatever, beyond its momentary excitement and gratification, to that which imitates it, and is its theatrical reproduction; the dramatic is the *real*, of which the theatrical is the *false*" (9). Too much self-consciousness about the process of performing renders actors "theatrical" in contrast to "dramatic" performers, who, like children, are "only theatrical when they become aware that they are the objects of admiring attention; in which case the assuming and dissembling capacity of *acting* develops itself comically and sadly in them" (10).

In the analysis that follows, I want to contradict Kemble's assessment of her aunt's "treatises" as "feeble and superficial," arguing instead that Siddons did indeed possess a mind that was "reflective and analytical" (17–18). Kemble failed to appreciate this fact because, like many contemporary theater practitioners and theorists, she insisted upon separating the intellectual from the emotional and bodily: "If that great actress had possest the order of mind capable of conceiving and producing a *philosophical analysis* of any of the wonderful poetical creations which she so wonderfully embodied," Kemble wrote, "she would surely never have been able to embody them as she did" (17; my emphasis).

Siddons's theory of acting, which can be induced primarily from her "Remarks on the Character of Lady Macbeth" and her notes on playing Constance in *King John* (both contained in Thomas Campbell's *Life* [1834]), reveals that she paid careful attention to the performative features of women's experiences both on and off the stage. It is as if she embodied Anna Jameson's perception that when one talks of the legal situation of women, whether actresses or not, "one stage is not worse than another" (*Winter Studies and Summer Rambles* 60–61). Siddons's "Remarks on the Character of Lady Macbeth" provide perhaps the best-known instance of a pre–twentieth-century actress "humanizing and feminizing the fiend" (Julie Carlson, *In the Theatre* 165). Instead of alienating her public, Siddons sought to create female characters that seemed plausible to her but also adhered to an ideal in which women were viewed as custodians of their family's moral health. In reference to Siddons, Ellen Donkin writes that, "although audiences demanded from the text the comfort and familiarity of the norms of Womanhood, *what in fact they responded to in performance was something that potentially ruptured that comfort and familiarity*" ("Mrs. Siddons" 278), and indeed, Siddons's notes suggest that by highlighting those moments when her female characters were oppressed by the dramaturgy of a particular play, she could—as a stage performer—comment, even if obliquely, on the problematic features of these very limitations.

Although she followed the eighteenth-century tradition of portraying Lady Macbeth as fiendish and hellish, as a femme fatale or "belle dame sans merci," in her written remarks Siddons suggests that, when on stage, she enacted a kind of cultural critique by also envisioning the lady as a supportively agonized eighteenth-century wife, "fair, feminine, nay, perhaps even fragile" ("Remarks" 124), whose selfishly needy husband neglects to appreciate the quiet stoicism she has to exert in order to bear him through his "pusillanimous" moments (132). Of Lady Macbeth's behavior in act 3, Siddons writes:

> [S]mothering her sufferings in the deepest recesses of her own wretched bosom, we cannot but perceive that she devotes herself entirely to the effort of supporting him. . . . Yes; in gratitude for his unbounded affection, and in commiseration of his sufferings, she suppresses the anguish of her heart, even while that anguish is precipitating her into the grave which at this moment is yawning to receive her. (129)

Here is summarized the silently suffering, self-effacing nurturer of others' feelings who, by "writhing thus under her internal agonies" (130), demonstrates the difficulties for women in the Romantic period of conforming to a feminine ideal that advocated a daunting and frequently debilitating self-control, where influence on the public sphere is exerted largely through a man.[30]

Siddons's remarks reveal the arduous "private study" that was required to act on stage the following range of emotions when playing Lady Macbeth: the "terror, the remorse, the hypocrisy of this astonishing being, flitting in frightful succession over her countenance" (131). The annotations by G. J. Bell to a script of *Macbeth* imply that Siddons successfully rendered this spectrum of emotion in breathtakingly short spaces of time.[31] The vocal variations that Bell heard and recorded—Siddons speaking one phrase loudly and another softly within the space of a single line—also suggest the emotional turmoil and complexity of motive that the actress sought to create in her most famous acting role. Instead of performing

Lady Macbeth in a way that held the character out at arm's length, as if to assure spectators that the actress shared in traditional readings of the character as unfemininely ambitious and deplorably shrewish, apparently Siddons looked for contradictions that complicated past readings. Describing her interpretation of the following lines uttered by Lady Macbeth— "He has almost supp'd: why have you [Macbeth] left the chamber?"—Bell writes the following words: "Eager whisper of anger and surprise." This moment, Bell tells us, was quickly followed onstage by Siddons's "inimitable expression of emotion": the "sudden change from animated hope and surprise to disappointment, depression, contempt, and rekindling resentment, is beyond any power but hers" (cited in Jenkin 46).

Siddons's notes provide additional information that can be used to formulate her system of acting. They show that she read the script of *Macbeth* not only from the perspective of Lady Macbeth but from that of her husband as well, a technique that allowed her to inhabit several subject positions in the process of revising her characterization of the wife. In other words, by considering how actors traditionally interpreted Macbeth during the late eighteenth century, she concluded that such interpretations required the Lady to be performed accordingly: as a beautiful and captivating woman, devoted to her husband, willing to listen to his agony, capable of "tenderness and sympathy" ("Remarks" 128), of nobility and graciousness, "of filial as well as maternal love" (127). For such "a combination only, respectable in energy and strength of mind, and captivating in feminine loveliness, could have composed a charm of such potency as to fascinate the mind of a hero so dauntless, a character so amiable, so honourable as *Macbeth*,—to seduce him to brave all the dangers of the present and all the terrors of a future world" (124).

Siddons's apparent desire to let the text dictate her portrayal—rather than vice versa—allowed her to discover, as Lady Macbeth becomes increasingly "agonized by the complicated pangs of terror and remorse" (130), that the character learns to sympathize with another person and to attend to feelings not her own. Siddons's portrayal—at least in her written analysis of the character—suggests that even the seemingly depraved may exhibit in a crisis "striking indications of sensibility" (128). Of the scene between husband and wife in act 3 Siddons writes:

> It is evident, I think, that the sad and new experience of affliction has subdued the insolence of her pride and the violence of her will; for she comes now to seek him out, that she may at least participate in his misery. She knows, by her own woful [*sic*] experience, the torment which he [Macbeth] undergoes,

and endeavours to alleviate his sufferings. . . . Far from her former habits of reproach and contemptuous taunting, you perceive that she now listens to his complaints with sympathizing feelings; and, so far from adding to the weight of his affliction the burthen of her own, she endeavours to conceal it from him with the most delicate and unremitting attention. (128–29)[32]

An additional value that emerges from Siddons's notes on Lady Macbeth is the importance of looking *off* the stage, away from the actual script, in order better to explain some of the reasons why characters are instructed in a particular way. In this sense, closet and public stages are treated as equally important to the process of creating character. Siddons's remarks suggest that the actor playing Lady Macbeth will benefit from imagining the "girlhood" of her heroine, an exercise in which Anna Jameson and Mary Cowden Clarke participated later in the nineteenth century by attempting in their prose narratives to "flesh out" the lives of female characters from Shakespeare. Just as actors today are frequently urged to construct character histories in order to gain a stronger sense of how their character is behaving in the present tense of the play, so Siddons tells us that she put together what might be termed a "past history" for Lady Macbeth, through which she could explain to audiences—and understand for herself—the character's changing behavior during the course of the play. "Let it be here recollected," Siddons writes in reference to Lady Macbeth's intensifying empathy for her husband, ". . . that she had probably from childhood commanded all around her with a high hand; had uninterruptedly, perhaps, in that splendid station, enjoyed all that wealth, all that nature had to bestow; that she had, possibly, no directors, no controllers, and that in womanhood her fascinated lord never once opposed her inclinations" (129).

Because Siddons sought to complicate rather than flatten her characterizations, she was able, by the example of her approach to reading plays, to espouse a method of acting that had implications for living a more enlightened life off the stage. Schooling herself to tolerate negative characters in order to make herself more capable of empathizing with the strange, the threatening, and the despicable, she confessed that she had for several years "perceived the difficulty of assuming a personage [Lady Macbeth] with whom no one feeling of common general nature was congenial or assistant. One's own heart could prompt one to express, with some degree of truth, the sentiments of a mother, a daughter, a wife, a lover, a sister, &c, but to adopt this character must be an effort of the judgment alone" (134). Yet Siddons persisted in trying to suspend her judgment about Lady

Macbeth in order to inhabit the character in a way that would make more humanly explicable her variety of behaviors. Siddons's theory of acting suggests that she shared with Joanna Baillie an affinity for what Baillie described in her theory as "sympathetic curiosity," an approach to viewing character that assumed "the subject or self can be constructed only in relation to other selves, and that knowledge is produced, not from 'objective' or detached observation, but rather from empathetic identification" (Mellor, "Joanna Baillie" 561). When an audience can be persuaded to watch with fascination the inner workings of a threatening character's mind—as in the case of Siddons's Lady Macbeth—it has inevitably to become tolerant long enough to experience the complexity of the tortured soul. Siddons's system of acting implies that the performance of complicated characterizations on the stage can educate spectators in a mode of observing that is more conducive to tolerating the strange, the alarming, and the traditionally ostracized.

In short, Siddons's theory of performing character can be summarized as follows:

> 1. The serious actor spends hours reading a script numerous times and—if playing the role continually—over a period of years, in order to expose the play's subtext, which would include clues about the character's past.[33]
>
> 2. Once in the theater building, the actor does not differentiate between the spaces of "offstage" and "onstage," but instead stays in character throughout the play in order to concentrate on another life and world not the actor's own. (In the memoranda that Siddons gave to biographer Thomas Campbell, she stressed the importance of this technique: "if the representative of Constance shall ever forget, even behind the scenes, those disastrous events which impel her to break forth into the overwhelming effusion of wounded friendship, disappointed ambition, and maternal tenderness . . . [s]he must inevitably fall short of that high and glorious colouring which is indispensable to the painting of this magnificent portrait" [cited in Thomas Campbell 1:244]).
>
> 3. Aware of her audience's expectation that a character's gender identity will be performed according to a prescribed cultural script, Siddons suggested that the actor must refrain from judging a character as much as possible in order to describe, rather than prescribe, a particular mode of behavior.

By recording how she selected particular movements, gestures, and vocal dynamics that captivated her audiences on stage, Siddons gave to subsequent eras invaluable information through which we can still glimpse this particular actor in her closet study as she prepares her performances for the public stage. And because Siddons's approach to acting urges readers to complicate their close readings of both male and female characters, her theory provides us with a perspective that encourages both the literary critic and the actor to adopt some of the skills of the other in the process of exploring the space between text and performance. In this sense, her remarks anticipate the current trend among closet drama revisionists to query how distinctions made between closet and stage have impeded our appreciation of the drama and theater of the early nineteenth century.

Theorizing Acting in Social Space:
The Williams–Jordan Interviews

When studying the contexts surrounding the production of British Romantic women's theater theory, one soon realizes that much of this theory did not survive because women's theorizing about the stage largely occurred during oral exchanges in domestic spaces.[34] Although male writers produced much of their theory in this way—Coleridge comes immediately to mind—little attention has been paid to the fact of this "lost theorizing" or to those texts that describe for us how Romantic theories of the stage were actually created. In the case of women's theorizing, we are more likely to encounter instances such as Charles Lamb provides in his essay, "Barbara S——," in which the narrator *tells* readers, rather than cites directly, the words that "Barbara" (professional actor Frances Maria Kelly) supposedly used in conversation to articulate her approach to acting. Desiring to know the extent to which an actor actually feels emotion on stage, "Elia" narrates how "Barbara" corrected his assumptions:

> She indignantly repelled the notion, that with a truly great tragedian the operation, by which such effects were produced upon an audience, could ever degrade itself into what was purely mechanical. With much delicacy, avoiding to instance in her *self*-experience, she told me that so long ago as when she used to play the part of the Little Son to Mrs. Porter's Isabella (I think it was), when that impressive actress has been bending over her in some heart-rending colloquy, she has felt real hot tears come trickling from her, which (to use her powerful expression) have perfectly scalded her back. (181)

But though Lamb is clearly interested in what "Barbara" says, he leaves out the words she actually spoke, praising instead her "delicacy" in "avoiding to instance in her *self*-experience." Even Kelly's own name is avoided in preference for the fictional "Barbara 'S.'"[35]

By contrast, Kelly's own journals recast certain biographical moments in dialogue form, a move that allows her to chronicle exactly how she asserted her rights as an actress when faced with the theatrical ignorance of a coercive provincial manager. "On one occasion," she wrote, "it was announced that 'Miss Kelly will sing by particular desire the favourite song of "Hope Told a Flattering Tale,"' in character." Kelly records the subsequent exchange as follows:

> "How is it, sir," I said to the manager, "that you have announced me for a song without giving me notice of your intention, or even asking me if I would sing it?"
>
> "The fact is, miss, the song is a great favourite of the Doctor's lady, who was the bespeaker, and it was not until very late last night that she sent to me about it."
>
> "Very well. But what in the name of all that's absurd do you mean by singing 'Hope Told a Flattering Tale,' *in character*?"
>
> "Why, miss, one does sometimes announce a song in character."
>
> "Certainly, when it happens to be a character song. There is no character in this."
>
> "True, miss, but since we have announced it. . . . Oh! I have it. Couldn't you come on leaning on an anchor, a wooden anchor?"
>
> "I told him I should do nothing so ridiculous, but eventually reluctantly consented, in order to fulfill my unsought obligations." (cited in Holman 19–20)

That Kelly writes her story in dialogue form not only gives readers a sense of how she may have sounded when she spoke, but this choice also invites readers in subsequent historical moments to enact Kelly's position without interference from a mediating voice, especially one full of those undisguised biases characteristic of most celebrity memoirs. While the reader can supersede Kelly by interpreting the sound of her voice as written on the page in a variety of ways (none of which may come close to approximating the speaker's actual sound), the dialogue form forces recognition of the fact that there once was a voice that we now associate with a particular actress. We no longer only hear *about* Frances Maria Kelly; we are given a rhetorical form that puts us more fully in her "presence."

It is precisely what Lamb dismisses as "self-experience"—and the recording of that experience—that I have been looking for when studying Romantic women's theater theory. The rarity of documents that describe how women actually went about theorizing the stage, or enacting this process, makes highly important the survival of certain editions of the anonymously written and undated celebrity memoir called *Public and Private Life of the Celebrated Actress . . . Mrs. Jordan*.[36] The Jordan memoir is valuable because particular versions contain the transcriptions of a series of dialogues between Helen Maria Williams (1762–1827) and actress Dorothy Jordan (1761–1816), which took place in the last years of Jordan's life after she fled to France to escape her creditors. Williams's documented admiration of Jordan as the "preeminent" practitioner of naturalistic acting, spontaneous body movement and seemingly unstudied performances, is notable for showing one woman attending to another woman's acting style in a way that expresses her appreciation for the actress's specific memories and generalizations about acting and that also preserves the "theory" of the era's great comedienne. That Williams's and Jordan's theories of the stage survive in a transcription of two women talking together in the privacy of a domestic setting reminds us of where the majority of the theorizing between women in the British Romantic period occurred: in oral exchanges performed on the closet stages of social theater.

Consciously directing her writing to a public audience, Williams explains to readers how this text was composed. After interviewing Jordan at different intervals, she then transcribed both women's words from memory when she returned home, saying at one time to Jordan, "with your permission [I] will, at our next meeting, bring the manuscript for your perusal, in order that you may correct any inaccuracies of which I have been guilty in the progress of the detail" (215). Thus, the text that we have today preserves Williams's *recollection* of her discussions with Jordan, subsequently corrected by Jordan when the actress was permitted to look over the manuscript. Though the extent to which Jordan modified Williams's text or the amount of license she took when writing down these interviews is not clear, Jordan supposedly read and approved them as being an accurate reflection of her views on acting and other stage practices. What we read today, a series of conversations as Williams recalled them from memory, animates the "onstage"/"offstage" distinction I discussed earlier in this chapter. An informal interview is reconstructed in a private setting for a public readership, and thus we see the woman writer negotiating several spaces in an effort to theorize the formal stage.

Early in the first interview, Williams describes herself as employing several strategies apparently calculated to coax Jordan into theorizing about her own performances. One involves her expounding her own thesis on the differences between French and English approaches to tragedy and comedy in an effort to encourage Jordan to concur or disagree. Given that Jordan was the most distinguished British comedienne of her generation, Williams's opening statements about the superiority of French comic actors are rather provocative: "In the walk of comedy," Williams postulates, "I certainly think that the natives of France have to boast *a far greater number of real proficients* than grace the English boards;—there is scarcely a minor theatre in Paris which cannot produce what may justly be termed clever comic performers" (202–3; my emphasis). Tragedy is another case, however, since, according to Williams, "sorrow and melancholy do not form component parts of the Gallic character" (203).

Williams's rather lengthy reflections on the differences between French and English dramaturgy seem designed primarily to lead Jordan comfortably into discussing her past performances. Yet it is interesting to observe that Williams's strategy temporarily places Jordan in the position of interviewer. Thus, initially, we find Jordan (rather than Williams) formulating questions to be answered, such as the following: "May I now inquire what is your estimate of the personification of genteel comedy," Jordan asks, "when drawing a comparison between the two countries?"

One soon discovers, however, that the women move between the two positions during the course of these interviews, sharing the roles of interrogator and respondent until a less formal exchange develops in the shape of a dialogue in which both women are featured as theorists. To start this dialogue in the first interview, Williams responds to Jordan's question cited above by saying: "You now propose a question, Mrs. Jordan, which is not quite so easily answered, because the manners and customs of the two nations vary so much in the common intercourse of society that they may be said to form two stiles particular to themselves." Tracing the contours of the Romantic debate about acting style, she continues:

> For instance, let the leading performers of Sheridan's "School for Scandal," (supposing them perfectly au fait at the French language) undertake the representation of a sterling comedy of this country, and I am thoroughly convinced a complete failure would be the result, and in the same manner reverse the characters, substituting French comedians as representatives of the piece adverted to, and a similar incompetence would be observable.

Jordan replies by restating Williams's thesis: "You therefore give it as your opinion that in genteel comedy each country possesses its peculiarities, and that on the score of histrionic excellence one does not surpass the other." And Williams enthusiastically concurs with Jordan's rephrasing: "I should certainly to the best of my judgment, come to that conclusion, as far as my humble talents can lead me to appreciate between the excellencies in England and France, in the walk of legitimate comedy."

Perhaps owing to the relative succinctness of Williams's answer, it is at this point that Jordan shifts from her position as questioner and begins to assert her own opinions, divulging her views on acting comedy, which Williams has evidently desired to elicit all along. Thus, Jordan:

> Your elucidation of this subject, Miss Williams, has brought to my mind a host of ideas which I had conceived were for ever buried in oblivion. There is, however, no accounting for circumstances, and I really feel at this moment a partial return of that predilection for the theatrical pursuit which was many years back, the predominant characteristic of my life. Ah! those were entrancing days which like pleasing visions of youth are passed away, leaving satisfaction arising from popular applause,—conceive, for instance, an actor in full health, perfectly satisfied with his own acceptation of a character having become spirit, progressing in perfectability of acting in proportion to the rounds of applause that greet his ear at intervals. The piece at length closes, and as he makes his bow, incessant peals of approbation salute him. Place such a scene, Miss Williams before your imagination, and then judge what internal exultation must animate the frame—yes, stimulate the sense to delight bordering upon exstacy.

As Jordan launches into a monologue that reads momentarily like a soliloquy (because Jordan tells us she feels transported and Williams seems temporarily forgotten)—"Ah! those were entrancing days which like pleasing visions of youth are passed away"—the actress seems to seize the stage for herself. But almost immediately she brings her back to the fore by insisting that Williams "[p]lace such a scene . . . before your imagination."

Not only does this directive indicate the value Jordan seems to place on the role of the imagination in making critical judgments but—more significantly in terms of my discussion here—it shows how she, in a kind of collaborative move, attempts to bring Williams into her moment of theorizing. By urging Williams to whip herself up into a sensory frenzy—"stimulate the senses to delight bordering on exstacy"—Jordan invites her to experience some of the pleasurable sensations that Jordan herself evidently enjoyed when she performed for enthusiastic audiences.

Yet Jordan's intensity nearly reduces Williams to silence. In the face of Jordan's experiential authority, Williams can only observe, "How often, my dear madam, has such been most deservedly your envied lot." When reading—and perhaps enacting—this first interview, one could certainly render in a taciturn way Williams's short reply. That is, one could interpret her response to Jordan's monologue as a (grudging) surrender to a competitive conversation in which one person's melodrama effectively inhibits—or cools—the other's fire. But it is equally reasonable to regard Williams's

response as but one example of a number of moments in these two interviews when she and Jordan encourage a mutually supportive scene of theorizing. That is, once Williams has moved Jordan to speak at length about
her own experiences as an actor, she seems content to curtail her initial
volubility, to turn instead to a brief but vivid description of how Jordan
"pronounced . . . conclusive words"; of "the tones of her voice"; of how
she looked as she spoke.

Indeed, Williams's attempts to describe for readers how Jordan looked
and sounded when she spoke about her craft reveal how invested she is in
helping her reading audience to appreciate (and to experience vicariously)
the actual scene in which Jordan creates her theory: "As Mrs. Jordan pronounced these conclusive words," Williams writes, "the tones of her voice
which were all sweetness, obviously faltered, and on fixing my regard upon
her woe-worn countenance I saw the big tear stealing down her cheek,
which she hastily wiped away, and endeavouring to assume an appearance
of sprightliness that ill accorded with her external demeanour, observed"
(and the words that follow are Jordan's): "But I think no more of such
scenes; old women, like myself who are fallen into the sear and yellow leaf,
should count their beads, and betake themselves of prayer and medita-
tions" (203–5). Quoting Jordan, who in turn quotes Shakespeare, Williams
at this juncture resembles an early-nineteenth-century theater manager,
whose task it was to make sure the lead actor was positioned to advantage,
downstage and in full view of the audience. Several times during this first
interview, in fact, it seems as if the self-exiled and heartbroken Jordan—
having fled her creditors and the memories of her abandonment by the
new king—is once again ensconced on a stage where she can let her acting
gifts flow unchecked. And, interestingly, this is a stage in which the tragic
or melodramatic rather than the comic mode dominates, as if Williams had
coached Jordan into experimenting with a new style of performance.

In the second interview, though Williams again sets the scene for Jordan's remarks by telling readers that she and Jordan engaged in "introductory conversation on the leading topics of the day," she does not transcribe
these conversations. This is because her focus is twofold: to help Jordan
theorize about her past performances; and to share with readers how Williams succeeded in getting Jordan to do so. It is unclear what criteria Williams used to determine which comments would later be cited verbatim
in her transcription of the interviews. But what interests me about this
second conversation is the information it gives about how Williams persuaded a depressed actor to share her views about the stage. It is also inter-

esting to examine how Williams, as a writer, attempted to construct her text in a way that would persuade her reading audience to care about what Jordan has to say. By stepping back from the interview and commenting on Jordan's speeches as well as by continuing to ask questions designed to encourage her to reminisce about her former performances, Williams exposes her readers to some of the strategies by which she prompted Jordan to consider her theater career more analytically than she might otherwise have been inclined to do.

In the transcription of this second interview, Williams uses her position as scribe to inform readers about *how* this interview was constructed in the first place: in "order to give a turn to the conversation which I perceived would lead to painful retrospections," Williams tells us, "I immediately resumed the former topic" (208). She does so "by observing" the following to Jordan: "'When alluding to the excellent qualifications of your relation, Mrs. Bland, your own merits in the ballad style should not be passed over in silence, since what is allowed on all hands must necessarily be founded in truth.'" Williams then tells readers that she persisted in her argument in spite of Jordan's seeming desire to change the subject, evidently because she wanted to turn the interview again to the subject of Jordan's own performances:

> —Our actress was on the point of stopping short my remarks, which, however, I would not suffer, but thus continued:—'Nay, nay, you will permit me in turn to utter something in praise of British talent, as you have hitherto wholly engrossed that subject. With all due deference therefore, to the vocal abilities of Mrs. Bland, there is a syren who with equal justice claimed the wreath of fame, and that was no other, Madam, than yourself;—whether for pathos, archness, or persuasion, you stood unmatched on the English boards, and when asserting thus much, what competition can the French adduce in giving utterance to simple and ballad harmony?—As well you might expect from the pen of Helen Maria Williams an epic poem comparable with the effusions of the divine Milton, or a production equally erudite and profound as the "Essay on the Human Understanding," of the philosophic Locke, as to think of hearing a strain warbled with English *naivete* on the boards of a French theatre; ere such a metamorphosis can take place, we can almost expect a revolution in nature, as even simplicity on the theatres of France, is coupled with a species of affectation wholly unconnected with the personification of the peasant's life in our own country.—Such, Mrs. Jordan, are my opinions voluntarily offered from the heart, and however prejudiced you may conceive me to be, from a long association with public manners and customs, I have, nevertheless, I trust, sufficient judgment to discriminate the prominent excellencies existing on either side of the channel. (208–9)

Overriding Jordan's apparently sincere desire to have Williams direct the conversation away from either praise—or analysis—of her acting style, Williams appeals to her reading audience and urges it to compare Jordan's performances favorably to the artificial and mannered style of the French.

To accomplish this aim, Williams ties herself to the deficient French as a means of prompting Jordan to elaborate on the features that defined her performances, and, apparently persuaded, Jordan delivers one of her more forthright statements:

> To say that I was devoid of talent as an actress, would be only begging a compliment; I feel that I must have possessed some share of the ability, or never could the results have ensued, that actually took place; raising me, as I may with truth affirm, from a state of exigency to an ample fortune, and the very pinnacle of popular favor. Notwithstanding all this, my scenic endowments appear to me to have been attended with so little study, and even the points eliciting most applause, were such ebullitions of the moment, that I must regret, as I before stated, they did not merit the comendations [sic] heaped upon them by a generous and open hearted public. (209)

Evoking the opposition between art and nature that structured debates about performances during this period, Jordan describes her own acting as spontaneous: "my scenic endowments appear to me to have been attended with so little study. . . ." But it soon becomes clear that Jordan uses this opposition to devalue her own approach to acting. Like Williams, who describes her potential as an epic poet unfavorably in order to give Jordan the opportunity to theorize center stage, Jordan seems to defer to Williams's opinion by suggesting that good acting requires more study than she found it necessary to do—or at least the appearance of more "art."

That Williams politely ignores Jordan's self-criticism gives the writer another opportunity to celebrate Jordan's naturalistic acting style—what James Boaden called, in reference to the comedienne, "heart in action" (*Life* 1:iii). Prefacing her remarks with a line from the first act of *Hamlet*, "Springes to catch woodcocks," Williams transcribes her response to Jordan's self-criticism at some length, attempting more forcefully than before to describe the kind of performance style she believed Jordan embodied:

> I have now caught you, my dear madam, in the trap laid for you by nature herself;—those very involuntary ebullitions you speak of.—those flashes of intellect, the sterling offsprings of a legitimate talent, were the talismans that ensured the encomiums of a discerning public. Kemble and Siddons commanded applause, and very justly, for their merits were transcendent; but they were excellencies acquired by art and study; all they produced was the

effect of mannerism;—the start, the emphasis, the elevation of the arm, were never varied; once seen, every after attendance presented only a repetition, and for this sterling reason, nature had nothing to do with representation; it was grand, imposing, and I may say at times tinctured with the sublime, and yet it was not what I call the thing—it wanted the finishing, the master touch, TRUTH—the soul of all true acting, NATURE. Mark the difference in Mr. Cooke, who, though an incessant slave, and I may say, constantly bestial-ized by liquor, who never knew the manner in which he should accept a speech until he burst upon the scene; his readings and conceptions being constantly varied, and as uniformly astounding; like a shock of electricity they worked upon his hearers, in short, it was not the performer Cooke but "Richard," "Iago," or the "Pierre" in "Venice Preserved," that stood before you. Such I call the true touchstone of the histrionic art, and in producing this excellence, you, Mrs. Jordan, ranked preeminent; for depend upon it a British audience cannot be entrapped by an ephemeral flash, a mere ignis fatuus:—there must be sterling merit of some description to ensure anything like brilliant success, and all the powers of skepticism to refute. (209–10)

Holding "Nature" as the "soul of all true acting," as "the true touchstone of the histrionic art," Williams's aesthetic portrays Jordan's style of perfor-mance as the antithesis of the Kemble school, with its emphasis on "art and study," "mannerism," codified gesture. Instead, variation, surprise, the appearance of *being* a character, and the ability to perform in a way that frequently worked "like a shock of electricity" upon the audience—these are the qualities in Jordan's acting that Williams attempts in her interview to feature, even to advocate.

Because Williams performed as an appreciative audience for the re-hearsal of Jordan's reveries—because she "crossed the very threshold" into the actor's closet space, to use Anne Mathews's words—she ensured that Jordan's perspective on her past performances would be available to future generations. Personal and philosophical modes converge in this transcrip-tion of narration and dialogue, both forms of which invite the reader to participate in a shared theorizing produced by two women conversing upon the stages of social theater. Had Williams not worked so carefully to engineer a series of interviews that would reveal the particular character of Jordan's commentary, and then to transcribe their dynamic in a way that attempts to capture the actual scene, her view of the importance of Jor-dan's contributions to the British comic acting tradition would have been lost to us, as would the theory of acting that Jordan espoused.

Mary Berry, Social Theater, and "Domestic Drama"

The setting for the Williams–Jordan interviews and the way in which this theorizing was produced remind us to look closely at those qualities and experiences which female social actors shared with their professional counterparts. How did the necessity of cultivating a specific performance of femininity cause some women theorists to consider the facts of their cultural identity as determined by their spatial position? How did these perceived similarities between female professionals and social actors structure women's theoretical discourse and move them to write critically about the extent to which social stages produced their own "private theatricals" and "domestic dramas"? [37]

To bring these questions into focus, I want to end this chapter by looking briefly at excerpts from the writing of one of Joanna Baillie's good friends, biographer and social historian Mary Berry (1763–1852). Not only do sections from Berry's journals and letters help us appreciate more clearly how the cross-pollination of social and professional theaters occurred, but they also provide us with an important context for my subsequent discussion of how Baillie theorized acting.

Like Mary Wollstonecraft (whose use of theatrical metaphors I discussed briefly in Chapter 1), Berry is not a writer who typically comes to mind when one thinks of British Romantic theater, even though she wrote a play, *The Fashionable Friends* (1802), which was performed as both a private theatrical and a professional production in London, and she did act, on occasion, on private stages. Yet she is especially interesting in the context of this study of women's theater theory for having sought outlets for theatrical expression by holding salon-like gatherings in the privacy of her English home. Berry's journals and letters contain numerous instances when—in addition to describing formal plays attended—she also recorded scenes she had witnessed (and participated in) in social theaters, those forums held in domestic space created to encourage improvisational performances among nonactors, whose major focus was the creation of artful conversation.

The editor of Berry's papers, Lady Theresa Lewis, summarized these gatherings as follows:

> For an unusually lengthened period of years she [Berry] formed a centre round which beauty, rank, wealth, power, fashion, learning, and science were gathered; merit and distinction of every degree were blended by her hospitality in social ease and familiar intercourse, encouraged by her kindness and

enlivened by her presence. She was not only the friend of literature and of literary people, but she assiduously cultivated the acquaintance of intellectual excellence in whatever form it might appear, and to the close of her existence she maintained her interest in all the important affairs in life, whether social, literary, or political. Without any remarkable talent for conversation herself, she promoted conversation amongst others, and shed an air of home-like ease over the society which met under her roof. . . . (Berry, *Extracts* 1:xiii)

Lacking, in Lewis's estimation, "any remarkable talent for conversation herself," Berry is nevertheless described as someone who "formed a centre" around which distinguished social actors gathered, and as someone who performed a number of skills—she "blended," "encouraged," "enlivened," "cultivated," "maintained," "promoted," and "shed"—in order to show others' conversational talents to best advantage. Called by Germaine de Stael "by far the cleverest woman in England" (cited in Kunitz 49), Berry set the stage for others' intellectual development "under her roof"—that place of "home-like ease"—and worked "assiduously" to shape the improvisatory discourse of live bodies in relation to a "social, literary, or political" context that she made an object of study throughout her life. Like the English bluestockings of the late eighteenth century,[38] Berry was one of a number of women during the Romantic period who used domestic settings to create a more dramatic and intellectually challenging environment and who encouraged others to explore their own theatrical bent in offstage arenas.

Berry's actions constituted what Sue-Ellen Case has called "personal theatre," in reference to women's attempts throughout history to construct performance rituals in the domestic spaces of their own homes. In Case's view, the eighteenth-century European salon, which Berry's gatherings resembled, was theatrical in the following ways: the "audience was composed . . . of personal friends and interesting acquaintances, who came specifically to engage in social dialogue with one another," and actors . . . who created their own lines and listened to the original dialogue of the others" replaced the playwright and the "passive audience member." The predominant feature that distinguished the salon from stagings in traditional theaters was the fact that the women in charge "played all the parts involved in theatrical production" (*Feminism and Theatre* 47). In contrast to British private theatricals, which though hospitable to women's participation followed a formalized script, Berry's "salons" encouraged the cultivation of what Case calls "the dialogue of present time" (46). This is an interchange "built on mutuality and intersubjectivity," which "operates not by mimesis but by enactment"[39] and is "an engaged dialogue, rooted in everyday life" (47). Such an improvised dialogue, as I have suggested above in discussing the interviews between Helen Maria Williams and Dorothy Jordan, was especially conducive to the production of women's theater theory because it encouraged a shared, spontaneous discourse in a relatively familiar and privatized setting.

Berry did not, of course, possess Case's positive perspective on her creation of personal theater. She could not readily appreciate how her social involvement partook of a theatrical tradition of women experimenting with space and form to create alternative approaches to formal stages, and therefore she was deeply confused about the cultural worth of those activities over which women presided in the domestic sphere, even as she stated that she longed for the cultural validation that a fulfilling life in the private realm could provide. Yet the dramatic monologues contained in Berry's journals and letters reveal a strong strain of awareness that a certain class of women who desired "regular employment" had to deal with what it means culturally to be identified as a "feminine woman" during the early nineteenth century. While this realization seems only to have intensified the often despairing tone of Berry's private discourse, her personal writings are remarkably revealing about the fact that she regarded her social position as a role she often hated performing.

Contemplating ways to be "useful," productive, indeed "powerful," Berry imagined turning from social theaters to practicing the art of poignantly chronicling her own desires and subsequent disappointments. "O for the power of involving myself in fiction and throwing aside (for the time at least) all the dull realities of life!" (2:314), Berry apostrophized in one of her letters. Yet she was conflicted about the worth of writing at all. As Strachey observed, "Had she been a man . . . *she would not have shone as a writer*, but as a political thinker or an administrator; and a man she should have been; with her massive, practical intelligence, she was born too early to be a successful woman" (cited in Kunitz 50; my emphasis). "I have hitherto avoided [keeping a journal]," Berry confessed, "because I felt ashamed of the use, or rather *the no-use*, I made of my time,—of the miserable minute duties and vexations which at once occupied and corroded my mind—of the manner in which I have let my life slip by me, and missed its present enjoyments, by always aiming at and acting for some indefinite future" (2:318; my emphasis).

On the one hand, Berry's inability to regard her social theater as substantive and productive contributed to her feeling that her existence was "long and insignificant" (2:4). Yet, on the other hand, Berry confesses in her journals that she had at one time, when believing she would eventually marry, "looked forward to a future existence which I felt, for the first time, would have called out *all the powers* of my mind and all the warmest feelings of my heart" (2:3; my emphasis). This belief in marriage as the greatest repository for the energies of the woman who wants both bodily and mental challenge partakes of the early-nineteenth-century view of "home . . . [as] the chief focus of women's mission" (Anthony Fletcher 399) and colors Berry's description of an imaginary couple in her biography of Lady Rachel Russell:

> surely, . . . intellectual beings of different sexes were intended by their Great Creator to go through the world together;—thus united, not only in hand and heart, but in principles, in intellect, in views, and in disposition—each pursuing one common and noble end, their own improvement, and the happiness of those around them, by the different means appropriate to their sex and situation;—mutually correcting, sustaining and strengthening each other; undegraded by all practices of tyranny on the one part, and of deceit on the other; each finding a candid but severe judge in the understanding, and a warm and partial advocate in the heart of their companion; secure of a refuge from the vexations, the follies, the misunderstandings and the evils of the world, in the arms of each other, and in the inestimable enjoyments of unlimited confidence and unrestrained intimacy. (2:4)

Portraying marriage as a union of "intellectual beings" whose "common and noble" goal is "their own improvement, and the happiness of those around them," Berry imagines a pairing of different (but politically equal) sensibilities, the wedding of which eradicates "degradation," "tyranny," and "deceit" and fortifies the couple against "the evils of the world." It is through such a marriage, Berry suggests, that she might have been able to do her best "work," and this work would not necessarily have involved writing or managing social theaters.[40]

Berry's personal reflections in her journals and letters provide a dramatic backdrop for her theoretical formulations, which turn on a paradox common to Romantic women writers who generalized about the London stage: whereas Berry's personal writing pictured actual domestic stages as arenas in which women played their most important and fulfilling roles, her formal theater theory devalued domestic drama. Berry's journals and letters reveal that she viewed plays about "private sufferings" and "the herd of griefs unparticipated by the world" as incapable of elevating the human spirit or of inspiring audiences to value a "higher" sensibility. Her generalizations about French neoclassicism—her resistance to the growing trend to stage melodramas in England ("the staple fare of working-class theatres" [Booth, *English Plays* 25]) and the *comédie larmoyante* and *drame bourgeois* in France—resulted in a theory of dramaturgy that echoes many of the major treatises on theater written during the eighteenth century.

In the first volume of *A Comparative View of the Social Life of England and France: From the Restoration of Charles the Second to the French Revolution* (1828), a study that combines historical, sociological, and anthropological perspectives, Berry heralds French neoclassicism's emphasis on the general (or universal) and the "elevated." To formulate her definitions of tragedy and comedy, which she then uses to demonstrate why France surpasses England when it comes to creating tragic drama, Berry writes that Shakespeare may be "a great moral teacher" (191), but he is an exception. By contrast, his Renaissance contemporaries—"Johnson [*sic*], Massinger, Shirley, Decker, Rowley, Beaumont and Fletcher, Ford, Webster, Field, and Marlow [*sic*]" (192)—chose subjects that "seem often to have been determined only by an excess of crimes and cruelties in the conduct of their principal personages, without sufficiently considering whether the action which calls them forth is *dramatic* as well as *natural*" (195). French dramatists, however, in treating horrific subjects, tend to concentrate their "whole art . . . in concealing" their subject, "as in nature such crimes must always seek concealment, and betray themselves only as the author exhibits them, in their dreadful effects on the moral being and happiness of his personages" (197). It is the French, Berry argues, who appropriately

> boast of the conduct and tone of their tragic muse; the elevation of her sentiments, the delicacy with which they are always expressed, the purity of her morals, and the dignity of her tone, always completely separated from that of her comic sister. It is true that, for a long time, she [the muse] never spoke but from the mouths of heroes, kings, or ministers, and is accused by her English detractors of being often, in her long-winded tirades, as tedious and as little interesting as those illustrious personages have, in subsequent ages, sometimes in reality appeared. . . . However true these accusations may be, and however the French theatre, in times subsequent to those of which we are speaking, may have advanced nearer towards the truth of what may be called *theatrical nature*, it is certain, that, on our theatre, some subsequent attempts to *unbuskin* tragedy, and to strip her entirely of the "gorgeous pall," which the pure taste of Milton (in spite of his republican severity) required for her attire, have been completely unsuccessful. (197–99)

Recapitulating the English critique of French neoclassicism as "long-winded," "tedious," antidemocratic, and uninteresting, Berry nevertheless prefers French drama for its dignified conduct and tone, its "elevated" sentiments, its moral "purity," its strict delineation of comic and tragic genres. Though French dramaturgy "may have advanced nearer towards the truth of what may be called *theatrical nature*"—that is, an artificial acting style in which declamation dominates—Berry is thankful that English stages have thus far been unsuccessful in posing a challenge to the principles of the classical tradition, even though they have tried to "unbuskin" tragic plays.

In a subsequent passage, this bias in favor of French neoclassicism causes Berry to view the domestic tragedies of George Lillo as problematic because they are "founded on catastrophes which had actually taken place in private life" (199). "The close adherence to individual and unelevated nature," Berry writes, "undignified by any previous distinction, and unaccompanied by any ennobling circumstances; the poverty necessary to be observed in the dresses and the absence of all species of decoration from the scene; although all strictly natural and obligatory, according to the subject chosen, were in direct opposition to dramatic effect, and essentially lessened the interest of [Lillo's *The Fatal Curiosity*]" (199–200).

For Berry, the problem lies not in the realism of domestic drama but rather in the fact that domestic subjects strike her as insufficient to instruct spectators in the development of moral sympathy. "Even *The Gamester*," Berry writes, "a story that comes home to every bosom, and which is likely to occur every day in the circles around us, as a drama, wants that previous elevation of sentiment and situation which is requisite to ennoble our sorrows and the misery of those who excite them."

> Could it be possible for *private sufferings, and the herd of griefs unparticipated by the world*, to become the subjects of tragedy, tragedy would immediately cease to be resorted to as an amusement. What human being may not inwardly say, "Too much *such* sorrow hast thou had already?" The most acutely-feeling minds will, therefore, always be those who require the greatest degree of elevation of sentiment, in fictitious calls on their sympathy. (200–201; my emphasis)

Berry here summarizes a prominent view in eighteenth-century British theater theory—lofty subjects supposedly elevate the human spirit—in order to argue that a focus on "private sufferings," the "herd of griefs unparticipated by the world," has no place in tragedies that would instruct "the most acutely-feeling minds" or the finer sensibilities of a discerning audience. Her bias for French dramaturgy, her disapproval of the realistic and domestic strains of the English dramatic tradition, places Berry in the unlikely position of seeming to align herself against the paradigm that associated France "with excessive faith in theory" as well as with feminist radicalism and sexually explicit German plays (Simpson 82, 91).

Yet, even as Berry seems to eschew domestic dramas and the display of "private sufferings" on the stage, the problem of women's domestic sorrows figures prominently in her most vivid private writing, as we have seen. Her willingness to explore the dramatic contours of her own melancholy complicates her more public assertions about domestic drama and reveals that an alternative theory of the stage emerges from her closet, one in which domestic dramas are deeply valued for at least seeming to provide talented women like Berry with productive and creatively fulfilling roles. That Berry's formal theory appears alongside her social commentary, one context complicating the other, reminds us to look closely at how Romantic women writers drew upon their experiences of closet stages in order to analyze their relationship to public theater.

Mathews's exploration of celebrity, Siddons's remarks on performing female characters, Williams's and Jordan's interviews about acting, Berry's discussions of neoclassicism and domestic drama—these are only a few instances of a pervasive, if largely implicit, pre–twentieth-century women's theater theory waiting to be discovered in, and collected from, the closet spaces of a variety of genres. As scholars continue to investigate the work done by women in late-eighteenth- and early-nineteenth-century theater, we will come to understand more fully the extent to which numerous women analyzed playwrighting, staging, managing-directing, costuming, acting, and theatre reviewing in both overt and indirect ways. We will also begin to appreciate in more detail how this theory influenced the rhetoric of Romantic writers as they explored their relationship to public and private arenas. By focusing on the preface writing of Joanna Baillie, one of the period's most important theater artists, and discussing it in the context of other female playwrights who contemplated their gendered position in public theater, the next chapter sets the stage for an analysis in Chapters 4 and 5 of some of the ways in which Baillie's dramaturgy enacts a theory of acting and provides a dramatic example of how the closet/stage dichotomy has been used since the Romantic period to hide from view the exciting range of Romantic women's theater theory.

3. Joanna Baillie's Theater of the Closet: Female Romantic Playwrights and Preface Writing

> . . . Our Author is a Female; once before,
> The culprit dar'd your Mercy to implore.
> To splendid Talents she lays no pretence,
> But writes, what Nature dictates, *Common Sense*.
> . . . If scenes domestic, can afford delight,
> You'll not withold your suffrage on this Night.
> Critics, for once, relax the censor's frown—
> It were not manly, Sirs, *to strike a woman down*!
> Confirm those Hopes, which Truths have long convey'd,
> By pard'ning Errors, which *ourselves* have made.
>   —E. J. Eyre, "Prologue," Marianne Chambers's *Ourselves* (1811)

When, in E. J. Eyre's prologue to Marianne Chambers's (fl. 1799–1811 or 1812) comedy *Ourselves* (1811), the speaker announces that the author is female, a set of statements follows that tropes the woman writer as a "culprit" for "daring" to appear before an audience: she has no "splendid Talents" but only takes "dictation" from Nature by writing "common sense"; her dramatic focus is predictably the domestic sphere; critics demonstrate their "manliness" by showing "mercy" toward this female trespasser, by "relaxing" their standards of judgment, and by permitting her to make "errors" in front of a theater audience.

That British female playwrights were still being regarded as "culprits" during the late eighteenth and early nineteenth centuries caused some of them, in their play prefaces, dedications, and advertisements, to portray themselves as "anxious" and "trembling" before the prospect of public representation.[1] Whether or not Romantic women perceived the London stage as accessible (based on their personal experiences), many prefaced their plays with language that alluded to—if not directly addressed—the difficulties women encountered when they chose to offer their work up to public scrutiny. Although Charlotte Smith (1749–1806) tried to assure those who "have a Turn for Dramatic Composition, that the formidable and repulsive Tales of Delay and Difficulty, incident to a Communication with Managers, are not always to be credited,"[2] Felicia Hemans, by contrast, stated in 1828 that "in this age . . . dramatic triumph seems of all others the most difficult" (cited in Chorley 1:229). And in an earlier letter to H. H. Milman, as she readied one of her plays for production, Hemans used language that implied her initiation into the theater business had been traumatic: she confessed "a most devout horror of the whole race of managers" and told Milman that "I begin to look at them very much in the light of so many Ogres, and to feel that it will be almost sufficient cause for self-gratulation, if I put my head into the wolf's jaws and escape unhurt" (1:65–66). More succinctly, in her preface to the *Moral Dramas Intended for Private Representation* (1790), Anne Hughes (fl. 1784–1790) complained that the "Stage is accessible to few." Sophia Lee (1750–1824), author of the financially successful *The Chapter of Accidents* (1796) starring Sarah Siddons, wrote of her "awe" and "deference" in "ventur[ing] . . . to bring a Tragedy before the Publick" and of her discouragement with managers of the stage (whom we would today call "producers"): "life opened gradually upon me, and dissipated the illusions of the imagination," she says, when she "learnt that merit merely is a very insufficient recommendation to managers in general . . . and as I had neither a prostituted pen or person to offer Mr. Harris, I gave up, without a trial, all thoughts of the drama, and sought an humble home in Bath, resolving to bury in my own heart its little talent, and be a poor anything, rather than a poor author" (iv). That Lee would give up all thoughts of the drama when her play made enough money to help finance a school in Bath with her sister Harriet[3] suggests how disturbing the process of play production could be for women, even when lucrative. In the Advertisement to her first play, *The New Peerage* (1787), Harriet Lee (1757–1851) epitomizes the notes of anxiety sounded in women's play prefaces composed in the late eighteenth and early nineteenth centuries by writing that the "Apprehensions that must ever attend a Woman on making a first Effort in the Drama, become justly heightened when one thinks of committing it to the Press, Precluded, by Sex, from the deep Observation of Life, which gives Strength to Character, or Poignancy to Expression, it will be difficult, even in her own Opinion, to supply the Deficiency; and it is from the Indulgence of the Publick only that she can hope, what she dares not expect, from their Judgment."

It is helpful for a moment to revisit the fiercely articulated antagonism toward the stage of one of Baillie's unexpected admirers, Lord Byron, since his responses help to explain to some degree why many women who either wrote plays, acted on stage, or simply liked seeing dramas performed felt the necessity of trying to come to terms with the role of spectatorship in their professional lives. As I will discuss below, while Baillie asserts herself more confidently in her preface writing than a number of the women referred to here, she shares with them a willingness to express her trepidation about play production, confessing in her "Introductory Discourse" that she was "about to bring before the public a work with doubtless, many faults and imperfections in its head" (1). When her plays were first published anonymously, Hester Piozzi commented that the tone of Baillie's preface "caused the critics to decide that the dramas were written by a learned man" (Carhart 70). Yet Baillie's discourse clearly shows her to be a product of the same cultural context that caused many women playwrights to write disparagingly of their efforts to participate in the theater arts. If even Byron expressed fears about the responses of playgoers—he who expertly manipulated social spectators until, when he could push them no longer to tolerate his exploits, dramatically and flamboyantly withdrew to a self-enforced exile on the Continent—then it should be easier to understand why some women would view the theatrical medium as potentially detrimental to their social reputations and emotional well-being. Conditioned not to seek public attention, women playwrights and actors often found it particularly unnerving to meet the critical gaze of certain vociferous individuals. But even more daunting was the possibility that an entire auditorium could decry a woman's political allegiances or personal behavior.

Coupled with their sense of trespass as women traversed the boundary that tried strictly to delineate public from private stages was the fact of the traditional, and (by a number of accounts) increasing, rambunctiousness of London theater audiences, a feature of play production that evidently cowed even such a self-dramatizing personality as Lord Byron. Having been what we would today call the literary manager for Drury Lane theater in 1815 (the year he tried to get Baillie's play *De Monfort* remounted), Byron knew from firsthand experience how vulnerable playwrights were to audience approval, and in his preface to *Marino Faliero, Doge of Venice* (1821) he wrote that he preferred not to endure "the trampling of an intelligent or of an ignorant audience on a production which, be it good or bad, has been a mental labour to the writer" (499). What contemporary British director Peter Brook has famously heralded as the aim of his theatrical productions—"immediacy"[4]—seems to have frightened Byron. The "sneering reader, and the loud critic, and the tart review, are scattered and distant calamities," he wrote. In contrast, onstage production is "a palpable and *immediate* grievance, heightened by a man's doubt of [the audience's] competency to judge, and his certainty of his own impudence in electing them his judges" (my emphasis). "Were I capable of writing a play which could be deemed stage-worthy," Byron continued, "success would give me no pleasure, and failure great pain" (499).[5] This antipathy to sitting through an audience's live responses to his dramatic work resulted in Byron's advocating what he called "mental theatre," a phrase contemporary critics have variously interpreted to mean (*a*) plays that focus on the drama of the inner life; and/or (*b*) the reader's act of creating theater in the mind by reading drama in the privacy of the closet study.[6]

The degree to which Byron's plays are antitheatrical is subject to debate. But the point I want to make here is that his theoretical retreat from the stage to the closet underlines an important aspect of women's participation in British Romantic theater: although there were many discouragements to doing so, a number of women faced the challenges of moving from their private closets to public stages and back again, arguing the importance of both stages for educating audiences about the performative features of gender.[7]

In order to defend their position as transgressive women, in their dramatic prefaces Romantic women playwrights anticipated the recent trend among (feminist) historians and theorists to precede their critical analyses by discussing their cultural position, or "positionality."[8] While it would be misleading to suggest that Romantic writers theorized their gendered relationship to the London stage with the same self-reflexivity as late-twentieth-century writers, their discourse does convey a nascent consciousness of how the necessity to behave as "feminine" affected their relationship to the theater arts, and for this reason their writing merits close analysis for the information it yields about the degree to which Romantic writers perceived of gender as something that was "practised"—to recall Hannah More's word—or performed, to use a more contemporary term.

Jill Dolan and Sue-Ellen Case, both of whom have produced a body of rich theoretical material about the theater, have been especially vigilant about confronting ways in which their socially constructed position in a cultural matrix informs their critical narratives. Here is Dolan using "the mode of address of positionality" (Case, *Performing Feminisms* 6) in the preface she wrote to *The Feminist Spectator as Critic* (1988). "In publication," she asserts, "it seems equally important to take a stand and to state it at the outset of one's writing." For this reason, she explains, she has "tried continually to clarify my stance and my ideological, political, and personal investments in the studies that follow. I write from my own perspective as a white, middle-class woman, with every effort to stay aware of and change my own racism and attitudes about class. As a Jew and a lesbian, I also write from my own awareness of exclusion from dominant ethnic and heterosexual discourse" (x).

Although not nearly as explicit as Dolan's statements, the prefaces of Romantic women playwrights reveal that they similarly sought to establish a "connection" with readers before their texts were negotiated, one that would draw empathetic attention to their experience, as women, in professional theaters. In her "General Preface" to the eleven-volume edition of her collected works (1830), for example, Hannah More writes that "between him who writes and him who reads there must be a kind of *coalition of interests*, something of a *partnership*, however unequal the capital, in mental property; a sort of *joint stock of tastes and ideas*" (my emphasis). The establishment of this "partnership" is often the focus of the woman preface writer, who—like an actor stepping out of character to address the audience about what it sees on stage—seeks to create an alliance by confessing her anxieties about the public nature of her enterprise.

The anxiety of Romantic women playwrights emerges as prescient when one realizes that, as recently as the last fifteen years, women have written a good deal about the emotional strains encountered by late-twentieth-century women playwrights. Using the trope of the closet to describe the process of emerging as a playwright into public view, dramatist Michelene Wandor confessed in 1981 that "theatre is plainly a difficult field for women to write in": "the playwright must in a sense 'come out' more publicly than the novelist" (126). Yet even when "coming out" into the public forum has been achieved, other inhibitions on women's creative expression still persist. Gayle Austin's 1990 study of how feminist theory can enrich dramatic criticism tries to explain why "we are not used to associating women with playwrighting": it is because the "writing of plays requires mastering to some degree a male-dominated, public production machinery, something that relatively few women have been able to do over the long history of the form, and consequently there is not as large a body of extant plays by women as there is of novels" (2).

As recently as 1993, Ellen Donkin and Susan Clement wondered why, even among feminists working in the theater, "women are persuaded to abandon their truths" (3) when directing classical dramas that would reinforce sexist assumptions about women. Their conclusion is that women are still laboring under "a powerful desire to please, to be pleasing" (3), which is "connected to a presence" that they call "Big Daddy" (after the character in Tennessee Williams's play *Cat on a Hot Tin Roof*)—that is, "a form of cultural conditioning that floats in and among real men and women and has profound implications for their artistic work and their relationships with each other" (4). Women in particular have "internalized" the "cultural formations" that have disempowered them, "even when the overt exclusion of women wanting professional access and identity is no longer an issue" (4). That today it is not unusual to find women theater artists inhibiting their own progress and that of other female colleagues by adhering to traditional models for feminine behavior may help us better understand why Romantic women who wrote about their relationship to London theater were so preoccupied with *the act* of emerging from private into public space.

In discussing Romantic women's play prefaces, we must not forget that tradition demanded from both male and female playwrights a certain amount of performed obsequiousness. Using the occasion of publishing her collected works to express her cynicism about the authenticity of most prefatory voices, Hannah More expressed irritation about this tradition of self-debasement:

> It may not, it is presumed, be thought necessary to apologise for the publi-
> cation of this collection, by enumerating all the reasons which produced it.
> "Desire of friends," is now become a proverbial satire; the poet is driven from
> that once creditable refuge, behind which an unfounded eagerness to appear
> in print used to shelter itself; . . . The author professes his inability but he pro-
> duces his book; and by the publication itself controverts his own avowal of
> alleged incapacity. It is to little purpose that the words are disparaging while
> the deed is assuming. Nor will that profession of self-abasement be much re-
> garded which is contradicted by an act that supposes self-confidence. ("Gen-
> eral Preface" in *Works*)

But convention does not solely account for the frequency with which women artists cast themselves as innocents initiated into the world of experience by a sometimes kindly, often inattentive actor-manager (or male friend or relative) who urges them to appear before the public against their modesty or better judgment.[9] The authentic sense of trespass that many women artists communicated about the act of playwrighting provides a contrast with More's assumption that the person who publishes necessarily possesses "self-confidence."

The prominence of certain women in late-eighteenth- and early-

nineteenth-century London theaters can cause us to minimize the difficult position of the majority. But if we skim over women's complaints and
concerns about their position in British theatrical culture, we may fail to
register that the articulation of this anxiety was a potent rhetorical strategy
adopted by women writers to discuss theatrical politics indirectly, as well
as a way to theorize about the culture's representation of female actors,
characters, and playwrights. Because prefaces yield moments "in which
social attitudes about gender [can] be made visible" (Diamond 91), these
documents emerge as significant repositories of a female-authored theory
in which enculturated fears about participating in theater were identified
and subtly critiqued.

In 1854, thirty years after Mary Russell Mitford (1787–1855) composed
four dramas for the English Romantic stage, she described the prefatory
tradition as follows:

> The Prefaces of the great Laureate indeed would be difficult to imitate, inas-
> much as they contain some of the finest prose in the language. They consist,
> for the most part, of noble and generous criticism, strangely mingled with
> theories dear to the merry Monarch, with vindications of the practice of inter-
> fusing licentious farce amidst real tragedy, and preference for the rhymes of
> Corneille to the blank verse of Shakespeare. . . . [This] forms the ground-
> work of most dramatic Prefaces, largely blended with skilful specimens of the
> noble art of self-justification, with vehement attacks upon critics, and per-
> petual grumblings against managers and actors, and all that was done and all
> that was not done for the pieces that follow. (*Dramatic Works* 1:vi–vii)

Mitford identifies Dryden's critical generosity, political astuteness (his in-
clusion of "theories dear to the merry Monarch"), his "vindications" and
defense of certain "preferences," as the means to characterize preface writers
in general, many of whom—in Mitford's view—overpraise themselves, re-
taliate against their critics, and complain about how their plays are staged.
The preface she attached to her collected dramas takes a different approach
by placing centerstage the story of Mitford's relationship to composition
and publication.[10] Mitford also employs the persona of the ambivalent
woman writer as a means of foregrounding the conditions under which
Romantic women playwrights produced their art. "How he [Francis Ben-
noch] chanced upon these plays of mine, I hardly know," Mitford begins.

> I think he picked them up in the library of a great country-house where he
> was visiting. They had fallen into such utter oblivion, that I also might have
> forgotten them, but for an occasional dream, too vague to be called a hope,
> that in the brief moment of kindly indulgence, which follows the death of any
> one who has contributed, however slightly, to the public amusement, some

friend might gather them together in the same spirit that prompts the string-
ing verses into an epitaph. To edite these tragedies to myself, seems a kind of
anachronism, not unlike engraving the inscription upon my own tombstone.
I can only pray that my poor plays may be mercifully dealt with as if they were
indeed published by my executor, and the hand that wrote them were laid in
peaceful rest. (*Dramatic Works* 1:vi)

Though one could read these words playfully—a little later, in fact, Mitford tells the reader that she has "no mind to forfeit so pleasant a privilege"
as the tradition of indulging "in the permitted egoism of a rambling preface" (1:vi)—the vocabulary and images that she uses suggest a more somber
performance of these lines. Here the preface writer creates a persona clearly
conflicted about the desirability of publishing her "poor plays." In one
breath she entertains the "dream" of having died so that she might "merit
a brief moment of kindly indulgence" from her male friend, Francis Bennoch,[11] who—fulfilling the office of executor—will take all responsibility
for publication from her shoulders. Yet she also identifies her discovered
plays as residing in a country-house library, rendering them part of the
established male literary tradition. In one sense Mitford's plays are out of
circulation even as they are housed comfortably, but in another they have
been "canonized" as part of a valuable cache of books that will be passed on
to future generations. By synecdochizing herself as "the hand that wrote
[these tragedies]"—which she imagines "laid in peaceful rest"—Mitford
creates an image that isolates her desire both to distance herself from and
call attention to the fact of her authorship. Both solely—and only—a composing hand, in Mitford's fantasy the female playwright is also imagined as
de-composing, in the sense of having been "laid to peaceful rest" in some
sepulchre.[12]

   Such an image, while troubling, perfectly captures the ambivalence of
female playwrights toward participating in London theater. Even as they
sought shelter in the small, enclosed rooms of domestic spaces where a
long tradition of female theater and drama has been produced, women like
Mitford nevertheless put themselves forward into the public eye, describing, often forthrightly, their terror at such a move.

Elizabeth Inchbald's Critical Prefaces and the Position of the Female Critic

Referring to the 125 prefaces that Elizabeth Inchbald composed for John
Bell's *The British Theatre* (1806–9), Katharine Rogers writes that they are

"most interesting for what they reveal about [Inchbald] herself—as an individual and as a woman who had achieved great success in a man's world and yet was intent on maintaining femininity as her contemporaries defined it" (278).[13] I am also drawn to these documents, but because of what they reveal about Inchbald's view of the position of the early-nineteenth-century female critic, a perspective that contextualizes my discussion below of Joanna Baillie's prefatory remarks. Inchbald's portrayal of herself as a critic is often in conflict with her preference for dramatic heroines of self-effacing rectitude, who—rather than challenging the critical establishment—submerge themselves in the task of supporting the creative and intellectual endeavors of men. Her analysis of her own criticism, on the other hand, shows her challenging the standard of femininity in which critical assertions by a woman in any field of study were considered not only useless but harmful to women's emotional health and political stability.

When playwright George Colman the Younger became upset with Inchbald over the comments she made on his plays, she printed the letters they exchanged as a means of defending herself against his accusations. Like Wollstonecraft in *A Vindication of the Rights of Men* (1790)—who tried to distance herself from Burke's arguments by performing with her prose style a critique of his "courtly insincerity" ("I have not yet learned to twist my periods," wrote Wollstonecraft, "nor, in the equivocal idiom of politeness, to disguise my sentiments, and imply what I should be afraid to utter" [5])—Inchbald defended her critical choices by satirizing Colman's feigned gallantry even as she genuinely worried about having offended him.

First, she presents us with Colman's faux chivalry: he writes that his dramas have "had *the honour* [my emphasis] to be somewhat singed, in passing the fiery ordeal of feminine fingers . . . which it grieves me to see destined to a rough task, from which your manly contemporaries in the drama would naturally shrink. Achilles, when he went into petticoats, must have made an awkward figure among females;—but the delicate Deidamia never wielded a battle-axe to slay and maim the gentlemen."[14] Colman goes on to ask why Inchbald did not "apply" to him first before pointing out faults in his work. If she had only done so, he writes in language suggesting that Inchbald should be absorbed with the rituals of courtship rather than of critical judgment, then Colman "should have been as zealous to save you trouble as a beau to pick up your fan—I could have easily pointed to *twenty* of my blots, in the *right* places, which have escaped you in the labour of discovering *one* in the wrong."

Next, in a very deft and poignant reply, Inchbald portrays herself as a female writer deeply sensitive to her precarious position in order ultimately to mock Colman's views. She wonders how "'my manly contemporaries in the drama'" could be so offended by "the illiterate" of which she, "an unlettered woman," is a member, even as she states (sincerely) that she rues the circumstances that resulted in her taking on this project. The following confession recalls the note of familiar anxiety that structures the prefaces of other Romantic women playwrights:

> In one of those unfortunate moments, which leave us years of repentance, I accepted an overture, to write from two to four pages, in the manner of preface, to be introduced before a certain number of plays, for the perusal, or information, of such persons as have not access to any diffuse compositions, either in biography or criticism, but who are yet very liberal contributors to the treasury of a theatre. Even for so humble a task I did not conceive myself competent, till I submitted my own opinion to that of the proprietors of the plays in question.

Because Inchbald "submitted her own opinion" to others in the case of assessing plays that had not "gone through various editions," she writes that she assumed "no one dramatist could possibly be offended"; after all, these "cursory remarks" were produced by "a female observer," and any "injudicious critique of such female might involve her own reputation, (as far as a woman's reputation depends on being a critic,) but could not depreciate the worth of the writings upon which she gave her brief intelligence and random comments." Rather than Colman's getting upset at the content of these critical remarks, Inchbald suggests that he should take comfort in the fact that these judgments were penned by a woman. Certainly the female critic has no inappropriate expectations of achieving any kind of critical authority: instead, the prefaces' "only hoped-for recommendation" lies in the "*novelty of the attempt*" (my emphasis).

Although Inchbald was genuinely upset about the possibility of having rendered what Colman believed was injudicious criticism—to the point where, as P. M. Zall has stated, she declined to write criticism after this incident[15]—in her letter to Colman she defended the idea that a woman could produce valuable critical commentary. Yet to assert the worth of her own enterprise, she called into question her own achievement as a female critic. We have encountered this strategy before in this study, in the interviews between Helen Maria Williams and Dorothy Jordan (see Chapter 2), when Williams aligned herself with a style of writing she devalued in order to point up Jordan's strengths as an actor. Inchbald

addresses Colman as follows: "Permit me, notwithstanding this acquiescence in your contempt for my literary acquirements, to apprise you, that
in comparing me, as a critic, with Madame Dacier, you have, inadvertently,
placed yourself, as an author, in the rank with Homer. I might as well aspire
to write remarks on 'The Iliad,' as Dacier condescend to give comments
on 'The Mountaineers'" (2:113). Adopting Colman's strategy of criticizing her by comparing her critical skills unfavorably with an allegedly more
accomplished female critic, Anne Dacier (1654–1720), Inchbald attempts
to expose Colman's pomposity by suggesting that she and Colman occupy
a similarly low artistic status. Yet in the process she also tries to demonstrate that women critics of the era can be positioned prominently, as
critics of such importance that they would not "condescend" to talk about
(even) male-authored plays. Such a rhetorical performance helps Inchbald
to assert—to use Anna Jameson's words cited in Chapter 1—the "value of
[women's] criticism," even while appearing to sacrifice her own achievement to make the point.

Throughout her prefaces, Inchbald gives us information about how
she believed dramatic criticism should be practiced.[16] One of her central
tasks as critic, she theorizes, is to teach her reading audiences to consider
the differences between public and private forums without ultimately eschewing (or devaluing) the other. It is the movement *between* closet and
stage that Inchbald models as a critic, for the purpose, it would seem, of
urging greater appreciation for two arenas often opposed and hierarchized.
Though she considers the perspective of the closet reader in her remarks,
she also assumes that such a reader wants to know more about the professional stage. To this end, Inchbald demonstrates her interest in the bifurcated character of dramatic literature—hovering between text and performance—by frequently citing the performance history of a particular play
and providing information about the playwright's life relevant to a play's
composition. She also includes anecdotes about actors' experiences in playing certain roles and her own observations about specific performances. In
formulating her theory of dramatic criticism, then, Inchbald suggests that
the experience of reading or seeing plays enhances the activity of doing
either, and that an understanding of the differences between closet and
stage—the ways in which these spaces are equally important for the theater
artist—are indispensable requirements for producing useful criticism.

Stating that her project is to "send forth" plays "from the stage to the
closet" ("Remarks on Richard Cumberland's *First Love*"), Inchbald would
seem to be echoing other critics of the era who preferred reading plays to

seeing them performed. But in many of her prefatory remarks, Inchbald suggests that her critical judgment about a particular play script has been formed as *both* a reader and a theatergoer, through a process in which she, like Anne Mathews, moves self-consciously between closeted and public spaces. Of John O'Keeffe's *The Castle of Andalusia* she writes that a "reader must be acquainted with O'Keeffe on the stage, to admire him in the closet." Edward Moore's *The Gamester* "is calculated to have a very different effect upon the stage and in the closet." Arthur Murphy's *The Grecian Daughter* has "been so rapturously applauded on the stage, and so severely criticised in the closet, that it is a task of peculiar difficulty to speak either of its beauties or its defects with any degree of certainty." The "power of delight" in Richard Cumberland's *The Jew* is not "confined to the circle of a theatre; it has nearly the same influence in the closet."

In these prefaces Inchbald distinguishes between one kind of space and the other, but without elevating closet over stage (or vice versa). George Colman's and David Garrick's *The Clandestine Marriage* is "pleasanter to *read* than to *see*." Nathaniel Lee's *The Rival Queens* is "calculated for representation, rather than the amusement of the closet." *The Winter's Tale* "seems to class among those dramas that charm more in perusal than in representation." "The characters which will amuse the most, in the reading of this play," she writes in her remarks on Richard Cumberland's *The Brother*, "are those most deficient of entertainment on the stage. The love-stories of the Belfield family are rather adapted to the closet, whilst Sir Benjamin Dove's cowardice, and ultimate victory, draw bursts of merriment and applause from every part of the theatre."

Yet at certain points in her prefatory remarks, Inchbald implies that closet space uniquely provides for the viewing of minute details that add to an appreciation of the psychological richness of certain characters, and in this sense, by depicting closet space as other than that place where one goes to escape a cacaphonous London audience, several passages resemble Joanna Baillie's theory. The closet is also the literal site for the development of a subtle and enriching psychological drama. In reference to Colley Cibber's *The Careless Husband*, Inchbald writes:

> The occurrences, which take place in this drama, are of that delicate, as well as probable kind, that their effect is not sufficiently powerful in the representation—whereas, in reading, they come to the heart with infinitely more force, for want of that extravagance, which public exhibition requires. The smaller avenues to the mind and bosom are often the surest passages to convey sensations of pain or delight; and the connoisseur in all the little touches of refined

nature may here indulge his taste, whilst, as an auditor, he might possibly be deprived of his enjoyment, by the vain endeavour of performers, to display, by imitation, that, which only real life can show, or imagination pourtray.

This perspective—that the "smaller avenues to the mind and bosom are often the surest passages to convey sensations of pain or delight"—is echoed in Inchbald's remarks about *Antony and Cleopatra*, the play on which Baillie based her tragedy on love, *Basil* (discussed in Chapter 4). Here Inchbald observes that "those minute touches of nature, by which Shakespeare proves a queen to be a woman, are, perhaps, the very cause, why Dryden's picture of the Egyptian court [in *All for Love*], is preferred, on the stage, before this. There are things so diminutive, they cannot be perceived in a theatre; *whilst in a closet*, their very smallness constitutes their value" (my emphasis).

While Inchbald does not, as Baillie does in her theory, extend this commentary to suggest that small spaces could serve as models for reforming the London stage, her recognition that the "very smallness" of certain "things" actually "constitutes their value," helps fortify the argument made in the collective discourse of many Romantic women writers that the theatricality of domestic spaces—where small things were housed—warranted serious analysis.

From Closet to Stage: Joanna Baillie's Theoretical Project

Late-twentieth-century scholars[17] have recently called attention to the similarities between the aims of two anonymous works published in 1798: William Wordsworth and Samuel Taylor Coleridge's first edition of the *Lyrical Ballads* and Joanna Baillie's first volume of a three-part collection of dramas, *A Series of Plays: in which it is attempted to delineate the stronger passions of the mind, each passion being the subject of a tragedy and a comedy* (1798–1812).[18] Baillie believed that her work was importantly innovative. Her plays, she wrote, are "part of an extensive design: of one which, as far as my information goes, has nothing exactly similar to it in any language" (1); to "trace [the passions] in their rise and progress in the heart, seems but rarely to have been the object of any dramatist" (10); "a complete exhibition of passion, with its varieties and progress in the breast of man, has, I believe, scarcely ever been attempted in Comedy" (14); "I know of no series of plays, in any language, expressly descriptive of the different passions" (17).

Although a long line of works preceding Baillie's dramas focus on "the passions,"[19] Baillie's project makes a unique contribution to dramatic history through its attempt to concentrate on these passions in an "infant, growing, and repressed state" (15), to trace them "in their rise and progress in the heart" (10). Through this attentiveness to feelings that have been repressed, closeted and hidden away in private chambers, Baillie's dramaturgy helps us regard Romantic closet drama anew, as resembling late-twentieth-century play scripts that focus on the problem of how to deal with crushing social imperatives to enact one's gender and sexual identity in extremely narrow ways (an idea explored at greater length in Chapter 4, where I discuss Baillie's early plays themselves).

Baillie's theoretical writing portrays her as a theater artist in search of an alternative mode of staging to those that already existed for showing forth the legitimate drama in London theaters. Especially in the preface she wrote to the third volume of the *Plays on the Passions* (1812), Baillie envisioned the following theatrical changes: a smaller stage to permit the subtler dramatization of both public and private realms; a more emotionally expressive, less exaggerated acting style to counter the stasis of neo-classicism; and a lighting design that would allow audiences to read the psychological shifts being performed by actors.

These suggestions for reforming the patent theaters were echoed throughout the era in, for example, Walter Scott's "Essay on the Drama" (1819) and Eugene Macarthy's open letter cited in Chapter 1, in which he wrote that "nothing but the complete extinction of *theatrical monopoly* can restore [English theatre] to a sound and healthy state" (5). Baillie's suggestions, however, are significant for the early date at which she articulates them and for the fact that her language links theatrical reform to "passion plays" forged in closet space. In an age when the Examiner of Plays tried to prevent the production of dramas that made politically charged allusions to current events both private and public, as early as 1798, Baillie's theory suggested that the closet play, rather than being antitheatrical and politically irrelevant, had the potential to dramatize publically the realities of closet life. Embracing both the private closet and the public stage, Baillie's dramatic work modeled the oscillating stance that characterizes much of Romantic women's theater theory.

Baillie printed her first volume of dramas before they had been performed, possessing "no likely channel to the former mode of public introduction [the stage]" (16). But even as she admits, in the "Introductory Discourse" (1798), that the opportunity to attach a theoretical essay to her plays "does more than over-balance the splendour and effect of theatrical representation," she also writes that it should not be supposed "that I have written [the plays] for the closet rather than the stage":

> If, upon perusing them with attention, the reader is disposed to think they are better calculated for the first than the last, let him impute it to want of skill in the author, and not to any previous design. A play but of small poetical merit, that is suited to strike and interest the spectator, to catch the attention of him who will not, and of him who cannot read, is a more valuable and useful production than one whose elegant and harmonious pages are admired in the libraries of the tasteful and refined. To have received approbation from an audience of my countrymen, would have been pleasing to me than any other praise. A few tears from the simple and young would have been, in my eyes, pearls of great price; and the spontaneous, untutored plaudits of the rude and uncultivated would have come to my heart as offerings of no mean value. I should, therefore, have been better pleased to have introduced them to the world from the stage than from the press. (16)

This desire to see her plays staged is expressed in a number of different places.[20] In the preface to her second volume of *Plays on the Passions* (1812), for instance, Baillie worries about the length of her two-part tragedy on ambition, *Ethwald*, and "other defects" that make it "not altogether adapted to the stage"; "I would fain flatter myself," she writes, "that either of the parts of Ethwald might, with very little trouble, be turned into an acting play, that would neither fatigue or offend" (105). A footnote to another tragedy, *The Stripling* (1836), tells her readership that she composed it when the boy actor, Master Betty, "was in highest favour with the public" in order to suggest that some young actor might find the play a pleasing vehicle. Arguing for *The Stripling*'s production, Baillie confesses: "It appears to me, in reading it again, after a long lapse of years, to be a play *not ill suited* to a very young actor, at the beginning of his career" (551; my emphasis).

Frances Anne Kemble's *Records of a Girlhood* (1879) contains an anecdote that attests to the fact that "the desire and ambition of [Baillie's] life had been to write for the stage" and that "the reputation she achieved as a poet did not reconcile her to her failure as a dramatist":

> I remember old Mr. Sotheby, the poet (I add this title to his name, though his title to it was by some esteemed but slender), telling me of a visit he had once paid her, when, calling him into her little kitchen (she was not rich, she kept few servants, and did not disdain sometimes to make her own pies and puddings), she bade him, as she was up to the elbows in flour and paste, draw from her pocket a paper; it was a play-bill, sent to her by some friend in the country, setting forth that some obscure provincial company was about to perform Miss Joanna Baillie's celebrated tragedy of "De Montfort" [*sic*]. "There," ex-

claimed the culinary Melpomene, "there, Sotheby, I am so happy! You see my plays can be acted somewhere!" Well, too, do I remember the tone of half-regretful congratulation in which she said to me, "Oh, you lucky girl—you lucky girl; you are going to have your play acted!" This was "Francis I.," the production of which on the stage was a bitter annoyance to me, to prevent which I would have given anything I possessed, but which made me (vexed and unhappy though I was at the circumstance on which I was being congratulated) an object of positive envy to the distinguished authoress and kind old lady. (350)

Baillie's emphasis on the successful production of her plays is a theme sounded as late as 1836, in the preface to the three volumes of plays she published under the title *Dramas*, in which she confessed that her intention was "that, after my death, they should have been offered to some of the smaller theatres of the metropolis, and thereby have a chance, at least, of being produced to the public with the advantages of action and scenic decorations, which naturally belong to dramatic compositions" (312).

Because Baillie's theory of play composition values the public performance of dramas found in private places, it points a directive for retrieving those experiences traditionally performed off stage and behind the curtains. Baillie's interest in representing the traditionally unseen and unheard by peering into the closet does not mean that she eschewed the public realm—in fact, she was fond of including processions and moments of spectacle in a number of her plays—but rather that she prefered a smaller theater space in which real-life closet dramas might be more realistically represented. By carefully considering the issue of how audiences are conditioned to view other people's individual traumas, Baillie tried to establish the need for certain modes of theatrical representation.

To do so, early in her "Introductory Discourse" Baillie reflects upon people's "intercourse with society" (2) and how their experiences of the world affect their experiences as spectators. Why would people be drawn to the spectacle of another's distress, she wonders, before speculating that "multitudes of people" are attracted to "a public execution" (2) because of the pleasures attendant upon reading the gestures of the prisoner's body, gestures that serve as clues to the degree of fortitude with which the prisoner is handling his or her emotional state. The same must hold true, she reasons, in the case of the "dreadful custom" among the "savages of America" of "sacrificing their prisoners of war" (2). This ritual could "never have become a permanent national custom, but for this universal desire in the human mind to behold man in every situation, putting forth his strength against the current of adversity" (2). For "what human creature is there," Baillie asks, "who can behold a being like himself under the violent agitation of those passions which all have, in some degree, experienced, without feeling himself most powerfully excited by the sight?" (3). Baillie's theory of drama emphasizes her belief that the capacity of her reader-spectators for "sympathetic curiosity"[21] will be enlarged if they can witness "what men are *in the closet* as well as in the field; by the blazing hearth and at the social board" (5; my emphasis). If they—as Baillie does—can gaze upon "even the smallest indications of an unquiet mind, the restless eye, the muttering lip, the half-checked exclamation and the hasty start," then this circumstance "will set [our] attention as anxiously upon the watch as the first distant flashes of a gathering storm. . . . If invisible, would [we] not follow him [the character] into his lonely haunts, *into his closet*, into the midnight silence of his chamber?" (3–4; my emphasis).

But how are spectators interested in this kind of character to follow him into his closet, especially as Covent Garden and Drury Lane each provided seats for over three thousand audience members? The answer begins to take shape midway through Baillie's introductory essay, when she poses a rhetorical question that serves as the capstone to her detailed characterization of Tragedy as a "person" whose responsibility it is "to unveil to us the human mind under the dominion of those strong and fixed passions, which, seemingly unprovoked by outward circumstances, will, from small beginnings, brood within the breast" (8):

> For who hath followed the great man into his *secret closet*, or stood by the side of his nightly couch, and heard those exclamations of the soul which heaven alone may hear, that the historian should be able to inform us: and *what form of story*, *what mode of rehearsed speech* will communicate to us those feelings, whose irregular bursts, abrupt transitions, sudden pauses, and half-uttered suggestions, scorn all harmony of measured verse, all method and order of relation? (8; my emphasis)

With this question, Baillie suggests that the playwright of tragedy will want to consider not only "what form of story" but also "what mode of rehearsed speech" might be required to follow "the great man into his secret closet." Here, and especially in her preface to the 1812 volume of the *Plays on the Passions*, Baillie raises questions about the kinds of architectural features and acting methods that would be needed to communicate her special brand of drama. She also focuses on issues of spectatorship, theatrical lighting, and blocking (or stage movement) as these elements contribute to or distract from the staging of her closet scenes.

In addition, by proposing with her plays to "lift up the roof of [a criminal's] dungeon," for example, and "look upon" him "the night before he suffers, in his still hours of privacy" (2), Baillie suggests a more literal meaning for the term "closet drama" than what it would come to mean after the Romantic period. Instead of describing a dramatic text that is unperformed or unperformable, "closet drama" as it derives from Baillie's theory refers to a genre that actually dramatizes scenes from a character's closet. This focus in itself was certainly not new; the domestic tragedies of Nicholas Rowe and George Lillo provided a context for Baillie's desire to create plays about private emotions in closeted settings. But Baillie's theory of the closet is notable primarily for its resistance to antitheatricality, its recognition of the closet's dramatic potential. Whether contemplating the behavior of prisoners, "the savages of America" (2–3), children, or "the fall of the feeble stranger who simply expresses the anguish of his soul" (6), Baillie's discourse conveys an intense desire not only to confront intellectually the fact that "many a miserable being . . . is tormented in obscurity" (14) but also to *see represented on stage* the closeted moments of middle-class characters.[22]

Reforming the London Theaters: Acting and Architecture

The fact that Baillie wanted to see her plays performed publically propelled her to suggest changes in theatrical representation that, because they place a value on smallness, seem to have been modeled on closet space. By the time she wrote her third preface to the third volume of her "passion plays" (1812) she had already endured the vicissitudes of public response to the staging of several of her dramas and, like many of her contemporaries, blamed their mixed reception on the size of the theaters:[23]

> The Series of Plays was originally published in the hope that some of the pieces it contains, although first given to the Public from the press, might in time make their way to the stage, and there be received and supported with some degree of public favour. But the present situation of dramatic affairs is greatly against every hope of this kind; and should they ever become more favorable, I have now good reason to believe that the circumstances of these plays having been already published would operate strongly against their being received upon the stage. (231)

For this reason Baillie was less concerned in 1812 with distinctions between the closet and the formal theater than with arguing for a transformation of the current theatrical environment that would allow for the representation of a different kind of dramatic fare:

> The Public have now to choose between what we shall suppose are well-written and well-acted plays, the words of which are not heard, or heard but imperfectly by two-thirds of the audience, while the finer and more pleasing traits of the acting are by a still greater proportion lost altogether; and splendid pantomime, or pieces whose chief object is to produce striking scenic effect, which can be seen and comprehended by the whole. (231)

Rather than pantomimic movement, Baillie would like to see the kind of "natural and genuine" (233) acting style practiced in the "small theatres" in which Siddons and "the most admired actors of the present time" (232) were trained, where they "were encouraged to enter thoroughly into the characters they represented, and to express in their faces that variety of fine fleeting emotion which nature in moments of agitation assumes" (232). Because the London theaters were so large, stage acting there was marked, in Baillie's observation, by falseness and exaggeration of body movement and facial expression, to "say nothing of expression of voice" (232). Therefore, her plays, with their emphasis on the discovery of the concealed passions of closeted characters, would inevitably be acted to ill effect in these larger spaces. In this environment, "what actor in his senses," she asks, "will then think of giving to the solitary musing of a perturbed mind, that muttered, imperfect articulation, which grows by degrees into words":

> that heavy, suppressed voice, as of one speaking through sleep; that rapid burst of sounds which often succeeds the slow languid tones of distress; those sudden, untuned exclamations, which, as if frightened at their own discord, are struck again into silence as sudden and abrupt, with all the corresponding variety of countenance that belongs to it;—what actor so situated will attempt to exhibit all this? No; he will be satisfied, after taking a turn or two across the front of the stage, to place himself directly in the middle of it; and there, spreading out his hands, as if he were addressing some person whom it behoved him to treat with great ceremony, to tell himself, in an audible, uniform voice, all the secret thoughts of his own heart. When he has done this, he will think, and he will think rightly, that he has done enough. (232–33)

This passage demonstrates Baillie's sensitivity to acting technique and indicates why she preferred a less "uniform" mode of speech and movement: such a style would allow for "the gradual unfolding of the passions" (232) during an actor's soliloquy, in Baillie's view one of the most important features of her plays.

This passage also shows Baillie confidently entering into the Romantic debate about whether "the actor [should] empathize to such a degree that his own personality would be overcome by the role, or, should he distance himself emotionally so as to enliven the role?" (Flaherty 126). It is not enough, in Baillie's view, for actors to plant themselves centerstage (as was the custom during soliloquys) to spread out their hands, and speak in the formal tones of someone "addressing [a] person whom it behoved [them] to treat with great ceremony." To make more credible the convention of speaking aloud one's inner thoughts would require a different approach to acting.

But first, a change in theater architecture must occur, a move from "over-sized buildings" which dwarf "the appearance of individual figures" and work against what Baillie calls "the proper effect" (233) of stage pictures. In current productions, Baillie complains,

> when many people are assembled on the front of the stage to give splendour and importance to some particular scene, or to the conclusion of a piece, the general effect is often injured by great width of stage: for the crowd is supposed to be attracted to the spot by something which engages their attention; and, as they must not surround this object of attention (which would be their natural arrangement), lest they should conceal it from the audience, they are obliged to spread themselves out in a long straight line on each side of it: now the less those lines or wings are spread out from the centre figures, the less do they offend against natural arrangement, and the less artificial and formal does the whole scene appear. (234)

The idea of a smaller stage attracts Baillie because she imagines it would allow audiences to appreciate her dramatization of "the progress of the higher passions in the human breast" (11). Certainly in the area of stage lighting the smaller stage would allow for technical subtleties that could reveal and emphasize nuances of character.

Yet the current construction of the London stages makes it "more difficult," she writes, "to produce variety of light and shadow, particularly the technique of "throw[ing] down light upon . . . objects," which she explains in a footnote will "present . . . a varied harmonious mass of figures to the eye, deep, mellow, and brilliant" (234). While Baillie hastens to tell her readers that she does not know "to what perfection machinery for the management of light may be brought in a large theatre," she uses her observations of theater practice as well as her imagination to conclude that "a great variety of pleasing effects from light and shadow might be more easily produced on *a smaller stage*, that would give change and even interest to pieces otherwise monotonous and heavy; and would often be very useful in relieving the exhausted strength of the chief actors, while want of skill in the inferior could be craftily concealed" (234; my emphasis).

At this point in her third preface Baillie attaches a lengthy footnote on stage lighting, which not only attests to a keen awareness of the features of Romantic theatrical production but also portrays her as a theater theorist compelled by her own dramatic vision to search for alternative modes of stage practice.[24] Currently, she writes, the "strong light cast up from lamps on the front of the stage . . . is certainly very unfavourable to the appearance and expression of individual actors" (234). Therefore, Baillie envisions the following solution to this problem even while, as in a refrain, she states that she is "not at all competent" to address this issue (234):

> I should suppose, that by bringing forward the roof of the stage as far as its boards or floor, and placing a row of lamps with reflectors along the inside of the wooden front-piece, such a light as is wanted might be procured. The green curtain in this case ought not to be let down, as it now is, from the front-piece, but some feet within it; and great care taken that nothing should be placed near the lamps capable of catching fire. If this were done, no boxes, I suppose, could be made upon the stage; but the removal of stage-boxes itself would be a great advantage. The front-piece at the top; the boundary of the stage from the orchestra at the bottom; and the pilasters on each side, would then represent the frame of a great moving picture, entirely separated and distinct from the rest of the theatre: whereas, at present, an unnatural mixture of audience and actors, of house and stage, takes place near the front of the stage, which destroys the general effect to a very great degree. (235n)

Providing her readers with insight not only into early-nineteenth-century London theater but also into her theoretical—and deeply theatrical—mind, Baillie carefully balances her observations of the specifics of Romantic theater practice with pragmatic and imaginative suggestions for how to represent closet drama. And when, at the end of this preface, she apologizes for being "impertinent" (235) and offers as an "excuse" an "almost irresistable desire to express my thoughts . . . upon what has occupied them considerably; and a strong persuasion that I ought not, how unimportant soever they might be, entirely conceal them" (235), Baillie paints herself as the impassioned soliloquizing character her dramatic theory purports to discover for spectators: since she cannot any longer "conceal" her thoughts, the process of producing prefaces to her projected dramatic oeuvre allows her to perform a heroine's soliloquy.

Turning to the Closet: Hannah More

Hannah More's theory of the stage resonates with my discussion of Baillie and the closet, especially when More turns to the subject of women and theater in her "Preface to the Tragedies" (1830). Here she seems to be responding directly to Baillie's project, which undertook to write dramas that would each delineate the effect of a single passion on a particular character; for More complains that, instead of glorifying "'charity, meekness, peaceableness, long-suffering, gentleness, and forgiveness'" (which form "the spirit" of Christianity), Romantic playwrights generally elevate emotions "into the rank of splendid virtues, and form a dazzling system of worldly morality," emotions such as love, jealousy, hatred, ambition, pride, and revenge (504). More believed that the glamorization of certain passions—many of which are the focus of Baillie's dramaturgy—had the effect of making young people dissatisfied with their real lives. "When it is recollected how many young men pick up their habits of thinking and their notions and morality from the playhouse," More worries, "it is not, perhaps, going too far to suspect, that the principles and examples exhibited on the stage may contribute in their full measure and proportion towards supplying a sort of regular aliment to the appetite (how dreadfully increased!) for duelling, and even suicide" (505).

But dissatisfaction with one's social role is especially harmful for women, whom More urges in conduct books to "practise" meekness and self-effacement at an early age so that the shock of having to perform such an identity in adulthood will not be nearly so profound. If women are frequently exposed to plays that fetishize—for example—the importance of passionate love, then these "feelings are easily transplanted to *the closet*: they are made to become a standard of action, and are brought home as regulators of life and manners" (507; my emphasis). Because women are directly threatened by the London stage when persuaded to admire the values dramatized there, More argues that it is necessary for women's practices in closet space—their attention to devotion and prayerbooks, to the "plain and sober duties of life" (508)—to inform (and reform) the current dramaturgy. But in the event that playwrights do not soon "correct" their plays, young ladies must be taught to appreciate the experience of reading, rather than viewing, drama. Women's "walk in life is so circumscribed" and their "avenues of information are so few" that plays such as Shakespeare's will allow them an introduction to the "dangers" of the world in a setting less likely to "ruffle" their imagination (508–9). Associating the female closet with confinement, then, More places women there as readers, rather than performers, of plays.

This argument suggests a more positive critical move than may at first seem the case and reflects what Christine L. Krueger describes as More's complex, at times even feminist (98), responses to social change. Her own successful theater career aside, it is surprisingly clear that More's theory argues for keeping women from going to public stages because she believes that live theater can have a powerfully destabilizing effect on their "circumscribed" existences by dislocating the female viewer from her commitment to performing gender in a culturally sanctioned way. Like the closet critics referred to in Chapter 1, More looks to closet space as a place of reading rather than acting plays. And yet, by urging women to engage theater in closet spaces, even if "only" through reading Shakespeare, More connects theater and drama with domestic and private settings and reminds us that the tendency during the Romantic period to link closet space with the reading of drama—at least in theory—actually serves to underscore the importance of looking more closely at a site where women have historically taken the lead in creating a variety of theatrical projects.[25]

Tracing Baillie's Critical Reception: From Closet to Stage

As in the case of Hannah More, Christianity was very important to Joanna Baillie, and one finds its doctrines shaping her theater theory.[26] In the preface to *The Martyr* (1826), for instance, Baillie wrote: "Of all the principles of human action, Religion is the strongest" (508); it is "the greatest and noblest emotion of the heart" (509). And in the second volume of her three-volume series called *Dramas* (1836), she treats seriously the "opinion entertained by many grave and excellent people, that dramatic exhibition is unfriendly to the principles and spirit of Christianity" (528). Yet, as I have already suggested, Baillie does not write out of nostalgia for the seventeenth-century tradition that linked private domestic space to upper-class religiosity (Hunter 282). Instead, she pays attention to "the phenomenology of the English closet" (282) in order to determine how to provide theatergoers with the model for a new approach to representation. Though Baillie's concern with what happens to young men and women in the theater prompts her to consider carefully the responses of "the grave and moral part of society" (529), she comes to the conclusion that we cannot "allege that dramatic representations are contrary either to the precepts or spirit of the Christian religion" (529). Rather, Christians need to see plays in order to counter the "bad tendency of the pieces exhibited there" and "the disorderly and worthless company who frequent playhouses" (529). Baillie's willingness to discuss the current theatrical scene in the context of her Christian beliefs as well as to speculate about the kind of theater required to dramatize her closet plays makes her discourse seem particularly robust, judicious, and far-sighted, especially when read in the context of the stage theory produced by pre–twentieth-century women.

Despite Baillie's achievements as a playwright and theorist, however, the fact remains that critics have had difficulty appreciating her contributions to theater history. Even those scholars who have seemed drawn to her prefaces and plays have often undermined her accomplishments by expressing ambivalence about her work. To broadly trace the outlines of some of the representations of Baillie's biography and writing that appeared between her death in 1851 and the revival of interest in her plays in the 1980s is to realize more fully the problems facing scholars seeking to construct a female-authored theater theory before 1850. If Baillie (whose theory survives in formal prefaces easily recognized as theoretical discourse and never inaccessible to scholars in this form) could so completely fall out of the canon, then women critics and theorists from the Romantic period (whose theory exists largely in passages scattered throughout their journals and letters) have stood little chance of being read, much less of being discussed in terms that take them seriously as theater theorists. Studying examples from the critical discourse used to sideline Baillie as a theater artist, from the time of her death to the latter third of the twentieth century, shows how her fluctuating reputation has been bound up with the obstacles to recovering women's theater theory which I discussed in Chapter 1: that is, with traditional uses of the term "theater theory" and its associations with masculine endeavor; with the pervasiveness of the closet/stage dichotomy; and with a tendency to separate social from formal theaters when searching for, and talking about, critical discourse.

Many of the articles written about Baillie before the recent revival of interest in her work often trivialized her as an eccentric, an anomaly, a "little Scotch spinster" (Carswell 285). Below I quote Donald Carswell from his book on Walter Scott at some length in order to emphasize the tone of hostile bewilderment that persists in Bailliean criticism throughout much of the twentieth century and that has, until recently, worked to eradicate her significance as a major theorist of theater. "What was the secret of her extraordinary vogue?" Carswell asked rhetorically in 1930, before supplying an answer in which he condemns both Baillie and the Romantics who first celebrated her:

> Her plays even at the height of her fame were never regarded as particularly actable, and now they are not even readable; yet, with the solitary exception of [Francis] Jeffrey, the opinion of the greatest generation of English letters since Elizabethans ranked her as a genius of the first order. . . . Perhaps no wholly satisfactory answer can be given. The case may be one of those literary oddities that simply happen. An undoubted factor in her success was that she made her appearance at a slack time where there was very little competition in the poetic world, and very moderate accomplishment, combined with the little novelty, was quite enough to win extravagant appreciation. Another factor may be suggested. Joanna Baillie's vogue was never popular: it was confined to literary people, and it is the amiable weakness of literary people that they are apt, if they are impressed by an author's aim, to overpraise his actual accomplishments. Joanna Baillie, rather before her time, had, in her old-maidish way, the brilliant idea of writing what in modern literary jargon is called "serious" or "psychological" drama. She succeeded because of the idea, and failed because the task was far beyond her. For one thing, however, she deserves a remembrance that in the general oblivion that has descended on her name has been denied her. She ranks after Burns and Hogg as third of the preserves and refurbishers of Scottish folk-song. Her contribution in this kind is small—only half a dozen pieces, but all perfect. . . . (295–96)

Although she had been compared to Shakespeare during the early nineteenth century, by the time that Carswell scrutinized her work it had become easy to dismiss Baillie as "third" in a line of Scottish ballad revivalists[27] as well as to mock those who once acclaimed the "old-maidish" playwright as preciously literary for ever having taken Baillie's work seriously.

The year before Carswell published his observations, Virginia Woolf wrote that "it scarcely seems necessary to consider again the influence of the tragedies of Joanna Baillie upon the poetry of Edgar Allan Poe" (45), a statement which had the (probably unintentional) effect of seeming to dismiss a writer whose work has barely begun to be explored in the 1990s.[28] In Baillie's case, this neglect is all the more striking given that her contemporaries readily acknowledged her significance as both a playwright and theater theorist. Mary Berry, to whom a copy of Baillie's first volume of plays was sent in 1798, summarized the tone of the early responses to Baillie's work by saying, "everybody talks in raptures (I always thought they deserved) of the tragedies and of the introduction as of a new and admirable piece of criticism" (88). The "rapture" of Elizabeth Inchbald survives in the introductory preface she wrote to Baillie's tragedy *De Monfort* in The British Theatre series (1806–9): "Amongst the many female writers of this and other nations, how few have arrived at the elevated character of a woman of genius! The authoress of 'De Montfort' received that rare distinction, upon this her first publication." Mary Russell Mitford voiced the following tribute in 1852, the year after Baillie's death: "Beloved, admired, appreciated by the best spirits of her time, it is with no little triumph that I, who plead guilty to some of that *esprit de corps* which may be translated into 'pride of sex,' write the name of our great female dramatist—of the first woman who won high and undisputed honors in the highest class of English poetry" (*Recollections* 1:241).[29]

Nevertheless, four years after Baillie's death, one can see emerging an interpretation of her life and work that: (1) emphasizes her failure as a dramatist; (2) portrays her theory and playwrighting as tedious; and (3) tropes her as masculine for seeking fame in theater. Sarah Josepha Hale's 1855 sketch of Baillie offers a good example of how this process began. First, Hale describes her not as a literary artist in her own right but as the "sister of the celebrated Dr. Baillie" (574), her famous anatomist brother. Even more detrimentally, she diminishes Baillie's achievement by wondering "whether, in selecting the drama as her path of literature, [Baillie] judged wisely" (574). In the fact of Baillie's dramatic career, Hale finds evidence of a woman having sought an inappropriate—that is, masculine—position: "as an essayist, or a novelist, she might have made her great talents more effective in that improvement of society, which she evidently has so deeply at heart"; she might "have won for herself, if not so bright a wreath of fame, a more extensive and popular influence." Instead, Hale suggests, Baillie's star has waned precisely because of her choice of medium. "[W]e would prefer," Hale addresses her readers, "that our own sex should rather be *admirers* of the fame of Joanna Baillie than *followers* in her own peculiar and chosen sphere" (my emphasis). The reason given is as astonishing as it is illogical: having "failed to reform the stage"—in spite of her "splendid talents, bold and vigorous fancy, and that calm, persevering energy of purpose, which none but minds of the highest order display"—Baillie should have refrained from trying to write innovative plays. "[L]et no other woman flatter herself with a hope of succeeding" (574), Hale writes, echoing those Romantic memoirs about actresses discussed in Chapter 2, which often equated female ambition with irresponsibility toward domestic life and public service.

What is often described in the latter part of the nineteenth century as Baillie's masculinity, the result of her desire for success in theater, is sometimes the subject of praise from Victorian writers. In 1871, for instance, Sarah Tytler and J. L. Watson wrote that "Joanna Baillie was a born leader. She was physically very courageous. . . . She knew how priceless were the privileges she had enjoyed in this respect . . . she would eagerly recommend to dainty and horrified English matrons the entire wholesomeness and happiness of letting their petted children run barefooted in summer" (188–89). And in a related observation written in the late Victorian period, Catherine Jane Hamilton asserted that "while some women authors were graceful and amusing and fanciful, Joanna Baillie had a condensed strength and a grasp of her subject such as few men have" (129).

Still, these positive assessments of Baillie seem not to have checked the negative influence on twentieth-century criticism of a sketch like Hale's. By describing Baillie in terms of a series of oppositions between closet and stage, mind and body, thought and feeling, Hale's biographical study created perceptions of Baillie's writing that were perpetuated in subsequent analyses and prevented readers from valuing the dramatic and theatrical qualities of her work. Hale wrote:

> In truth, it is when alone, in the quiet sanctuary of one's own apartment, that the works of Miss Baillie should be studied. She addresses the heart through the understanding, not by moving the fancy or even the passions in any strong degree; she writes to the mind, not to feeling; and the mind of the reader must become concentrated on the drama at first, by an effort of the will, before its singular merit will be fully apparent. (575)

This view of Baillie as a writer whose drama will appeal only to the "concentrated" reader in his or her quiet closet space also appears in later constructions of "Joanna Baillie," biographical subject.[30]

In 1922, for instance, Alice Meynell resurrected the playwright only to damn her work as dull and erudite. Blithely stating that Baillie "knows well what she is about, this at any rate is certain," Meynell suggests that those who read Baillie's plays will suffer tedium: "when she addresses herself with a most simple sense of responsibility to the tragic presentation of Hatred, Remorse, Jealousy, and Fear, her good faith and gravity, and the admirable manner in which she puts the murderer to school, *nearly quiet the reader's natural resentment and inclination to revolt*" (56–57; my emphasis). But since the phrase "nearly quieting" suggests that some of the reader's "resentment" and "revolt" will remain, one must conclude that, for Meynell, Baillie's success is debatable.

Meynell's ambivalence about Baillie is echoed by Margaret Carhart in her critical biography written a year later (1923), the only full-length study of Baillie that we have to date. This is an important work for providing extensive analysis of Baillie's life and writing, in addition to including chapters about Baillie's reading list, the performance history of her plays, and a list of songs that appear in her dramas. The last chapter, however, titled "Joanna Baillie's Place in Literature," reveals Carhart's conflicted attitude toward Baillie's theater career. Carhart waffles between stating the importance of Baillie's project and undercutting her achievement, thus echoing critics in the middle and late Victorian periods who expressed confusion about how this female playwright—whom William Wordsworth called the "model of an English Gentlewoman" (cited in Carhart 3)—could have produced such "masculine" (in the sense of impassioned and violent) literature, especially when she was known to have lived a quiet and decorous middle-class life. Here is an example from one of Carhart's laudatory paragraphs:

> No woman, according to [Francis] Jeffrey, was capable of understanding human passions, or of depicting the soul of a man swayed by the baser emotions. Yet Joanna Baillie attempted this very task, and, in a large degree, succeeded. Her life was sheltered from all harsh contact with the world; she herself was never shaken by any of the passions that stir the soul of a man to the depths. And yet she devoted the best years of her life to delineating these emotions which were personally unknown to her, and produced characters whose chief fault is that they show too plainly the power of emotion. (190)

On the one hand, Carhart refutes Francis Jeffrey's misogynist statement by asserting that Baillie "attempted" to understand the human passions and later in the chapter goes on to praise Baillie's ability to inhabit the minds of her male characters. In reference to the tragedy *Henriquez*, she writes that Baillie's "grasp on her subject is almost masculine" (196), and although criticizing her neglect of "the masses," Carhart notes that Baillie anticipated Wordsworth in the "Preface to the second edition of *Lyrical Ballads*" (1800) by trying to render "middle-class people speaking middle-class language in unusual circumstances" (203). However, she cannot refrain from condescending to her subject by expressing the astonishing assumption that Baillie "was never shaken by any of the passions that stir the soul of a man to the depths" (190). "It is hard to believe," Carhart exclaims, "that her most successful heroes were conceived by a woman, and an unmarried Scotch woman at that" (196). In addition, Baillie's plays lacked "expert treatment" and are thus not "interesting" (203); they "failed on the stage, but succeeded in the closet" (205). Furthermore, Carhart suggests that

Baillie's plays are problematic because her moral aims overshadowed her own observations about life, a life that was too narrowly circumscribed: none "of her heroes is sacrilegious or profane; adultery is almost unknown; dishonor of parents is rare; and one's neighbor's goods are secure" (203). In short, Carhart admires Baillie's ambition but not her actual accomplishments; Baillie is to be recognized for her "tenacity to a noble purpose" (206) but not for her theatrical innovations.

The same year in which Bertrand Evans called for a revaluation of Baillie's plays (1947),[31] M. Norton observed that the tendency of Romantic dramatists to imitate Elizabethan playwrights had not prevented Baillie's work from achieving a measure of originality. This essay recapitulates the pattern of earlier criticism, however, by using Baillie's own words to label her characters generally "'altogether insipid and insignificant'" (135) and calling her dramaturgy riven with "simplicity," "few intricacies" (136), and "unreality" (138). "When one considers the actors who dominated the theatrical world during Miss Baillie's lifetime, and whose approval was necessary prior to production," writes Norton, "it becomes increasingly obvious that something in the plays prevented their being good theatre" (139). This "something," it turns out, is that Baillie's characters lack "humanity": in "seeking to reveal the passion, she loses sight of the man" (143).

The complaint that Baillie's characters fail to move us largely because they embody her theoretical principles appears consistently since the time of her first reviews. Reflecting upon the 1800 production of *De Monfort* at Drury Lane, which starred Siddons and John Philip Kemble, James Boaden, one of Siddons's biographers, wrote:

> Mrs Siddons did her utmost with the Countess Jane. But the basis of the tragedy was the passion of hatred, and the incidents were all gloomy, and dark, and deadly. On the stage, I believe, no spectator wished it a longer life, and it is to the last degree mortifying to have to exhibit so many proofs, that the talent of dramatic writing in its noblest branch was in fact dead among us. (2:330)

In recent years P. M. Zall has drawn attention to other critiques of Baillie's stagecraft written by her contemporaries. Recalling Siddons's performance of Jane De Monfort in the same production, Thomas Campbell observed that, although Baillie's tragedies "were regarded by the reading world as the sweetest strains that hailed the close of the eighteenth century" (2:255), she did not know "the stage practically"; if she had, "she would never have attached the importance which she does to the develop-

ment of single passions in single tragedies" (2:254). Campbell also shares
with readers of his Siddons biography a paraphrase of Edmund Kean's
comments about *De Monfort* after a revival of the play in 1821: "though a
fine poem, it would never be an acting play" (2:257). In a letter written in
1800, Inchbald concluded that "De Montford" while a "fine play" is "both
dull and highly improbable in the representation; and sure it is, though
pity that it is so, its very charm in the reading militates against its power in
the acting" (cited in Boaden, *Memoirs* 2:34).[32]

Twentieth-century critics echo these remarks. Allardyce Nicoll complained that "neither Count Basil nor De Monfort is a great tragedy" because Baillie "has not studied the subtler intricacies of dramatic technique"
(*Eighteenth-Century Drama* 225). Although Nicoll situates Baillie as a theatrical innovator in the tradition of Ibsen and Maeterlinck (*Nineteenth-
Century Drama* 1:163) and allots substantial space to a discussion of her
plays (conceding that an adaptation of her play *Constantine Paleologus*,
called alternately *Constantine and Valeria* and *The Band of Patriots*, showed
that she "possessed more of the theatre sense, and of the will to theatre, than the majority of her poetic companions" [1:159]), he concludes
that "as her works stand, we can only account her an interesting historical figure whose works are now [in 1930] to be read rather for the light
they throw on contemporary conditions than for any great inherent merit"
(*Nineteenth-Century Drama* 1:162–63). In 1961, A. G. Insch wrote that the
plays are "a distinct disappointment," even though Baillie's theory evinces
"bold originality" (116), and in 1978, Om Prakash Mathur ignored the numerous passages in Baillie's play prefaces—in which she makes it clear that
her fondest wish is to create plays that will be performed on stage after her
death—asserting that she "could not make her plays stage-worthy" because
she was not nor cared to be "familiar with the stage." Suggesting Baillie's
imaginative bent by speculating that she "probably wrote for a stage of her
own conception" (319), Mathur nevertheless concludes that Baillie "must
take her place not in the playhouse but in the closet" (319). Echoing Insch
and Mathur several decades later, Robert Uphaus and Gretchen Foster included a headnote to Baillie's "Introductory Discourse" (reprinted in their
anthology of eighteenth-century women writers), which reads: "[t]oday
we find the plays *unperformable* and *generally unreadable*, but the theory of
passions elaborated in her preface remains of interest" (343; my emphasis).

Among the comments recorded by Baillie's contemporary friends and
critics, I have found only a few passages that offer a substantial defense of
Baillie's talent for creating dramas that worked well on the stage. Unsur-

prisingly, one is written by Mary Russell Mitford, who a year after Baillie's death published recollections that proclaim: "Mrs. Joanna *is* a true dramatist, . . . although it has been the fashion to say that her plays do not act" (242). Recalling a moment in her early-nineteenth-century girlhood when, at the age of thirteen, she first saw Baillie's *De Monfort* performed with John Kemble and Sarah Siddons, Mitford writes that she (and a friend with whom she saw the play) agreed forty years later, when they encountered Baillie at a social gathering, "that the impression which the performance had made upon us remained indelible. Now, the qualities in an acted play that fixed themselves upon the minds of children so young, must have been purely dramatic" (*Recollections* 1:243).

The tone and content of Mitford's commentary resembles the criticism that sought to revive interest in Baillie's work during the 1970s. Joseph Donohue ushered in a new age for Romantic drama scholarship by demonstrating how characters created by Romantic playwrights were both innovative and derivative from the dramaturgical experiments of Beaumont and Fletcher. When referring to Baillie, Donohue echoed some of the critical notes in the scholarship that had preceded him. Of the 1800 production of *De Monfort* he wrote that "no amount of scenery and lighting, even when complemented by the musical *savoir faire* of [Michael] Kelly and the acting virtuosity of Kemble as De Monfort and Mrs. Siddons as the noble Jane, could apparently compensate for the lack of theatricality implicit in the fact that the essential conflict of the play is severed from objective reality and entombed within the mind and heart of its chief character" (82). Yet in contrast to the critical positions described above, Donohue stated that he would refrain from "taking a vindictive attitude toward playwrights who write from theory rather than first-hand experience" (*Dramatic Character* 78) and therefore began to restore Baillie's reputation as an innovator: "she has single-handedly . . . effected on the stage a transformation in the nature of dramatic character whose repetition in the closet drama of subsequent years appears unmistakably evident," he wrote. She also redefined the "Fletcherian disjunction of character and event" as "an ethical disjunction of human virtue from human acts" by having *De Monfort* internalize the Gothic convention of "an event that took place years before and continues to exert its effects thereafter" as "a psychological process" (81). Donohue's follow-up study of English Romantic theater, published in 1975, explained Baillie's contributions to the evolution of dramatic character more precisely: "This exceedingly ambitious play [*De Monfort*] has an estimable importance in the history of the drama despite its failure on the stage, for it stands at a critical point between the late eighteenth-century Gothic drama and nineteenth-century innovations in that genre, particularly in the developing psychological complexity of the villain-hero" (*Theatre in the Age of Kean* 133–34).

Interest in Baillie's dramas began to intensify during the 1980s, along with the determination to fix her in theater history and Romantic studies as important for both her age and ours. While P. M. Zall and Marilyn Gaull repeated some of the same criticisms leveled at Baillie's plays throughout the century—she "was unfamiliar with her medium, one whose knowledge of plays came from the page rather than the stage" (Zall 17); her plays "were too subtle, too introspective, and philosophical for contemporary taste, too eccentric for the ritual requirements of popular drama" (Gaull 260)—other critics were equally certain that Baillie was an important playwright who had once encountered relative success on the Romantic stage and whose work might perform well in certain late-twentieth-century theaters.

For instance, Aloma Noble's 1983 dissertation on Baillie's artistry aimed "to clarify Joanna Baillie's role in the theatre of her period, and subsequently to establish her place in the history of the drama" (*Dissertation Abstracts International* 1974-A). Stuart Curran and Marlon B. Ross's discussions of Baillie in the context of other Romantic women writers (published in 1988 and 1989, respectively) made the case for her influence on Wordsworth's 1800 Preface, an argument that William Brewer (1991), Judith Page (1994), and Mary Yudin (1994) have since extended. That Priscilla Dorr's 1988 assessment of Baillie's status as "currently . . . that of a virtual unknown" (16) sounds strange today indicates the speed with which literary critics such as Jeffrey Cox, Anne Mellor, Marjean Purinton, and Daniel Watkins have attempted to revise Baillie's unjustified reputation as the writer of unreadable and unactable plays. Indeed, it is this period of critical reevaluation that seems likely to bear out Mary Berry's words to Baillie in 1844, when she predicted that Baillie's work "will flourish ever green, and will rise in importance as you recede from the present generation" (cited in Carhart 66).

Baillie's Legacy to Late-Twentieth-Century Theater Theorists

The theatrical innovations implied by Baillie's "closet-theater theory"—a smaller stage that permits the more subtle dramatization of public and private realms, a more naturalistic acting style, a lighting design that would allow audiences to read psychological shifts—foreshadow the experiments of late-twentieth-century women with "language, space, and the body" (Hart 13) as a means of showcasing more dramatically their particular experiences as an oppressed class. Baillie's observations in her prefaces about Romantic staging comprise a theory of theater that, if implemented, would bear a resemblance to those that have informed experiments in late-twentieth-century theaters with how most effectively to dramatize the particular experiences of actual women. For this reason, then (although this is a complicated issue, as I will discuss in the next chapter), Baillie may be said to fit within a feminist tradition of heralding women's theater in domestic settings. For even though her discourse focuses primarily on male characters and those issues that concern a middle-class spectatorship, her closet-theater theory shares certain impulses with those who would perform the marginalization of society's less powerful characters, who would enact the offstage, backstage, private experiences of different races, classes, genders, and sexualities that have, until recently, been revealed perhaps most startlingly and effectively through the nontraditional venues of contemporary performance art.

While acknowledging the transhistorical and heterosexist dangers of suggesting affinities between the discourse of a nineteenth-century middle-class Scottish woman in Romantic theater and late-twentieth-century feminists, I am struck by some of the similarities between Baillie's theoretical remarks and those of certain lesbian theorists who have recently written about the stage. Because some theater artists have found it helpful to explore their closet revelations in front of audiences restricted to lesbians, or in spaces not easily accessible to heterosexual spectators who may be alternatively curious, empathetic, or even openly hostile to the works at hand (Case, *Feminism and Theatre* 76), they have also found it necessary to explain and advocate their practical experiments through an extensive body of theoretical discourse that offers exciting possibilities for theatrical innovation.

In a now classic essay, "Toward a Butch-Femme Aesthetic" (1989), Sue-Ellen Case proposed that, in order to present on stage a feminist subject "endowed with the agency for political change," theater artists might want to consider that "the lesbian roles of butch and femme, as a dynamic duo, offer precisely the strong subject position the movement requires" (283). First, however, "the lesbian subject of feminist theory would have *to come out of the closet*, the basic discourse or style of camp for the lesbian butch–femme positions would have to be clarified, and an understanding of the function of the roles in the homosexual lifestyle would need to be developed, particularly in relation to the historical class and racial relations embedded in such a project" (283; my emphasis). Whereas Case's projects have concentrated on theoretical and theatrical activity designed to place this feminist subject centerstage—to bring the lesbian subject out of the closet—other feminist theorists have produced theories that suggest the value of closeting.

Like Case, Judith Butler has concentrated on butch/femme role playing (as well as drag and cross-dressing) to demonstrate, paradoxically, that the performance of gender implies "a certain radical *concealment*" ("Imitation" 15). "If I claim to be a lesbian," Butler writes, "I 'come out' only to produce a new and different 'closet'" (15):

> Conventionally, one comes out *of* the closet (and yet, how often is it the case that we are "outted" when we are young and without resources?); so we are out of the closet, but into what? what new unbounded spatiality? the room, the den, the attic, the basement, the house, the bar, the university, some new enclosure whose door, like Kafka's door, produces the expectation of a fresh air and a light of illumination that never arrives. Curiously, it is the figure of the closet that produces this expectation, and which guarantees its dissatisfaction. For being "out" always depends to some extent on being "in"; it gains its meaning only within that polarity. Hence, being "out" must produce the closet again and again in order to maintain itself as "out." In this sense, *outness* can only produce a new opacity; and *the closet* produces the promise of a disclosure that can, by definition, never come. (16)

With its references to Kafka, this passage can be read as a grim description of how the complicated process of "coming out" inevitably produces the false expectation that this process will eliminate the need for closeting. And yet Butler's assertion that "closets" are unavoidable can help theater historians appreciate more readily the historical significance of actual closet spaces.

Teresa de Lauretis, Leslie Rabine, and Eve Sedgwick have each written about gender identity in ways that suggest the concept of "the closet" can be disencumbered of some of the negative associations that the term has historically accrued.[33] Playing with the fact that the phrase describes a physical or psychic space to which people may feel pressured to consign an authentic "self," in various ways these theorists imply that the act of moving "inside and out" of closet ideology is potentially empowering: through this comparative movement a person can learn to appreciate the privacy that the closet affords for improvising, and experimenting with, a series of identities in preparation for presenting a(n) (in)coherent "self" to public view.

De Lauretis and others have cautioned that one can never be outside of ideology altogether. Yet Leslie Rabine has suggested that one's very awareness that gender stereotypes function to disenfranchise both male and female bodies can help a person cultivate what she describes as a politics of "oscillation" between a number of different positions, "in which the necessity of adopting a position in a given situation would include simultaneously calling it into question" ("A Feminist Politics" 27). By virtue of allowing one to dodge others' efforts to affix him or her with specific labels, this act of oscillation between political positions—and positionalities—may offer an individual a measure of freedom for challenging oppressive regimes. The stance that Rabine describes shares something with the situation of the theater performer who is inevitably aware of "being" both a character and an actor at the same time. James Boswell's essay "On the Profession of a Player" (1770) uses the language of the closet to describe this double-consciousness or "double-feeling": the character's passions "must take full possession as it were of *the antechamber* of [the actor's] mind, while his own character remains in *the innermost recess*" (469–70; my emphasis).[34]

By providing those of us who write about theater with new tools for rereading theater history, contemporary gay and lesbian critics sensitize us to the importance of closet drama for helping us to examine more critically particular categories and terms in theater history and to establish links between the contributions of those who perform a homosexual identity and those who identify themselves as "straight" actors. In *De Monfort* (1798), one of the first three plays in Baillie's "passion" series (discussed in the following chapter), Jane De Monfort speaks several lines to her brother that might easily serve as the epigraph to Baillie's closet theory:

> Come to my closet; free from all intrusion,
> I'll school thee there; and thou again shalt be
> My willing pupil . . ."
>
> (II.ii)

(Re)reading Baillie's prefaces can indeed "school" us in how her rhetoric of the closet can help give women in theater—lesbian or otherwise—a better sense of the tradition that informs our current inquiries into representation, spectatorship, mimesis, and performance.[35] By highlighting those moments when Baillie's dramaturgy reinforces her theoretical ideas about performance,[36] the next two chapters offer examples of how Romantic women writers used the play form to articulate and critique their gendered position on social theaters and formal stages. These chapters also extend my analysis of women's theories of acting in Chapter 2 by locating in Baillie's early plays a debate about gender identity and performance style.

4. Conflicted Performance Styles in Baillie's First Volume of *Plays on the Passions* (1798)

Conflicts over acting style in Joanna Baillie's early tragedies, *De Monfort* and *Basil*, reflect some of the tensions that were central to late-eighteenth- and early-nineteenth-century theater artists, whether their spaces for performance were located on social or professional stages. Although these plays depict the private/domestic sphere as allowing the improvisational approach to performance that Baillie's theoretical discourse would seem to advocate, both also tie fears about improvisation and excessive theatricality to fears of effeminacy. When Gay Gibson Cima observes that "acting styles reflect, enforce, and critique cultural models of behavior" (1), she directs us to look at some of the ways in which the dramaturgy of *De Monfort* and *Basil* draws on eighteenth-century and early Romantic modes of performance to criticize restrictive gender roles. Both plays suggest parallels between the main male characters and actual mid-eighteenth-century male actors, who, in Kristina Straub's words, were associated with "sexual 'deviance'" and who considered "sexually other to dominant masculinity" ("Actors and Homophobia" 259). *De Monfort* is especially striking in featuring one man's search for a style of social performance through which to express his wildly bewildering responses to another man.

In order to critique the repression of De Monfort's desire to let his passionate responses to Rezenvelt show all over his body, the play sets in opposition two styles of performance that competed for audience attention during this era and that, as Richard Hornby observes, still characterize debates over acting theory in the late twentieth century (143): the mode of statuesque stasis cultivated by the French neoclassicists and the emotive school of acting characteristic of German Romanticism, or—to put it differently—styles of performance that derived from "the war between Sentiment and Calculation" (Sennett 114).[1] Another way of dichotomizing these approaches is to think of them in the context of what Martin Meisel identifies as "the rise of a new pictorial dramaturgy" in the early nineteenth century: the "arrested motion" of the dramatic tableau, on the one hand, and the "stillness-brought-to-life" of the *tableau vivant*, on the other (47).[2] Hornby calls these two styles the "Technique and Method," the former now associated with British acting ("the mechanical") and the latter with American techniques ("the organic"), especially those derived from the Actors Studio (143). As this chapter will argue, the degree to which Baillie's dramaturgy advocates and distances itself from Sarah Siddons's style of acting reflects the play's ambivalence about a culture that would equate particular styles of acting with acceptable enactments of gender identity in social theaters.

Owing to the stage triumphs of David Garrick and Charles Macklin, British acting had moved by 1741 toward a more spontaneous style, in contrast to the declamatory mode of James Quinn. But when Sarah Siddons made her second London debut six years after Garrick's retirement in 1776, a public more interested in the conscious performance of artistry was ready to embrace her highly stylized gestures and speech patterns as well as those of her brother, John Philip Kemble, who gave his name to the acting "school" that he and Siddons embodied. That the "grand manner" style (Duerr 282) of the Kemble school actually dominated the stage in the first part of the nineteenth century—until Edmund Kean's and Eliza O'Neill's debuts in 1814—may strike us as surprisingly retroactive for an age called "Romantic," not because of the large gestures this style encouraged but rather because this acting approach emphasized a series of transforming "poses" and idealized stage "pictures" over spontaneity and inspiration (traits associated with Kean's performances).[3] Yet, just as British law and politics generally became more conservative in the wake of the French Revolution, so London's major theaters also enshrined conservative practices in the theatrical monopoly, the aggressive censorship of plays, and a taste for neoclassical acting. By the end of the eighteenth century, even as Coleridge (via the German theorists Friedrich and August Wilhelm Schlegel) was arguing for the principle of "organic unity" in opposition to neoclassical doctrine, English acting was becoming temporarily more "ordered, refined, elevated by elocution" (Duerr 268). As in the era's discussion of the visual arts, the "tension between classic principles and traditional English practice" (Marvin Carlson 120)—a practice that paired tragedy with comedy, high with low character, pleasure with moral instruction—is everywhere apparent in the theater theory produced by British writers during the Romantic period.

Baillie's Theory of Acting

Baillie's interest in acting was tied to the aim of her dramaturgical project, which was to teach moral behavior by encouraging her audiences to contemplate how "the passions" work on the soul. The better the performance, the more likely that spectators would carefully attend to the emotional struggles of her characters. Especially because the London patent theaters were so large and a number of her plays are filled with crowd scenes in order to provide the spectacles that thrilled Romantic audiences, on occasion Baillie expressed concern about how well the actors chosen to embody her characters could execute the emotion required. In a footnote attached to the end of the fourth act of *Ethwald, Part Two* (1802), for instance, Baillie contemplated whether, given such a large group of performers, the "expression of strong passion" could be consistently achieved in a particular scene:

> Should this play ever have the honour of being represented upon any stage, a scene of this kind, in which so many inferior actors would be put into situations requiring the expression of strong passion, might be disadvantageous to it; I should, therefore, recommend having the front of the stage on which the Thanes are, during the last part of the scene, thrown into deep shade, and the light only to come across the background at the bottom of the stage: this would give to the whole a greater solemnity; and by this means no expression of countenance, but only that of gesture, would be required of them. (190n)

Rather than endure bad acting, Baillie suggested that certain scenes from *Ethwald* be "thrown into deep shade," and in the stage directions to the second act of *The Homicide* (1836), she also focused on lighting effects to solve the problem of how to deal with less talented actors: the "whole light should proceed from one part of the deck; viz. the binnacle," so that "want of expression of countenance in the underactors will not be discovered, as none need come within the gleam of its light but those who can give expression" (651).

Baillie's plays are designed for actors capable of performing in a style that would come to be called "romantic," making use of "muttered, imperfect articulation, which grows by degrees into words"; "that heavy, suppressed voice, as of one speaking through sleep"; "that rapid burst of sounds which often succeeds the slow languid tones of distress"; "those sudden, untuned exclamations . . . with all the corresponding variety of countenance that belongs to it" (232–33). Preferring emotional and "naturalistic" acting (a relative term, of course), Baillie wrote in a footnote to *The Stripling* that one of the reasons the play might be good for "a very young actor" was that it contained "no false, overstrained passion in it, to mislead him into ranting or exaggerated expression, either as to gesture, voice, or face. Were there more characters *of a simple nature*, adapted to young actors, to be found in our dramatic stores, they would not at first acquire those bad habits which so often prevent their after excellence" (551; my emphasis).

Perhaps Baillie's most overt statement of her theory of acting appears in the preface she attached to the third volume of the *Plays on the Passions* (1812). Here Baillie stated that she valued the "natural and genuine acting" cultivated in the smaller "country theatres" because this mode allowed for "that variety of fine fleeting emotion which nature in moments of agitation assumes" (232–33). As an antidote to the "exaggerated but false" (232) acting style encouraged on the London stage, Baillie argued for the preservation of rural training grounds that would develop in actors a method analogous to what she spoke of in her "Introductory Discourse" as "a rough forest of our native land," the "oak, the elm, the hazel . . . the bramble" and the "humble cottage" (6).

Emphasizing the importance of small theaters, naturalistic performance, and the simple fact of the actor's countenance as a major site of drama, Baillie was both responding to and helping to shape the period's interest in physiognomy, the belief that the body could be read for information about the quality of human character. This belief lay behind a number of late-eighteenth-century treatises on acting, which approached performance as primarily the task of managing countenance. For instance, writing in her memoirs (1826) that the "theatre is only a representation of what passes in the world" (1.235), private theatrical playwright Elizabeth Craven observed that "powerful acting" required the physiognomy to be fully seen, else the performance of passions (increasingly the aim of actors during the Romantic period) would be lost. "All the movements of the soul should be displayed on the physiognomy," Craven wrote: "the muscles which extend, the veins which swell, the skin which reddens, prove our interior emotion, without which it is impossible to exhibit great talent. There is no part which does not require great management of countenance, to listen well, to show by the motions of the eye the soul which moves within, is a part of acting as necessary as that of speaking" (1:235–36).

A passion for helping actors manage their faces and bodies lay behind the publication of Henry Siddons's acting manual—called *Practical Illustrations of Rhetorical Gesture (1807)* and adapted from Johann Jakob

Engel's *Ideen zu einer Mimik,* 1785–86)[4]—which attempted to do for acting what scientists like Baillie's brother, Matthew, were doing for the study
of disease.[5] In the same way that Matthew Baillie conducted experiments
in his anatomical theater and attached engravings of "some of the most
important parts of the human body"—including the uterus, vagina, and
clitoris—to the numerous editions of his *The Morbid Anatomy* that followed its publication in 1793, so Henry Siddons studied how an actor's
assumption of particular gestures could produce in an audience specific
emotional responses. Siddons recommended Joanna Baillie's plays—especially *De Monfort*—to "every lady and gentleman of the theatres, desirous
to improve themselves in the art which they profess" (82). Stating that he
is bent upon "examining every different *ramification* of gesture" (24) and
collecting "different physiognomies" (25), Siddons seems to draw directly
on Baillie's rhetoric in her "Introductory Discourse," in which she writes of
tracing the passions in their rise and progress in the heart, by asserting that
the "player who wishes to be accomplished in his art should not only study
the passions on their broad and general basis; he should *trace their operations
in all their shades*, in all their different varieties, as they act upon different
conditions, and as they operate in various climates" (10–11; my emphasis).

Erika Fischer-Lichte has observed that movements to quantify gesture as "the means indicative of the interior operations of the soul" have
paralleled a cultural nostalgia for "theatre as a corrective force in the civilizing process" (27–28). Perhaps sensing the conservatism of his enterprise,
Siddons argued for his project's relevance by drawing an analogy between
himself and the natural historian:

> But you will doubtless say, What is the use of this scrupulous mode of ex-
> amining every different *ramification* of gesture? . . . While reflecting, says
> Sulzer, that by the sole examination of drawings and descriptions, an ama-
> teur in natural history is able to imprint the shape of many thousand plants
> and insects in his mind, with such exactitude and precision, that he can mark
> the slightest variations in their structures—the most minute deviation in their
> anatomical parts—we may with reason conclude, that a collection of differ-
> ent physiognomies, collected and classed with the same industry, is a scheme
> equally possible, and that a new art would result from the attempt, not less
> important in its kind. (24–25)

Though in theory trying to help actors develop a scientific method with
which they could claim acting as "a new art," Siddons's concern with
whether his manual would have any "use" raises the question of whether

the impulse to codify gesture—or, as in Joanna Baillie's case, to delineate "the passions"—inhibits or attempts to liberate human behavior. Whether one views Baillie as tracing a generic path through how "the passions" work on the psyche—and therefore confining characters to certain pre-scribed responses—or as freeing her audiences from traditional gestures by providing them with an intensely intimate look into the closeted aspects of "the soul" depends to a degree on how one reads her problematic rela-tionship to feminist issues.

Baillie's "Feminism"

Baillie's "off-stage documents"—that is, her letters and nonfictional prose writings—suggest that she cultivated a conservative perspective on women's rights, even though one can also draw out the feminist implica-tions of her theory and dramaturgy. When referring specifically to women, Baillie's nonfictional prose writings reveal her to be less interested than we might expect in subtle or in-depth explorations of female psychology. Typical of this lack of interest is the sentence that appears in her preface to the second edition of *Miscellaneous Plays* (1805): "Of the characters of the two principal women in this piece [Rayner] . . . I shall say nothing" (389). Though Baillie's theory opens up ways of appreciating women's contri-butions to both public and private stages, her prose expresses a stronger concern with shaping male character. In her preface to the second volume of *Dramas* (1836), for example, she quickly dispenses with the problem of what might happen to young women attending plays, since they "go to theatres protected and kept out of the way of witnessing anything proper," in order to focus at some length on "the effect which coming into con-tact with such company [i.e., prostitutes in the patent theaters] may have on young men" (529). Likewise, Baillie's plays are more often attentive to heroic and noble actions of men in war than to women's domestic lives. Rarely does a female character lend her name to a play's title or become the dramaturgical focus, and most of the dialogue and action revolves around men.

Like the female celebrity memoirists discussed in Chapter 2, in the preface to *Metrical Legends of Exalted Characters* (1821) Baillie confessed that she struggled with the problem of how to write women's lives: "[I]n preferring a heroine of this class for my Legend," Baillie wrote, "I encoun-tered a difficulty which, I fear, I have not been able to overcome";

the want of events, and the most striking circumstance of the story belonging
to the earlier part of it, while the familiar domestic details of her life, which so
faithfully reveal the sweetest traits of her character, are associated in our imaginations with what is considered as vulgar and mean. I have endeavoured by
the selection I have made of things to be noticed, and in the expressions which
convey them to the fancy, to offend, as little as might be, the fastidious reader;
and I beg that he will on his part receive it with indulgence. (*Works* 709)

Even though Baillie advocated looking to domestic space for interesting drama, she simultaneously worried about offending her readership
with "what is considered as vulgar and mean," the "domestic details" of
female biography. It was this concern with giving inappropriate information about a woman's private life that caused her to assess Mary Berry's
book, *A Comparative View of Social Life in England and France* (1844), as
an offense "to that delicacy which is expected in the writings of a woman"
(cited in Berry, *Extracts* 3:371).[6]

Yet a number of Baillie's female contemporaries praised her for creating female characters whose independence of spirit they could admire.[7]
When Baillie anonymously published the first volume of the *Plays on the
Passions* (1798), Berry guessed that the author was female because of the
admirably intellectual female characters she had created: "I say *she*," Berry
wrote in a letter dated March 21, 1799, "because and *only* because no man
could or *would* draw such noble, such dignified representations of the
female mind as the Countess Albini and Jane De Monfort. They [male
playwrights] often make us clever, captivating, heroic, but never rationally
superior" (*Extracts* 2:90).[8] Felicia Hemans admired Baillie for "her general
idea of what is beautiful in the female character":

There is so much gentle fortitude, and deep self-devoting affection in the
women whom she portrays, and they are so perfectly different from the pretty
"*un-idea'd* girls," who seem to form the *beau ideal* of our whole sex in the
works of some modern poets. The latter remind me of a foolish saying, I think
of Diderot's, that in order to describe a woman, you should write with a pen
made of a peacock's feather, and dry the writing with the dust from butter-
flies' wings. (cited in Chorley 1:99)

Eschewing peacock feathers and butterfly wings, the dramaturgy of
De Monfort daringly anatomizes the passion of hatred in order to explore
the problem of homoerotic love. Baillie seems to have sensed the boldness
of her enterprise. In reference to *De Monfort*, she explained that because
hatred is a passion "less frequent than any other of the stronger passions,"

to "endeavour to interest the mind for a man under the dominion of a passion so baleful, so unamiable, may seem, perhaps, reprehensible" (16). That she felt compelled to defend her interest in how hatred works on a confused man's mind indicates her awareness that delving into the psychological manifestations of this emotion tested the bounds of feminine (and Christian) behavior. For this reason, she begged "it may be considered, that it is *the passion and not the man* which is held up to our execration; and that this and every other bad passion does more strongly evince its pernicious and dangerous nature, when we see it thus counteracting and destroying the good gifts of Heaven, than when it is represented as the suitable associate in the breast of inmates as dark as itself" (16; my emphasis).

Cynthia Burack could very well be describing Baillie's work when, in 1994, she identified "a more recent development in feminism," the "resuscitation of the place of the passions" (2). Indeed, rather than "avoiding" or "marginalizing" "disagreeable passions," as Burack complains late-twentieth-century feminists have tended to do (3), in her plays Baillie featured a range of emotions—including hatred, anger, and jealousy—and in this sense placed herself in the vanguard of those Romantic women who used literature to reconceptualize "the nature of the self to include such aspects of human being as emotion, nurturance, and affiliativeness" (Burack 107) and to document some of the ways in which "disagreeable passions . . . threaten to disturb natural hierarchies of power" (27).

Uncloseting Unspeakable Love: Baillie's Play on "Hatred," De Monfort

With its vision of secret souls coming uncloseted, Baillie's theory of performance cried out for the acting methods of the impassioned Edmund Kean, and indeed *De Monfort* predicts Keanian acting through its portrayal of the title character. Read from a feminist perspective, the tragedy is concerned with how acting styles indicate the degree to which a particular performance of gender must—in the terms that the culture has set—be closeted away. At various moments in the play, the improvisational gesture allows the character of De Monfort to express a weariness with, and even a distrust of, those performance methods favored in social theaters. These moments recall an important essay by Judith Butler in which she uses a phenomenological approach to assert that the successful social actor, like the actor on the stage, has managed to memorize a script in which the boundaries for the performance of gender identity have been carefully delineated.⁹ This circumstance occurs as a result of a difficult process similar to the rehearsal period preceding a play, a process through which a culture's "directors" shape the body of the social performer to meet spectatorial demands. Butler stresses the community effort behind this project, the social rather than the individual aspect of gender performance, in order to remind us that one does not perform his or her identity in isolation—as a role put on and discarded as easily as one might exchange a theatrical costume: the "act that gender is, the act that embodied agents *are* inasmuch as they dramatically and actively embody and, indeed, *wear* certain cultural significations, is clearly not one's act alone" (525). Rather, the performance of gender constitutes and is the product of a complex act shaped by many people. Butler exposes the difficulties—and punitive consequences (527–28)—that can result from resisting cultural imperatives to perform gender in scripted ways.

Turning to *De Monfort* with Butler's perspective in mind, certain features of the plot emerge with stronger force, especially those moments when De Monfort is punished for violating his culture's conventions of social performance. The play that received the most stage productions during Baillie's lifetime (Aloma Noble documents fourteen different mountings), *De Monfort* is set in Germany in an unspecified era, in keeping with the tendency of English plays in the 1790s to draw upon German culture for translations, technique, and stage devices.¹⁰ Ostensibly, the drama concerns De Monfort's ungovernable disdain for Rezenvelt, a man whose talent for performing the cultural code of polite behavior arouses his fury, and it begins with De Monfort's arrival at the Frebergs' estate: he has found it necessary to flee his home and beloved sister, Jane, because Rezenvelt has made De Monfort beholden to him by sparing his life in a duel. Described from play's start as the consummate social performer, Jane soon follows De Monfort to the Frebergs' and urges him to make peace with Rezenvelt, who has also arrived on the scene. But although De Monfort tries to please Jane by going through a public ritual in which he expresses his intent to behave according to the cultural code, his performed reconciliation with Rezenvelt is short-lived. When Conrad, "an artful knave," repeats to De Monfort rumors about an attraction between Jane and Rezenvelt, De Monfort no longer makes any effort to closet his overwhelming passion and ends up murdering Rezenvelt in a wild wood.

Apprehended and taken to a convent, De Monfort endures his greatest trial when he must confront his sister, who persists in trying to persuade him to behave according to her vision of the manly man and noble brother. After nursing him for a short interval until he dies, supposedly from remorse, Jane eulogizes her brother as someone who should be remembered, although the play does not make it clear on what basis he merits such adulation. The final scene—which Baillie later suggested might be unnecessary in a future staging, perhaps because she sensed the problems with Jane's eulogizing a murderer [11]—seems indispensable in light of the play's preoccupation with how styles of acting express cultural concerns about closeting (and uncloseting) gender identity: it shows Jane performing a eulogy of De Monfort in which she lauds him as "noble" (a synonym in the play for the admirable—and appropriately masculine—social actor), in spite of his having committed an inexcusable crime.

That the play is titled *De Monfort* should not, as Jeffrey Cox has suggested, compel readers to focus solely on the way in which the dramaturgy moves the male sibling of the De Monfort family through the culture of the play; why Jane De Monfort has so much at stake in De Monfort's performance of the politely aristocratic and emotionally repressed man is one of the play's more interesting questions. One can certainly sympathize with Jane's compulsion to act as guardian of a particular code of behavior even while observing that her commitment to a restrictive style of social performance oppresses both her and her brother. For Jane seems so bent upon assuring herself that De Monfort has indeed performed according to her ideal that she spends time telling others how to interpret his public scenes. When, for instance, Freberg calls De Monfort "suspicious grown" at the start of the play, Jane counters with language that suggests De Monfort is only masking his true identity, urging the Count toward an alternative interpretation:

> Not so, Count Freberg; Monfort is too noble.
> Say rather, that he is a man in grief,
> Wearing at times a strange and scowling eye;
> And thou, less generous than beseems a friend,
> Hast thought too hardly of him.
>
> (II.i.251) [12]

Jane also wrests from De Monfort's murder of Rezenvelt an interpretation that maintains the illusion of his heroic stature. Knowing that he has killed a man because he hates him so intensely, still Jane distinguishes De Monfort from more common criminals: "He died that death which best becomes a man, / Who is with keenest sense of conscious ill / And deep remorse assail'd, a wounded spirit. / A death that kills the *noble* and the brave, / And only them" (V.iv.312; my emphasis). Straining on, she ends the play with an epitaph that rings hollowly: De Monfort's "nameless tomb" will be consecrated to one "Who, but for one dark passion, *one dire deed*, / Had claim'd a record of as noble worth, / As e'er enrich'd the sculptur'd pedestal" (V.vi.104; my emphasis).

Of course, this "one dire deed" is one too many. Jane may try to minimize De Monfort's murderous action in the interest of proclaiming his "dignity," but her words do not convince. Instead of speaking "what we feel, not what we ought to say" as Edgar urges at the end of *King Lear* (V.iii.322)—the play to which Baillie alludes several times and which, perhaps more than any other Shakespearean drama, argues against the use of "pomp" and empty rhetoric—Jane seems driven to control public opinion about her brother's identity, to cast De Monfort in the mold of an idealized hero whom the play never shows us. This is because the play's focus is elsewhere: the charting of discrepancies between the noble manly figure whom Jane desires and De Monfort's oscillation between a narrow range of masculine behaviors, all of which preclude his expressing something other than hatred for the man who so obsesses him.

From the beginning of the play, De Monfort is described in ways that forecast the typical Romantic hero, also prefiguring Byron's antisocial and melancholy protagonist in *Manfred* (1817) (Donohue, *Dramatic Character* 81) and Emily Brontë's Heathcliff. De Monfort's "violent conflict of mind" (V.iv.310), his sporadic desire for oblivion—"I now am nothing," he says toward play's end, "I am a man, of holy claims bereft; / Out of the pale of social kindred cast" (V.ii.302)—comprise, from Donohue's perspective, an innovation in the English theater's development of dramatic character for which Baillie is responsible. She redefines the "Fletcherian disjunction of character and event" as "an ethical disjunction of human virtue from human acts," internalizing the Gothic tradition of allowing "an event that took place years before . . . to exert its effects thereafter" (*Dramatic Character* 81). Reminiscent also of the Gothic villain-hero that Ann Radcliffe popularized in *The Mysteries of Udolpho* (1794) and *The Italian* (1797),[13] De Monfort is presented as a personality whose agony is self-inflicted and sense of identity confused. If, as Eve Sedgwick argues, the Gothic novel is "the first novelistic form in England to have close, relatively visible links to male homosexuality" (*Between Men* 91), the same may be said for Gothic drama, the genre to which *De Montfort* belongs.[14] In contrast to Jane's seemingly unreflective enactment of her social role of noble womanhood, De Monfort arrives on the scene a self-consciously troubled person, and others recognize the change: from "comely gentleman," his hatred for Rezenvelt has transformed him into one who now possesses "that gloomy sternness in his eye / Which sullenly repels all sympathy" (I.i.237).

De Monfort protests against the kind of cheerful social theater that his acquaintances perform, and he often tries to read bodies for the discrepancies between what they reveal and conceal. In his view, Rezenvelt *must* mask a soul corrupt in proportion to the zealous consistency with which he enacts the effeminately fluttering, chivalric courtier. That others do not seem to mind Rezenvelt's exaggerated gestures causes De Monfort no end of agony, as in them he sees reflected his own impulses. The ecumenical Freberg, for instance, wants the two men to reconcile, exulting that Rezenvelt is "so full of pleasant anecdote, / So rich, so gay, so poignant in his wit, / Time vanishes before him as he speaks, / And ruddy morning thro' the lattice peeps / Ere night seems well begun" (I.i.241). Nor can Jane appreciate De Monfort's desire to wear openly his hatred for Rezenvelt, even though she begs him to confess his feelings to her. At the start of the drama De Monfort has left Jane precisely because he knows that, in her presence, he may not experiment with his need to perform as the spoiler of social play because she directs his behavior with an eye to audience approval. Once at the Frebergs, however, he does try on a number of performance modes that confound his audience and, by act 3, when he duels with Rezenvelt, he dares to shout, "now all forms are over" (III.iii.286).

These "forms" refer to what Freberg has earlier called the "culture of kind intercourse" (III.i.274), a system requiring an upbeat cheerfulness to mask "open villainy" (III.iii.286) or any expression not in the social repertoire. While De Monfort's rebellion against the "forms" finds its most extreme expression in his repressed attraction to, and subsequent murder of, Rezenvelt, this rebellion may also be read as either a conscious or unconscious resistance to imitating the performance style embodied by Jane De Monfort, a style grand and classical, indeed antithetical to the performance mode that Baillie discusses in her prefaces as conducive to bodying forth the subtleties of a character's most intimate passions.

De Monfort's oscillation between hidden and uncloseted pensiveness is also contrasted with the consistently cheerful actions of the revel-loving Frebergs, who seem to live from one "midnight mask" to another.[15] Theirs is a world of flattery, of false, feigned, and indiscriminate friendships, of hyperbolic and superficial discourse. "[A]ll men are thy friends" (I.ii.246), De Monfort complains to Freberg, whose grand gestures are evocative of the "exaggerated" and "false" acting style indigenous to the large, licensed London theaters that Baillie criticized in her preface to the third volume of the *Plays on the Passions* (1812). Daniel Watkins observes that "in the conduct of the Frebergs is seen the predictable last fling of a social class that has lost its commanding position in society" (47). But it is important to note that because the Frebergs are revelers and party-goers—often attending masquerades—they offer De Monfort the opportunity to improvise his identity at least momentarily, an opportunity he never takes because he is confused about how to express himself in defiance of Jane's expectation. In the eighteenth century, Terry Castle tells us, masks were "in the deepest sense a kind of collective meditation on self and other, and an exploration of their mysterious dialectic":

> From basically simple violations of the sartorial code—the conventional symbolic connections between identity and the trappings of identity—masqueraders developed scenes of vertiginous existential recombination. New bodies were superimposed over old; anarchic, theatrical selves displaced supposedly essential ones; masks, or personae, obscured persons. . . . One became the other in an act of ecstatic impersonation. The true self remained elusive and inaccessible—illegible—within its fantastical encasements. The result was a material devaluation of unitary notions of the self, as radical in its own way as the more abstract demystifications in the writings of Hume and other eighteenth-century ontologists. (4)

It was precisely this disorienting aspect of the masquerade, as G. J. Barker-Benfield has noted, that served the eighteenth century as "a metaphor for a life" and that "eighteenth-century moralists saw as modern because of the vanity and sexual games-playing to which they believed a better past had degenerated." The masquerade was viewed as "a manifestation of eighteenth-century consumerism—one in which women asserted themselves in pursuing pleasure—" and "the criticism leveled against it was exactly the same as the criticism leveled at consumerism's other manifestations—novels, boarding schools, and wearing fashionable clothing" (183).

Because she is thus associated with the mask—is hostess of an event in which women are not only allowed but encouraged to pursue their pleasure—the gaudily dressed Lady Freberg bears the taint of vulgarism and impropriety that serves as a foil to Jane's aristocratic propriety. In one sense culturally suspect, in another Lady Freberg can be read as someone who embraces improvisation and therefore represents an approach to social performance that would help to liberate a gender-bound culture. By contrast, Jane's enactment of what Mary Poovey has at length described as the early-nineteenth-century "proper lady"—self-censoring, self-effacing, and self-sacrificial—allies her with conservative forces, a condition symbolized by her "homely" dress (II.i.251). This costume arouses the envy of Countess Freberg, because other characters (especially the Count) respond to Jane's plain clothes with enthusiasm: "Such artless and majestik elegance, / So exquisitely just, so nobly simple, / Will make the gorgeous blush" (II.i.252), Freberg says, pointing directly to Jane's clothing. (Baillie repeats this sort of sartorial coding in *The Tryal* when she signals Harwood's virtuousness by having him wear "a plain brownish coat" to a ball in Bath [I.i.204].)

The Count's negative reaction to his wife's "gaudy" party costume and the dressing-room scene that follows in act 3 serves to set the Countess against Jane, for the purpose, it would seem, of underscoring the "desirable" traits of noble womanhood and suggesting that, in the world of *De Monfort*, a woman's true character can be known through the semiotics of costume.[16] When Jane exits to prepare for the Frebergs' party—dressing herself in the Countess's clothes in order to gain access to her brother's unguarded confessions—the Count expresses his dissatisfaction with his wife by berating her dress code: "How hang those trappings on thy motley gown?" he asks. "They seem like garlands on a May-day queen, / Which hinds have dress'd in sport" (II.i.253). This is but one of several instances when Freberg portrays the Countess as an unsuccessful performer of femininity, whose fashion blunders are emblematic of her failure to approach Jane's moral rectitude and propriety. The play even suggests that the Countess's gaudy taste signals a deceptive "nature," since she may be regarded as ultimately responsible for inflaming De Monfort to commit murder. (The lie she spreads about Jane and Rezenvelt kindles De Monfort's rage, which results in his killing Rezenvelt and then dying himself.) Yet the misogyny that lies just beneath the surface of characters' chuckles about the "art" of "female cultivation" (II.i.254), an art in which the much maligned Countess Freberg is well practiced, might caution us against condemning the Countess too readily. Though Jane De Monfort's comparatively "simple" and natural style of speech and dress is valorized, the play also questions her adherence to a code of behavior in which passionate outburst, improvisational acting—even gaudy costumes—are looked upon askance in social performance.

De Monfort's preoccupation with women's dress is significant from a feminist perspective, for throughout Western history, costume (both on and off the stage) has been used to gender the wearer and thus create and transmit messages about a person's political position. Anne Hollander reminds us of the cultural connotations of mid-eighteenth-century theater stage dress: classical drapery, for example, signaled that the wearer possessed an affinity for "simple truth" (276). Because Jane De Monfort wears simpler lines, in contrast to the opulently dressed Lady Freberg who enjoys her masquerades and other gatherings, the dramaturgy suggests that Jane is to be read not only as more tasteful but also as more trustworthy, the play's moral center and the voice of unshakeable virtue.

References to costume further establish the connections between Jane De Monfort and Sarah Siddons, which are significant in light of Baillie's dramaturgical valorization of an acting style at times antithetical to the way Siddons's performances have been generally described.[17] In 1789–90 Siddons "developed a taste for Greek sculpture"—perhaps under the influence of her "sculptress friend" Mrs. Damer (Nagler 415)—a taste that translated into her penchant for classical costume, which in turn signaled her aesthetic values. James Boaden, one of Siddons's biographers, underscored this connection between her costume, her performance style, and her attempt to assert a more neoclassical view of tragedy:

> Conspiring with the larger state to produce some change in her style, was her delight in statuary, which directed her attention to the antique, and made a remarkable impression upon her, as to the simplicity of attire and severity of attitude. The actress had formerly complied with fashion, and deemed the prevalent becoming; she now saw that tragedy was debased by the flutter of light materials, and that the head, and all its powerful action from the shoulder, should never be encumbered by the monstrous inventions of the hairdresser and the milliner. (cited in Nagler 416)

On the one hand, female costume and makeup in *De Monfort* are described as producing "grafted charms, / Blending in one of the sweets of many plants" (II.i.83), but, on the other, women who use theatrical techniques to embellish and disguise themselves are targeted as masking their actual loss of youth, physical attractiveness, naturalness, and "couth." As in *Basil*, discussed below, women's theatrical impulses evoke fears that female identity is unstable: the prude and the coquette might, through artifice, transform their physicalities into social bodies that appear either interchangeable or uncategorizable. At the Frebergs' party in act 2, for example, Rezenvelt describes the process by which theatrical devices can obscure the "true" identity of the female performer:

> Aged youth,
> With borrowed locks, in rosy chaplets bound,

Clothes her dim eye, parch'd lips, and skinny cheek
In most unlovely softness:
And youthful age, with fat round trackless face,
The downcast look of contemplation deep
Most pensively assumes.
Is it not even so? The native prude,
With forced laugh, and merriment uncouth,
Plays off the wild coquette's successful charms
With most unskilful pains; and the coquette,
In temporary crust of cold reserve,
Fixes her studied looks upon the ground,
Forbiddingly demure.

(II.i.254)

The dramaturgical ambivalence toward the play's dominant performance styles emerges more clearly in act 2, when De Monfort and Rezenvelt nearly come to blows over the issue of who may touch Jane's "thick black veil" (II.i.255). At this moment Jane's significance recedes in the face of the men's intense responses to each other as they move toward Jane's stark hymenal costume, reminding us of Eve Sedgwick's observation (from René Girard) that, in any erotic triangle, "the bond that links the two rivals is as intense and potent as the bond that links either of the rivals to the beloved" (*Between Men* 21). De Monfort may be dedicated to the idea that Jane is chastely devoted to him and, with pride, describe how she has become the "virgin mother of an orphan race" (II.i.257), but he is even more committed to the idea that Rezenvelt "woos" his hate. Certainly De Monfort seems most confused about his sexuality and gender identity when he is in his enemy's presence, casting him as a kind of Satan to his Eve—calling Rezenvelt "fiend," "devil," "villain," and "serpent"—and locating Rezenvelt's power in his potential not only to seduce his sister but also to cause De Monfort to lose control of the tenor of his social acting.

Indeed, Rezenvelt raises the possibility that De Monfort is fighting against his physical charms at the Frebergs' party. Smiling "archly" (according to the stage directions) because De Monfort refuses to be sociable, Rezenvelt says that, were De Monfort to "swerve" from his "native self" and "grace my folly with a smile of his," one might call him a "woman turn'd" (II.i.255). While De Monfort tries to distinguish himself from those who are "besotted" and "bewitched" by Rezenvelt, his obsession with the marquis signals a complicated, closeted longing for the knowledge of a (perhaps sexual) experience outside of his own, a desire that instead takes the form of a frenzied murder and, shortly to follow, De Monfort's expulsion from the "culture of kind intercourse."

After the murder, Jane again tries to inspire De Monfort to perform according to the culture's standard for the socially valuable "man." The stage directions tell us that De Monfort "endeavours to suppress his feelings" (V.ii.306) as he leads Jane from the convent to the prison. Perhaps because he has earlier failed to perform to her satisfaction in the reconciliation scene with Rezenvelt, De Monfort tries harder now. In act 3 he had resisted Rezenvelt's proferred bear hug ("I'll have thee [De Monfort] to my breast," Rezenvelt exults), having said throughout the play that he cannot act what he does not feel: "I will not offer you an hand of concord, / And poorly hide the motives which constrain me" (III.i.273). The public aspect of this third-act scene—the fact that spectators assemble to watch De Monfort perform his apologies—pleases Jane but is exactly what De Monfort rejects: "Must all the world stare upon our meeting?" he asks her before the Freberg's troop onto the stage (III.i.270).

Although at play's end De Monfort is so grateful for Jane's presence that he assumes a posture that she can describe as "noble," restraining his outbursts and behaving with enough classical stoicism to earn her posthumous praise, in the manner of the Kemble school of performance, his countenance and language throughout the drama indicate his recognition that social intercourse frequently requires the enactment of identities that cannot be anticipated, catalogued, or consistently defined.

One of the reasons De Monfort keeps butting up against the play's valuation of an ostensibly cheerful restraint that manifests itself in a stiff and carefully controlled gesture is that his spontaneous overflow of powerful feelings works against the cultivation of a single, unified identity with which to perform in social settings. Daniel Watkins observes that "the psychological confusion and the passion of hatred seen in De Monfort are, in the larger context of the dramatic action, signs of a radically divided subject" (57). De Monfort's general refusal to act in a familiar and consistent way challenges other characters' apparent desire to hold on to a society in which class and gender performances are carefully rehearsed, where the improvisational mode is contrasted unfavorably with what might be called a version of the Gothic tableau or French neoclassical style. De Monfort's is an interestingly uncomfortable character primarily because he will not let others forget that they have adopted performance modes that allow them to glide by each other without the trauma of confronting their closeted selves, their secret longings, their hidden responses to a power structure at odds with unmediated expression. It is as if he shares the position of eighteenth-century actors who were cast as "sexual suspects" even though "no longer closely associated with the homophobically constructed sexuality of the cross-dressed player-boy" (Straub, "Actors and Homophobia" 263).

De Monfort's repression of his homoerotically charged hatred, his attempt to meet the public with a "tamed countenance" (III.i.269), only ensures that he will, whenever he is alone, give vent "to all the fury of gesture" of which he is capable (I.ii.244). His resistance to performing a single identity in a socially sanctioned performance style ultimately results in the violent consummation he so fears: by murdering Rezenvelt, he knits together their fates; in the last scene the bodies of both men, swaddled in black, lie close to each other on a low table. It is this aspect of the play that suggests it is a "closet drama" in the contemporary sense—the story of sexual suppression and of the horrific consequences that follow upon it.

Another word about Jane De Monfort is necessary here before turning to *Basil*. By viewing Baillie's play as aligning Jane's mode of gender performance with Siddons's acting style, my reading of her character supports Jeffrey Cox's view that Baillie wrote with attentiveness to the "culturally coded responses Siddons, the actress, evoked" (*Seven Gothic Dramas* 55). According to Cox, *De Monfort* "can be read as an investigation of 'Siddons-mania,' the nearly hysterical response to the performances of Sarah Siddons," who was "the perfect actress for the Gothic dramas, for she was at her best in the two stances the Gothic demanded for women: women were either terrorized and mad or stoic and indomitable, but they were always passive" (53). Like a number of Baillie's male contemporaries, who, as Julie Carlson has argued in *In the Theatre of Romanticism*, were threatened by Siddons's onstage power, Baillie criticizes the style of acting that Siddons embodied by pitting the histrionics of De Monfort against his sister Jane for the purpose of highlighting her oppressive behavior, her extraordinary concern with what others think of her social performances. Representing the epitome of perfect womanhood by the standards of late-eighteenth-century middle-class London society, the character of Jane De Monfort is written to be performed in the world of the play with a carefully controlled gesture and speech; even her simple costume evokes the classical acting mode associated with Siddons and her brother John Philip Kemble, both of whom starred in *De Monfort* when it was first staged in 1800. By contrast, De Monfort's inconsistent and erratic performances

are filled with Sturm und Drang, anticipating the style of acting popularized by Edmund Kean in his fiery portrayals of Elizabethan and Romantic
heroes when he made his stage debut in 1814. (Kean, like Kemble, also
appeared as De Monfort, in 1821). For Cox to say that Jane eventually becomes "freed from the masculine gaze" and starts "to define herself beyond
the roles offered by a male-centered social system" (Cox 56) is perhaps to
overstate the situation at play's end. Jane does indeed more obviously take
control of events when De Monfort's guilt emerges; by the last act she
represents, in Daniel Watkins's view, "an individualism and subjectivity
over against aristocratic and religious structures of value—to display bourgeois sensibilities shorn of the ugliness associated with Rezenvelt's character" (56). But in her attempt throughout the play to ward off the angry,
hateful feelings that De Monfort cannot at times suppress and in trying
to control others' responses to his murder of Rezenvelt, Jane perpetuates
rather than escapes from a mode of performance that would present class,
gender, and sexual identity in clearly recognizable and bounded gestures.
From the perspective of the late twentieth century, one can read the target
of Baillie's dramaturgical critique as those cultural restraints that place inhibitions on a more spontaneous approach to social performance, one that
would allow an individual to cultivate different modes of acting, which
could shift according to the space inhabited.

It is difficult from this vantage point to determine the degree to which
Siddons's onstage performances actually reflected her system of acting,
which was discussed at some length in Chapter 2. Analyses from the period
suggest that her performances were generally regarded as more spontaneous and heartfelt than her brother's, but they were also consistently
faulted for their resemblance to statuary. Summarizing Henry Siddons's
descriptions of "the Kemble school of acting" in reference to Gothic
drama, Paul Ranger observes that this approach to performance consisted
of "an alternation of a series of static tableaux with an interlude of intense
activity": "the actor held each attitude for a length of time as he delivered
his lines, changing the pose as he became gripped by a new emotion" and
"the weight was placed on one leg; a wide stance using as much personal
space as was workable was adopted; one hand articulated at some point of
the body, whilst the free hand and arm broadly described the space around
the actor" (91). In other contexts, offstage performances that took place
in social theaters, some of Siddons's contemporaries objected to the kind
of grand gestures Ranger describes. Baillie's friend Mary Berry wrote with
pleasure in 1799 of the fact that Siddons put aside her mannered style when

attending one of Berry's private gatherings: "She (Mrs. Siddons) who was of a little party we had last night, spoke of [Baillie's plays] with a surprise and delight that did honour to her taste. She (by the bye) was at her very best last night; *had put off the Catherine, or rather not put it on* since her return from Bath, and sang to us after supper, and was agreeable" (2:89; my emphasis). Although Baillie thought so highly of Siddons that she wanted her to play the lead in *De Monfort*, it is one of the play's interesting features that the dramaturgy enacts ambivalence about Siddons's approach to performance through opposing her role (Jane De Monfort) to that of De Monfort who, because of being extremely dependent on Jane's good opinion, battles her throughout the play in an attempt to uncloset his need to express passionate, socially forbidden, desires for another man.

Baillie and Closet Space

Just as De Monfort struggles with how to perform his gender identity correctly for public audiences while still giving vent to his closeted desire, so in her preface writing (as Chapter 3 suggested) Baillie enacted her own conflicts about how to "be" a successful playwright: despite the fact that many of her male colleagues took what we might call "a feminine turn" by heralding the closet as a retreat from the vulgarities of the public stage, Baillie showed her ostensible robustness by arguing that only full-fledged theatrical productions could help her determine how successfully she had brought the drama of the closet into public view. Her whole body of work may be read as an attempt to negotiate the boundary separating text from performance—if not to heal the opposition between closet and stage that resulted in the elevation of plays read over plays acted, then at least to argue for the value of theater that experiments with, and participates in, both kinds of arenas.

   An example of how Baillie's dramaturgy sometimes parallels her theory in which she attempts to overturn the closet–stage dichotomy so that the closet is aligned with embodiment rather than reading, occurs in her comedy *The Election* (1802). At one point her character Charles Baltimore protests his mother's suggestion that he try "taking up a book and reading an hour before dinner" (117), and Mrs. Baltimore pleads with him to "try, for once in your life, what kind of a thing reading quietly for an hour to one's self may be. I assure you there are many good stories in it, and you will get some little insight into the affairs of mankind, by the bye."

When Charles insists that "no story read can ever be like a story told by a pair of moving lips, and their two lively assistants the eyes, looking it to you all the while, and supplying every deficiency of words" (117), the deficiency of plays read rather than staged looms into view.[18] Purportedly no fond book reader herself, Baillie suggests that reading is often a disappointing experience, especially in comparison to a live story:

> Charles sits down with his book; reads a little with one arm dangling over the back of the chair; then changes his position, and reads a little while with the other arm over the back of the chair; then changes his position again, and after rubbing his legs with his book, continues to read a little more; then he stops, and brushes some dust off his breeches with his elbow. (118)

Clearly resistant to this activity, Charles at last takes his mother's proferred book, but then complains that some people, "when they open a book, can just pop up a good thing at once, and be diverted with it; but I don't know how it is, . . when ever I open a book, I can light upon nothing but long dry prefaces and dissertations; beyond which, perhaps, there may lie, at last, some pleasant story, *like a little picture-closet* at the end of a long stone gallery, or like a little kernel buried in a great mountain of shells and husks. I would not take the trouble of coming at it for all that one gets" (117–18; my emphasis). By equating the possibility of discovering a pleasant story during the act of reading with coming upon a little picture-closet at the end of a long stone gallery, Charles not only places closet space in opposition to reading—a position underscored by the stage direction that describes him in the actual act of perusal—but he also allies closets with pleasantly theatrical experiences, a rhetorical move in the play that urges us to reconceive "the closet" half of the closet–stage dichotomy as a site for potentially exciting embodiment.

The settings of many of Baillie's dramas would suggest otherwise. Aware that audiences expected the London patent theaters to show dramas rich in spectacular effects, she structured the plots of her tragedies around social upheaval, religious conflict, political intrigue, and the geographical sublime. Her plays are often filled with crowd scenes, stage battles, armies, and outdoor adventures, and large groups of people periodically burst into choral song (even in her nonmusicals). The stage directions for *The Martyr* (1826), for example, call for the appearance of lions in an amphitheater, even though Baillie did not regard the religious content of her play as suitable for dramatization. *Ethwald, Part Two* (1802)—her version of *Macbeth*—contains a lengthy scene that forecasts Bertolt Brecht's *Mother Cour-*

age, in which women, babies, the sick, and the elderly flee the horrors of a war created by Ethwald's rage for glory; it also depicts a field of battle "strewed with slain" (175).

Yet Baillie's preference for the "private and domestic" is clearly stated in her October 1805 letter to her brother, Matthew Baillie, when she declined Sir John Sinclair's proposal to write a tragedy on the fall of Darius, saying that she would, instead, "write a tragedy upon some interesting, but more private and domestic story" (cited in Carhart 25). Indeed, though her plays are full of public ceremonies, a number of scenes take place in little rooms, and rarely does one or more of the characters in a given drama fail to refer to the fact that they have either been in, or are about to go visit, the closet spaces of the great houses that appear in many of Baillie's plays. Contrasts between theaters of war and closet spaces inform the dramaturgy of many of Baillie's dramas, including *Basil*, Baillie's tragedy about love, as if to underscore that her theory argued an equal value for two very different kinds of arenas.

Performing Resistance and Resisting the Performative in Baillie's *Basil*

One of the many plays Baillie wrote about the military during the lengthy period when England was at war with France, *Count Basil* (or *Basil*, as it has come to be called) depicts a male character who, like De Monfort, is faced with the challenge of adapting a rigid style of performing masculinity to differing performance venues. When removed from war's theater and facing a social drama for which he lacks training, however, Basil almost immediately loses his sense of how to enact "manliness." Baillie not only explores the plight of men searching for performance modes through which to enact a culturally acceptable "masculinity," but through the character of Victoria she also examines some of the difficulties faced by Romantic women theater artists who wished to experiment with the performance of femininity in both closet and public spaces. In Anne Mellor's reading, this play challenged "hegemonic constructions both of 'human nature' and of gender and offered an alternative account of the 'emancipatory' potential within social practices" ("Joanna Baillie" 561) through its valorization of the counterpublic sphere, that is, "a hitherto culturally marginalized 'women's realm,' the realm of feelings, sympathy, and curiosity" (563).

As in contemporary American society, the male bonding of military culture in *Basil* casts the performance of "the feminine" as an impediment to warrior might. Count Basil seems wedded to the approval of his soldier cousin, Count Rosinberg, until he becomes attracted to the Princess Victoria and, as in *De Monfort*, a crisis between men ensues. When Basil begins to pursue Victoria into the closet recesses of her domestic world, he must endure a barrage of criticism from Rosinberg, who portrays Victoria as the typical fatal woman all men must shun. The Countess Albini, Victoria's maternal mentor, also objects to the attraction, but for different reasons: she wants to teach Victoria how to develop a sense of self that does not derive from "the way in which women are constructed and constricted by the male gaze" (Cox, *Seven Gothic Dramas* 56). She urges Victoria to recognize that her physical attractiveness is the source of an "unreal pow[e]r": "For she who only finds her self-esteem / In others' admiration, begs an alms" (II.iv). Yet, though "endorsing genuineness and usefulness as characteristics more desirable in women than artificiality and ornamentation" (Purinton 145), Albini's words go unheeded. Victoria continues to flirt with Basil, and he commits suicide when he discovers that a battle has been fought without him—"A soldier's reputation is too fine," he says, "To be expos'd e'en to the smallest cloud" (II.i.23). Blaming herself for the fact that Basil has been attracted to her domestic idyll, Victoria promises to "spend my wretched days / In humble pray'r for [Basil's] departed spirit" (V.iii.48) as a punishment for supposedly enchanting him. This alleged seduction is indicted by the ever-watchful Rosinberg, who has wanted to keep Basil "pure" for war. The target of the dramaturgy's critique, however, is not only a culture that would prescribe a narrow range of performance styles with which to "do" gender; it also highlights the necessity of becoming aware of the performative features of social acting as a means for developing a space in which to further experiment with a wider range of performance styles.

Set in Mantua in the sixteenth century, "when Charles the Fifth defeated Francis the First" (18), *Basil* begins with two processions, Baillie's nod to "the popularity of extravaganza" (Tobin 195). Representing the "debate between two opposing methods of government" in the battle for "control of the public sphere" (Mellor, "Joanna Baillie" 563), one of these processions shows Basil and his men marching into town on their way to war; the other reveals Victoria leading her women to the shrine of Saint Francis to give thanks for her father's recovery. Both characters are introduced in performative modes amid crowds watching them, as if Basil and Victoria were part of "some show" (I.i), and the subsequent action of the play will make it clear that they are indeed as vulnerable to spectator approval as were actors during the late eighteenth century, whose professional success—especially in the case of women—depended on their ability to meet the culture's expectations for the performance of gender appropriate to one's age and marital status. That the play draws on features of the public stage to enact its cultural critique—"What opportunities for Mr. Cecil de Mille's particular genius!" M. Norton exclaims in reference to *Basil*'s processions, masked ball, and street scenes (137)—shows the degree to which Baillie's dramaturgy is based on a practical knowledge of the London stage as well as demonstrates her sensitivity to the uniquely fraught position of the late-eighteenth-century female actor, who, as I discussed in Chapter 2, had constantly to confront the problem of moving as a public woman between private and public arenas.

As the character in *Basil* who seeks creative outlets for self-expression by performing femininity melodramatically, the highly self-conscious Victoria eventually embodies the condition of the Romantic female theater artist, whose anxious condition often impeded her ability to improvise happily in a direction that did not confine her to cultural stereotypes. In contrast, Basil seems unaware that his version of masculinity is performative, and although he tries throughout the play to move from his military context to a different social setting, he seems helpless to discover modes of performance that would allow him to negotiate different arenas with ease. Basil is indeed a victim in the course of the play, not—as Rosinberg would argue—of Victoria's machinations, but rather of his allegiance to a world in which excessive emotion has no place other than in militaristic rituals that involve only men. Though Victoria flirts with the power of "inflict[ing] pain" on Basil and "emulates the masculine model of oppression," she is as much inhibited as Basil is by "their notion of separatedness" (Purinton 146). She cannot be blamed for Basil's unfamiliarity with how to perform his gender in a number of settings, an ignorance that prevents his comfortable movement between the closeted world of feminine domesticity and the public theater of men at war.

Rosinberg's obsession with Basil is similar to De Monfort's with Rezenvelt, suggesting that both of Baillie's early tragedies are fascinated by what happens to men for whom there is no socially sanctioned mode of expressing desire. Baillie emphasizes Rosinberg's intense preoccupation with Basil when the officers head for town for "an hour or so" in act 1: Rosinberg starts to exit the stage and then returns because he is worried that Basil, left to himself, will drift Victoria's way. Alarmed when Basil confesses that Victoria's train has "wak'd from sleep" his soul (I.ii.21), Rosinberg tries to respond with restraint, but he cannot repress an expostulation that reveals not only his misogyny but also his own personal investment in Basil's resistance to women: "What! 'midst the dangers of eventful war, / Still let thy mind be haunted by a woman, / Who would, perhaps, hear of thy fall in battle, / As Dutchmen read of earthquakes in Calabria, / And never stop to cry 'alack-a-day!' " (I.ii.22). Believing that the only female capable of the kind of tenacious devotion he exhibits toward Basil is Rosinberg's own mother ("I know her love will never change," he says, "Nor make me prove uneasy jealousy"), Rosinberg is so fearful of change that he reminds Basil of words he spoke earlier in life, words for which Rosinberg is now nostalgic, since they promised him a life of steady male comradeship, and perhaps erotic fulfillment:

>   —I shall never forget it!
> 'Twas at Vienna, on a public day;
> Thou but a youth, I then a man full form'd;
> Thy stripling's brow graced with its first cockade,
> Thy mighty bosom swell'd with mighty thoughts.
> Thou'rt for the court, dear Rosinberg, quoth thou!
> "Now pray thee be not caught with some gay dame,
> To laugh and ogle, and befool thyself:
> It is offensive in the public eye,
> And suits not with a man of thy endowments."
>   (I.ii.22)

Because Rosinberg views relationships with women as making a man impotent for military rituals—like contemporary American midshipmen at the U.S. Naval Academy, some of whom have been branded with a *W* on their buttocks for, in the words of a recent article, "dating women at the school" (Gelman 29)—he has a disdain for the sentimental gestures and emotionalism of lovers, even as he recalls Basil's focus on his own "endowments." In the mask scene in act 3, Rosinberg acts the part of a courtier to mock heterosexual infatuation; he enters the stage "fantastically dressed, with a willow upon his head, and scraps of sonnets and torn letters fluttering around his neck" in order to "make a jest of all true love" (III.iii.32). Men are to be chided for succumbing to what he will call, on Basil's deathbed, "cursed passion" (V.iii.47), and women are to be feared for "affecting" passion; their courtship performances are full of the changes

Rosinberg shrinks from: scolding, frowning, banishing and then recalling their lovers, caressing and chiding them—women who are not mothers of men endanger a man's attempt to stay stolid by behaving in unpredictable ways, assessed by Albini as "affected freaks" (III.iii.32).

While at first Rosinberg seems to have an ecumenical outlook on women—he praises "the varieties of lib'ral nature, / Where every kind of beauty charms the eye; / Large and small featur'd, flat and prominent" (I.ii.21)—the bulk of his commentary valorizes the late-eighteenth-century ideal of femininity, finding in any woman's performative impulse a public theatricality inimical to a man's peace of mind. The woman who behaves histrionically, who is linguistically and physically assertive, is to be avoided or labeled "proud," "captious," and "fatal." As in John Keats's famous ballad (1819), which *Basil* anticipates, Victoria is portrayed as "la belle dame sans merci," whose knight not only often wanders "alone and palely loitering" but—in Baillie's play—eventually takes his own life. "Confound the fatal beauty of that woman, / Which hath bewitch'd thee so!" Rosinberg shrieks toward play's end (IV.iii.39), in a desperate attempt to move Basil back onto his original trajectory. "Confound these women, and their artful snares," he sounds the refrain, "Since men will be such fools!" (IV.iv.41). "O curse that woman! . . . / She has undone us all!" (V.iii.46). Even "woman's grief" is suspect, Rosinberg tells Victoria as she sobs over Basil's body: it resembles "a summer storm, / Short as it violent is" (V.iii.48).

In reference to Keats's poem, Karen Swann has argued that romance can be "at least as fatal to the lady as the knight" (89), and this is almost the case with Victoria. She does not (like Basil) die at play's end, yet she dedicates herself to a kind of necrophiliac marriage: "I'll love [Basil] in the low bed of death" (V.iii.48), she says over his body, evoking the image of a dead nun in her projected act of self-immolation. Victoria's fate is to cast herself as Basil's murderer, a moment that was predicted at the end of the mask when the figure of Cupid is frightened away by "a band of satyrs," whose triumphal banishment of the god of love is capped in a "grotesque" dance (III.iii.35).

Victoria's mentor, Countess Albini, shares with Rosinberg an impulse to restrain Victoria from spirited behavior, although their motives differ: Rosinberg wants to "save" Basil for men of war and Albini to help Victoria learn independence from those who would anatomize her physicality, which Basil does after their first encounter when he praises "[h]er roundly spreading breast, her tow'ring neck, / Her face ting'd sweetly with the bloom of youth" (I.ii.21). Albini provides a counterpoint to Victoria's father, the Duke, who is particularly intolerant of femaleness: he describes Victoria's resistance to assisting in the scheme to prevent Basil from fighting in battle by saying: "[h]er mind, as suits the sex, [is] too weak and narrow / To relish deep-laid scenes of policy" (II.iii.25), an observation reinforced by Basil in act 4 when he observes to Rosinberg: "She is a woman, who avoids all share / In secret politics" (IV.iii.39). The effect of Albini's counsel, however, which evokes for Victoria inevitable comparisons with her dead mother (even more idealized than she throughout the play), is to undermine her self-confidence. Continually chastised for being vain and flirtatious, Victoria readily comes to identify with these critiques once Basil shoots himself.

Prior to this event, however, Victoria's biggest fault is that she aims to enliven her life by using her talent for performing hyperfemininity, a skill devalued by a culture that provides women with few appropriate outlets for spirited expression. "Were human passions plac'd within the breast / But to be curb'd, subdu'd, pluck'd by the roots?" Victoria asks Albini in one of her frustrated moments (II.iv.27). To effect more control over a world that would physically fetishize her, she tries to use that very physicality to her advantage. Not only does she rival Basil's procession with her own in the opening scene, but she conveys a spirited competitiveness when she confesses that she aims "[t]o make the cunning artless, tame the rude, / Subdue the haughty, shake the undaunted soul; / Yea, put a bridle in the lion's mouth, / And lead him forth as a domestic cur" (II.iv.27). Neither malevolent nor unselfconscious about the performative aspect of her actions, Victoria understands the degree to which she is experimenting with what it feels like to indulge "the freaks of thoughtless youth" (II.iv.27). It is too early in her life, she suggests, to start behaving like her sainted mother, about whom Albini and Geoffrey trill with passion, or to conform to the behavior of "a plain, good, simple, fire-side dame," with her hair in "braided locks" and a "white coif" (II.iv.27). If she were now—in the present moment of the play—to fulfill the culture's imperatives to behave as a dignified, useful person, Victoria seems to sense that she might have to relinquish even the ephemeral power she holds over suitors and courtiers who comply with her only because she is beautiful. Indeed, Rosinberg corroborates Victoria's sense that whatever power women might have in this culture is "a short-live'd tyranny / That ends at last in hatred and contempt" (IV.iv.41). Perhaps this recognition that her "empire" is only illusory prompts her to wear a guise in the mask scene that evokes the image of a "female conjurer": she is comfortable with sending up the fact that her performance of femininity has been blamed for magically enchanting men away from their more significant duties and their masculine identity. Therefore, like Prince Hal in *Henry IV, Part One*, who cultivates a mercurial persona with an eye to earning more respect from those confused by his adolescent forays with Falstaff and crew, Victoria tells Albini that, after having allowed herself one more scene with Basil, "folly of this kind / Will quite insipid and disgusting seem; / And so I shall become a prudent maid, / And passing wise at last" (IV.iv.42).

Unlike the princess, Basil has not yet learned to distinguish between acting an identity and being it. He does not possess the theatrical skills that give Victoria the temporary freedom to create a social performance through which she can self-consciously assess herself in relation to her culture. Unable to distance himself from any identity he assumes, Basil—like his prototype, Romeo—is physically shaken by the princess's very presence. He "changes countenance" when Victoria enters the room, sees a "dizzy mist that swims before my sight," and experiences a "ringing in my ears" (II.i.23). Later, he elicits Victoria's apparent disapproval when he runs up to seize her hand and "presses it to his lips" with these hyperbolic words: "Let this sweet hand indeed its threat perform, / And make it heav'n to be for ever dumb!" That Basil has difficulty expressing himself outside of his male military world is imaged strikingly in the moment when he woos Victoria through her little boy-pet, Mirando. As in *De Monfort*, homoerotic desire seems to drive Baillie's dramaturgy. Basil promises to sing underneath Mirando's window to lull him to rest but instead picks him up and kisses him "so furious rough" that Mirando protests to be let down (III.iii.35).[19] Completely unsure of how he is to perform, and also ignorant of the fact that his melodramatic speech and gesture constitute a performance in the first place, Basil confesses several times to Victoria, "I know not what I do" (II.ii.24).

In the soliloquy that follows the second scene of act 2, the uncertain Basil wonders whether he has "done well," and he wants to ask Rosinberg for his perspective on recent events. When Rosinberg calls him "weaker than a child," Basil counters with a defense of his feelings as a "noble weakness, / A weakness which hath greater things achiev'd / Than all the firm determin'd strength of reason" (II.ii.25). But the problem is not his childishness. As Terry Eagleton has observed in reference to literary theory, when the child asks why the world works as it does, s/he "unwittingly" creates the kind of "alienation effects" that Brecht valued in the "inept actor," who constantly defamiliarizes stage convention by refusing to operate within the rules of effective mimesis (*The Significance of Theory* 34). Basil's problem is that, once he arrives in Mantua, he finds himself in a world of adults who value performance skills that he has not yet managed to acquire—a self-consciousness about what is imitative or seemingly authentic, for example. Though Basil momentarily experiences "a new-born pow'r within me / Shall make me twenty-fold the man I've been / Before this fated day" (II.ii.25), he comes to realize that Rosinberg's training has actually taken the power of performance away from him. For one thing, Basil is poorly equipped to comprehend the artificiality of gender identity through the assumption of various performance styles for specific spaces, and as a result, he founders in the social dramas of this urban carnival.

As in *Romeo and Juliet*, however, one of the many Shakespearean plays that infuse Baillie's verse,[20] Basil and Victoria enjoy a brief respite from their adult supervisors in a "very beautiful" forest grove (IV.v.42), a scene that exhibits *Basil*'s focus on the efficacy of assessing gender identity as performative. Dressed as a huntress, thus evoking the image of Artemis, the vigorous goddess of the moon and protector of youth who looked after horses and other animals,[21] Victoria enters the grove with Basil "as if just alighted from their horses" (IV.v.42). Baillie's description of Victoria's equestrian skill suggests that the playwright may have felt an affinity with this character: Baillie's youthful ease around horses is often mentioned in the biographical accounts of her life. Catherine Jane Hamilton, for example, notes that Baillie "scampered heedlessly on any pony that came in her way," and that even "in her womanhood she was never a book-lover, never bookish, as her friend Lucy Aiken was. She gleaned inspiration from the sights of Nature, from old legends, and from the real life that was passing around her" (1:113–14). This relish of the outdoors is one of the features that makes Victoria a compelling figure, as she describes for Isabella her own appreciation of riding a horse:

> . . . I vault already on my leathern seat,
> And feel the fiery steed beneath me shake
> His mantled sides, and paw the fretted earth;
> Whilst I aloft, with gay equestrian grace,
> The low salute of gallant lords return,
> Who, waiting round with eager watchful eye,
> And reined steeds, the happy moment seize.
> (IV.iv.41)

To seize "the happy moment," Victoria and Basil dismount in the grove, which the imaginative Victoria describes in magical terms. This is the pastoral island where "little elfins dance, / And fairies sport beneath the summer's moon" (IV.v.42). However, when she portrays this landscape to Basil and her past delights there, Victoria's verbal facility overwhelms him, and all he can do is echo her language until she admonishes, "My lord, it is uncivil in you thus / My very words with mock'ry to repeat" (IV.v.42).

This moment draws attention to Basil's inability to find the "correct" gestures and intonations for enacting courtship ritual. His hyperbolic speech—though a match for Victoria's—vexes her (because it is uncontrollably rendered) to the point where she devises a new strategy that heightens the stakes of the moment before. She begins to "remember" a walk in this very grove with another man, information that renders Basil even more strident and awkward and leads him to disintegrate into the wild gestures that periodically inform his performance throughout the play: unable to finish his sentences, Basil is described in the stage directions as "clasping his hands, and raising them to his head," "drooping his head, and looking distractedly upon the ground," "tossing about his arms in transport." Hoping for more "courtly" behavior, Victoria "pretend[s] not to see him," and eventually exposes his moves as inappropriate by letting him know that the man she is speaking of is her brother. But once she does this, Victoria is no longer intrigued with Basil and exits the stage promising to remember him only as a "friend." Still mystified by how to behave and lacking the awareness to realize that he has not done well with Victoria—after all, "she said she would remember me," Basil reassures himself—he tries to scrutinize the gestures of Victoria's body as she walks into the distance. Do her "doubtful ling'ring steps" portend desire, he wonders in soliloquy; "will she look back?" (IV.v.43).

The answer is predictable given that this play is a tragedy, and Basil learns that while he has been cavorting with the princess, the battle against the French has been fought. The Duke's desire to delay him has been effected, and the tragedy reaches its denouement with Basil's suicide, a turn in the plot that caused Baillie's friend, Mary Berry, to write that "nothing to me can be more affecting than the end of that play" (2:90).[22] Countess Albini, who unapologetically criticizes Victoria's courtship flirtatiousness, does not appear in the fifth act to prevent Victoria from pledging her chastity to the memory of Basil's life.

As in the case of Jane De Monfort, however, a few more words need

to be said about Albini, who seems the play's most enlightened character in terms of the performance of gender. Mellor assesses her as "Baillie's
homage to Mary Wollstonecraft," the "embodiment of rational judgment"
(565), and indeed, Albini's main objective is to teach Victoria a way of relating to men that will allow her more control over her body and mind.
Throughout the play, Albini is distinguished from the other characters
for garnering the respect of both women and men through occupying a
culturally masculine position that allows her to speak her opinions forthrightly. Victoria tells Isabella that Albini's "nobler mind / Procures to her
the privilege of man, / N'er to be old till nature's strength decays" (II.iv.28;
my emphasis), and Rosinberg compliments her as "the one of all thy sex, /
Who wearst thy years with such a winning grace" (III.ii.33).

Yet by trying to hasten Victoria into a less "degraded" position where
she can reside safely protected from her culture's desire to sexualize young
women, Albini neglects to realize the following: precisely because Victoria's attempts to garner men's admiration are self-conscious, aggressive,
carefully staged, and temporary, she shows that she is busily involved in the
process of teaching herself—through an exaggerated performance of femininity—how to manage the "poor ambition" she feels as a result of living in
a culture that would curb her theatrical bent (IV.iv.42). While recognizing
her kinship with Victoria—Albini concedes that she "well remember[s] in
my youth / I felt the like"—still Albini expects Victoria to obey her directives and tear such ambition "indignant from [her] breast, / As that which
[does] degrade a noble mind" (IV.iv.42). From one perspective, Albini is
wise to urge Victoria to drop her excessively feminine performance. But
from another she is negligent in failing to appreciate that Victoria's experiments with performing her femininity do not necessarily express her real
values or her "true" "self." Albini's concern for how spectators will read
Victoria's body in the social space causes her to send Victoria the message
that structured much of the discourse of women who wrote about or for
the British Romantic stage in London between 1790 and 1840: especially
for women, the theatrical medium was fraught with dangers, not the least
of which was its threat to a woman's ability to perform her gender identity
with accuracy, moderation, and proper decorum.

This threat lay at the heart of the restrictions that governed the life of
the woman artist in Romantic theater, who had constantly to be concerned
with how spectators would interpret her performances of gender both on
and off the stage. Even someone as aware of the differences between acting and "being" a character as was Elizabeth Inchbald animated one of the

recurring themes of "the antitheatrical prejudice" (see Barish, 1981) when writing of Olivia in Hannah Cowley's *Bold Stroke for a Husband*; she worried that a woman's ability to "counterfeit" a role boded unhappiness for the prospective marriage partner: "In the delineation of this lady, it is implied that she is no termagant, although she so frequently counterfeits the character. This insinuation, the reader, if he pleases, may trust—but the man who would venture to marry a good impostor of this kind, could not excite much pity, if his helpmate was often induced to act the part which she had heretofore, with so much spirit, assumed" ("Remarks to *Bold Stroke for a Husband*").[23]

Yet in spite of the culture's tendency to confuse women's performances of character on stage with their gender performances elsewhere, women theater artists like Joanna Baillie worked to devise rhetorical strategies through which to call attention to their professional and personal concerns. By drawing on some of the experiences of Romantic women for the context of her closet play, *Basil*, Baillie asserted the value of a theatricality that often showed itself only within the confines of domestic architecture. This assertion is not unproblematic, however. As detailed above, Baillie often created plots in which the heroine who exerts her values in the face of challenges to her sense of rectitude is counteracted by martial men who "expatiate / On woman's weakness" (*The Separation* 536). A foil that makes more dramatic women's struggles to assert beliefs to which they can be unwaveringly true, nevertheless the frequent misogyny of Baillie's male characters cannot be explained only as descriptive of the era's ideology of femininity, which upheld a mode of behavior inhibiting to women's individual achievement.

It is possible to see these recurring moments of woman-bashing in Baillie's plays as reflective of her own ambivalence about the position of women, especially in the public spaces of formal theaters. As my reading of *De Monfort* suggested, Baillie's creation of a female character—which pleased Siddons (to Baillie she said, "Make for me more Jane De Monforts" [cited in Cox, *Seven Gothic Dramas* 56]) but which embodied a style of acting that Baillie suggested in both her theory and dramaturgy worked to limit the experimental and improvisational impulse—provided her with the means of critiquing stereotypical performances of gender roles even as she rendered these cultural stereotypes dramatically compelling. This is one of the reasons why homoerotic desire plays such a central role in both *De Monfort* and *Basil*. *Basil*'s inability to perform in another persona for the sake of heterosexual courtship ritual belongs to the spectrum that contains

De Monfort's general unwillingness to act in a manner that would please his sister-mother Jane. That the dramaturgy of both plays is dominated by De Monfort's and Basil's repressed desire for other male characters suggests that one of the reasons Baillie was interested in domestic spaces and closet drama stemmed from her curiosity about "closet issues."

Baillie's importance to the Romantic period and to our own era lies less in her identity as a female playwright per se than in her concept of the closet as a showcase for the subtle mechanisms that theater artists in the Romantic era developed for questioning the ideological restraints that governed—and still govern—gendered experience. This is one of the reasons that Agnes Withrington, in Baillie's first comedy, *The Tryal*, must animate the dialectic between closet theater and public staging in order to discern whether her future husband will love her when she is not acting up to the era's ideal. Whereas in *Basil* "the hour of trial came, and found [the hero] wanting" (V.iii.46), in this comic trial discussed in the next chapter Agnes proves to be more than a match for the social adversity she might have married into had she not thought to devise a plan by which to separate the authentic lover from the man who hunts a dowry. Through a dramatized exploration of the dynamics of the private theatrical—often the province of women—Baillie offers us another example of how a study of her dramaturgy can animate the theatrical contexts that structure women's writings for and about the early-nineteenth-century stage.

5. Private Theatricals and Baillie's *The Tryal*

No pay, we play, so gay, all day—
Curse the expense, chase care away!
—Richard Brinsley Peake, *Amateurs and Actors:*
A Musical Farce in Two Acts

If here our feeble powers
Have lightly wing'd for you some wintry hours;
Should these remember'd scenes in fancy live,
And to some future minutes pleasure give,
To right good end we've worn our mumming guise,
And we're repaid and happy—ay, and wise.[1]
—Joanna Baillie, "Epilogue to the Theatrical
Representation at Strawberry Hill"[2]

As the epigraphs above suggest, one of the primary aims of putting on plays in the upper-class British home was to amuse those who had enough money to buy off boredom. Private theatricals were often unabashedly elitist projects, not only in the sense that many took place in exclusive domestic environments, but because they required, in addition to time, a great deal of money to arrange. Sybil Rosenfeld writes that Lord Barrymore's expenses for cake alone at the opening night reception of his private theater at Wargrave in 1789 were "rumoured" to have been £20, small change after the £60,000 that was spent on building the theater itself (18–19). To overcome the luxury of boredom was the impetus behind the staging of Elizabeth Inchbald's 1798 adaptation of August von Kotzebue's *Lovers' Vows* (1791) in Jane Austen's *Mansfield Park* (1814), perhaps the best-known work of literature that features the late-eighteenth-century phenomenon of amateur acting. The eagerness with which most of Mansfield's youthful residents embrace John Yates's proposal to put on a play is not only indicative of "a love of the theatre," which the narrative labels "so general" (147); Yates has arrived onto an already indolent scene embodied by the frequently supine Lady Bertram, and his proposal to mount a private theatrical follows on a painfully aimless visit to Mr. Rushworth's country house, during which each person's "spirits were in general exhausted" (133).

From the perspective of a feminist theater historian, however, the exclusivity of those private theatricals which took place in aristocratic and upper-middle-class domestic environments was important for providing certain women (and sometimes their servants) with a forum for experimenting with the theater arts.[3] It would be misleading to suggest that British private theatricals constituted some sort of avant-garde movement at the height of their vogue (1780–1810).[4] Even though new works were performed on private stages, they often derived from the canonical plays that dominated eighteenth-century patent theaters and also constituted the bulk of private theatrical offerings.[5] But because private entertainments were often produced in isolated settings, making theatrical activity accessible to a group of people who were not necessarily theatergoers, they inevitably deviated from London productions in spirit; they were certainly more conducive to spontaneity. Often rehearsed in the context of a house party that could go on for several weeks, and in small spaces that rendered more permeable the customary barriers between spectator and actor, the private theatrical could offer its participants a deeply personal and imaginative experience, not only allowing for a great deal of playfulness and delight in the act of improvisation, but also encouraging a serious self-consciousness about the performative features of social acting. As Gillian Russell (1995) has observed, in the context of her discussion of the military's amateur theatricals in Georgian Britain, the "phenomenon of amateur theatricals was . . . part of a broader struggle for the definition and control of various kinds of sociability in late eighteenth-century Britain" (128).

Because scholars have been preoccupied with debating the degree to which the turn to the closet in the period's canonized theater criticism does—or does not—express an "antitheatrical prejudice," the actual theater that was produced in the closeted spaces of the private sphere during the Romantic period has often been overlooked. This theater of the closet, though not exclusive to women, was particularly friendly to women's creative endeavors, and it is this theatrical context that Joanna Baillie's earliest comedy, *The Tryal* (1798), explores. Written during the British private theater movement and considered for a private theatrical production at Bentley Priory in 1803, *The Tryal* probes some of the tensions created by the trend among certain aristocratic and upper-middle-class women to write and direct improvisational performances in domestic spaces. Through the character of Agnes Withrington, an heiress who directs two women in a plot designed to determine the motives of the men who would marry her, *The Tryal* looks closely at those "ordinary" and "familiar" circumstances that comprised "Characteristic Comedy," Baillie's term for plays like her own that featured emotional trials on domestic stages.

Although Baillie did not identify herself with the English feminist movement of the 1790s, her theoretical discourse suggests that the domestic sphere, rather than being merely a place to retreat from the problematic stage practices of London theaters, could offer women interested in theater and drama a space for creative development. Baillie's theory encourages us to look at Romantic theater and drama in ways that highlight women's contributions to the period. Her language privileges the closet of "the great man," but she also advocates the performance of those dramas forged in private space to suggest that closets are not only sites of reading—of unperformability, disembodiment, and masculine intellection—but that they also contain a rich performance history in which women have actively participated before, during, and since the Romantic period. In this way, Baillie can be seen as contributing to the eighteenth-century trend to focus on domestic space in order to celebrate women's cultural worth.

Women and the Private Theatrical

Defined as "performance wholly or mainly by amateurs [presented] to selected or invited audiences, as opposed to the general public" (Rosenfeld, *Temples of Thespis* 9), private theatricals are usually distinguished in narratives of theater history from those plays that were acted privately by professionals.[6] Therefore, as Sybil Rosenfeld notes, the first amateur actors in England may be considered the priests and guild members who performed church-sponsored mystery and morality plays (ibid. 8–9). By contrast, because the performers of early Tudor "household revels" were on retainer as specialists of acting, they corresponded to what we would today call "professionals."[7] As Keith Sturgess has written, by 1620 the word "private" in reference to theater meant that a play was to be performed "indoors" (3), and these private theaters—conceived along the lines of "a club, an academy, and an art-house" (4)—were attended largely by aristocratic audiences attempting to distance themselves from the rowdier playgoers of outdoor stages. The associations of aristocracy with theater in an exclusive domestic setting were reinforced by seventeenth-century masques and "aristocratic entertainments" such as John Milton's *Arcades* performed at Harefield in the early 1630s. Yet the rage for private theaters in England did not ignite until the eighteenth century, when this mostly aristocratic pastime was encouraged by developments in France, which had more than sixty private theaters by 1750 in Paris alone (Marvin Carlson 51), and during the last quarter of the century boasted variations on the private theatrical, such as the pornographic dramas often featured in "clandestine theatres."[8]

These "clandestine theatres" require a brief mention here, since the fact that French women "assumed great importance in the development of this theatre culture" (Toepfer 66) points to some parallels in Great Britain. Neither England, Scotland, Ireland, nor Wales produced a figure quite like France's Duchess de Villeroi, who—in a move presaging certain aspects of feminist theater in the 1980s[9]—sometimes excluded men from the audience for the purpose of featuring "plays glorifying lesbian love and setting the scene for huge sapphic orgies involving women from the opera and the Comedie Française" (66). But just as the private theater scene in mid-eighteenth-century France had its Marie Antoinette and Marie-Madeleine Guimard, and the German court theater its Charlotte von Stein in the 1770s,[10] so the British private theatrical community enjoyed the passionate commitment to private entertainment of many (primarily aristocratic and upper-middle-class) women.

By organizing, sponsoring, writing, and performing in private theatricals, eighteenth-century women were following the example set in earlier eras by English aristocrats such as Alice Spenser, Dowager Countess of Derby, who acted in Jacobean masques and attended country-house entertainments (Brown 15), Queen Henrietta Maria, who in the early seventeenth century took the then unusual step of appearing in two court pastorals (Sturgess 57), and the Princesses Mary and Anne, who performed in Crowne's *Calisto* in 1675. By the dawn of the next century it was not unusual to find wealthy women directing their children, grandchildren, or friends in an evening of theater of which they were the primary organizers, or writing plays for them, as in the case of the Countess of Hardwicke, whose *Court of Oberon* blended together a French piece with her original composition in order to "render it more suitable to her juvenile performers, the youngest of whom was but two years old."[11] An anonymous letter to the editor of the *European Magazine* written in 1788 indicates how firmly the private theater movement had taken hold by century's end:

> The practice of people of distinction and fortune to erect theatres, and commence actors to perform in them, *en famille*, is now so general, and is indeed, under certain restrictions, so very praise-worthy and innocent, that a sort of general account of all the play-houses and players of *ton*, to be continued occasionally, would perhaps be a pleasant, not to say profitable, companion

or vade-mecum to those places of resort: and it might, appositely enough, be called The Fashionable Rosciad. (66)

Among the amateur playwrights and actresses in Great Britain were Elizabeth Cobbold, whose memoirist wrote that not only was she "a very frequent attendant on the theatre," but she "herself also possessed much taste and skill in dramatic composition, and wrote several pieces of great merit" (Jermyn 16). Though it was not the case, as the character of Bombast says in Archibald Maclaren's play, *The Private Theatre* (1809), that "little theatres furnish actors for the great, as little rivers furnish salmon for the sea" (I.ii.12), nevertheless amateur performer Charlotte Twistleton received acting training on the private stage at Adlestrop House sufficient to launch a professional career. Between 1780 and 1805 Elizabeth Berkeley Craven either composed, translated, adapted, or altered nineteen plays.[12] As Lady Craven she organized and appeared in private performances in Warwickshire, and upon relocating with her second husband from Germany to England, as the Margravine of Anspach she supervised the building and operation of a private theater in the 1790s at Brandenburgh House in Hammersmith. Here she alternately performed the functions of actress, playwright, producer, translator, musician, and singer. "My taste for music and poetry, and my style of imagination in writing, chastened by experience, were great sources of delight to me," she wrote in her memoirs in 1826:[13]

> I wrote *The Princess of Georgia*, and the *Twins of Smyrna*, for the Margrave's theatre, besides *Nourjad* and several other pieces; and for these I composed various airs in music. I invented *fetes* to amuse the Margrave, which afforded me a charming contrast to accounts, bills, and the changes of domestics and chamberlains, and many other things quite odious to me. (2:106)

Craven's reference to the domestic context in which her comedies, pantomimes, and musical dramas were forged reminds us to pay particular attention to private settings in constructing women's theater history. For it is often in domestic spaces, far away from the traditional stage, that much of women's drama and theatrical art has actually been produced. For instance, Kirsten Gram Holmstrom's study of monodrama, "attitudes," and *tableaux vivants* devotes a large portion of the text to an analysis of a trend among upper-class European women to create "mimoplastic art" in the public spaces of their homes between 1770 and 1815 (128). Whether striking neoclassical poses and manipulating costume pieces, as in the case of Lady Emma Hamilton (whose stark gestures framed by special lighting effects anticipated photographers' models in the twentieth century), or miming scenes to music as did Ida Brun, or creating "art-historical etudes" (216) as did Henriette Hendel-Schutz (in which academic audiences could discuss with her the intellectual and artistic choices she had made), it is clear that the domestic setting was essential to these women for developing "a new genre on the borderline between pictorial art and theatre" (139).

Conceived and rehearsed on the home front and attended by a group of acquaintances, friends, and relatives theoretically inclined to tolerate women's ventures into acting and playwrighting, the British private theatrical gave those who would otherwise have had no theatrical experience a mode for exploring the theater arts. In the case of professional female actors, private performances also afforded opportunities for participating in theater in ways often unavailable to them on the public stage. Professional actress Harriot Mellon complained that "'there never was such a stupid task as drilling fine people!,'" but an evening of private theater at Strawberry Hill was nevertheless an occasion for her to manage the stage, in addition to occupying the position of "privy-councillor in all matters relative to costume and other little etceteras known only to the initiated in Thespian mysteries" (Baron-Wilson 1:280). Elizabeth Farren, another well-known actress of the period, frequently undertook the task of directing the amateur actors at Richmond House's private theatricals in 1787–88, "the most fashionable and exclusive . . . of their time" (Rosenfeld, *Temples of Thespis* 34).[14]

Private settings also helped some women inadvertently theorize acting. By focusing on the problem for the actress of being in the public eye while trying to adhere to cultural expectations for the proper performance of femininity, a number of women writers produced discourse that not only theorizes this problem as an indicator of the actress's heightened sensitivity to gender performances but also employs a mode of theorizing in which "onstage" and "offstage" documents at times intersect. Private playwright Elizabeth Craven, for instance, tells an anecdote in her *Memoirs* (1826) in which she focuses on the body of the amateur actor in a domestic setting to produce acting theory for a public audience. Craven recalls the following incident from her early teens when she was in Paris watching a performance that featured the famous actress Hyppolite Clairon:

> I remember, when I was thirteen years old, I was taken to the *Theatre François* at Paris, to see the performance of *Semiramis*. This character so much excited my laughter, that my mother ordered me to be taken home to the Hotel Beaufreau before the piece was finished, because my noise offended the *par-*

terre. I did not know that it was Mademoiselle Clairon who performed the part of *Semiramis*; but twenty years afterwards, when I was playing the part of the Sultan in *Almenorade*, my foolish memory recalled to mind *Semiramis*, and I imitated that declamation, which I then recollected. There were only twenty-five persons who composed the audience, all friends of the Margrave, who burst out into exclamations of my performance; and after the play was over, they declared that I must have seen Mademoiselle Clairon, whom, they said, I had so closely imitated. I protested that, to the best of my recollection, I had never seen her. They insisted that it was herself, and that I must have seen her repeatedly to have followed her manner so exactly. Declamation on the French stage was quite in fashion, and I had been so particularly struck with this kind of acting, that it had lain dormant in my mind till the occasion brought it forth. (1:217–19)

Late-twentieth-century performance theorist and actor Hollis Huston has recently (1992) observed that "only the actor's smart body can stand across the gap between theory and performance" (10), and in Craven's anecdote we see how the uncontrollable laughter of a teenage girl who witnesses a professional production sows the seeds for the adult amateur's subsequent performance in a private setting. Only when Craven goes to write about this private performance in a memoir aimed at a public audience, however, does she produce what can be described as a theory of performance, one that draws on the memory of girlish giggles to suggest her imitation of Clairon embodies Craven's critique of the French declamatory style.

Gender and Space

Feminist geographers and anthropologists have been especially interested in how the spatial features of women's lives structure their creative responses. Shirley Ardener's statement that "*behaviour and space are mutually dependent*" (2) informs Daphne Spain's thesis "that initial status differences between women and men create certain types of gendered spaces and that institutionalized spatial segregation then reinforces prevailing male advantages" (6). One way of segregating the sexes is through architecture, and a number of critics in a variety of fields have represented the eighteenth century as the period when the concept of using "architecture to reinforce prevailing patterns of privilege and to assert power" (Spain 7) began to have a significant impact.

Peter Brooks argues that eighteenth-century domestic architecture took its cue from the "new and intense concern for privacy in the Enlightenment" (49): the "well-demarcated private apartments, boudoirs, 'closets,' and alcoves of eighteenth-century upper- and middle-class hous-ing . . . supported the realization of new values attached to the individual and to the intimacy required for an individual's commerce with family, friends, and self" (28). Philippa Tristram reaches a similar conclusion—that the eighteenth-century house "made generous provision for those who wished to make their journeys privately, within the mind"—even though it was "essentially public with its absence of corridors and its interconnect-ing rooms" (3). This "new emphasis on the family and home as a refuge— as a personal world that afforded protection from the anonymity of indus-trial society" (Wekerle, Peterson, and Morley 9)—expressed a growing be-lief in the individual's right to govern private life. But the problem with any idealization of inwardness, of course, lies in the fact that, for women, there is often no individuality outside of their functioning relationship to domestic space, the "place" to which, since the industrial age, they have been consigned. As Doreen Massey has observed in relation to the concept of a public/private dichotomy, any attempt in the past to "confine women to the domestic sphere was both a specifically spatial control, and through that, a social control on identity" (179).

Although women who participated in private theatricals did not own their domestic dwellings or necessarily receive credit for their contributions to private entertainment, their role as organizers of domestic space gave them at least a measure of control over some of the ways in which their social identity was configured and represented. Reginald Brimsley John-son has noted, for example, how the English bluestocking circle arranged domestic space in specific ways—from Elizabeth Montagu's semicircle to Elizabeth Vesey's zigzags to Mrs. Ord's "chairs round a table in the centre of the room" (10–11)—in order to create different conversational modes.

In addition to providing nonactors with a theatrical playground, the private theatrical also encouraged audiences to appreciate domestic space for the fact that it allowed them to "indulge in delicacies and subtleties that would be thrown away at Drury Lane or Covent Garden" (Rosenfeld, *Temples of Thespis* 168), a fact that could make social issues more vivid. An-thropologist Victor Turner (1982) has written at length about the idea that "theatre is the most forceful, *active* . . . genre of cultural performance, . . . a play society acts about itself" (104). It is "this proximity of theatre to life," in Turner's view, that "makes of it the form best fitted to comment or 'meta-comment' on conflict" (105). "When we act in everyday life, we do not merely re-act to indicative stimuli, we act in frames we have wrested from the genres of cultural performance." It therefore follows, Turner writes, that stage acting should concentrate on "bring[ing] into the symbolic or fictitious world the urgent problems of our reality" (122).

Those who made theater in their homes between 1770 and 1810 confronted the performative aspects of their actual experience through the process of self-consciously adopting roles for the private stage. For women especially, whose performance of femininity was tested perhaps most stringently in the semipublic spaces of the domestic sphere, the private theatrical provided often unlooked-for opportunities to analyze how social identities are constructed and represented.[15] As Bruce Wilshire has observed, in *Role Playing and Identity: The Limits of Theatrical Metaphor* (1982), "theatre is an aesthetic detachment from daily living that reveals the ways we are involved in daily living—particularly our empathetic and imitative involvements" (ix). But it was just this potential to disturb domestic harmony by revealing "the ways we are involved in daily living" that made the private theatrical particularly problematic where women were concerned.[16]

In an essay called "Remarks upon the Present Taste for Acting Private Plays" (1788), playwright Richard Cumberland expressed his anxiety about amateurism by referring specifically to female actors in private theaters: the "Andromache of the Stage may have an infant Hector at home, whom she more tenderly feels for than the Hector of the scene; he may be sick, he may be supperless; there may be none to nurse him, when his mother is out of sight, and the maternal interest in the divided heart of the actress may preponderate over the Heroine's" (116). Disturbed by a trend in which the act of playwrighting appears to him demystified, is "thoroughly bottomed and laid open," and is "now done by so many people without any difficulty at all" (115), Cumberland warned that this fashion "should be narrowly confined to certain ranks, ages, and conditions in the community at large," and that "young women of humble rank and small pretensions should be particularly cautious how a vain ambition of being noticed by their superiors betrays them into an attempt at displaying their unprotected persons on a stage, however dignified and respectable." If they "have both acting talents and charms," Cumberland continues, "I tremble for their danger" (118). Professional actress Ann Catherine Holbrook sounded an equally pessimistic note about amateur acting in her memoirs published in the early nineteenth century: "The Metropolis, particularly, teems with this evil [private theatricals], which is of much greater magnitude than is generally supposed, as it tends to discourage industry in youth, and fill them with hopes, as shallow in foundation, as a fairy vision;—castle-building here is at its summit" (52).

The Tryal: Amateur Acting and Female Liberation

Joanna Baillie's associations with such "castle-building" extended back to her childhood, a reminder of the pervasiveness of amateur theatricals in late-eighteenth-century culture.[17] Sarah Tytler and J. L. Watson noted that at school Baillie became "the chief figure in something like private theatricals" (2:193)—school plays figuring as amateur performances. In the *Dictionary of National Biography*, George Barnett Smith wrote that Baillie—like her heroine in *The Tryal*, Agnes Withrington—"was early distinguished for her skill in acting and composition, being especially facile in the improvisation of dialogue in character" (1:886). Catherine Jane Hamilton made a similar observation: "at school, by her sister's report, she was principally distinguished in being the ringleader of all pranks and follies, and used to entertain her companions with an endless string of stories of her own invention. She was also addicted to clambering on the roof of the house to act over her scenes alone and in secret" (1:114). Perhaps owing to these personal associations, Baillie centered her earliest comedy, *The Tryal*, around improvisational acting as the means by which certain women struggle to assert themselves, even if only temporarily, over the plot that shapes their domestic lives.

It is interesting to contemplate the fact that Baillie's first comedy was almost performed for the first time on a private stage by amateur actors, since this mode of representation might have caused its participants to view *The Tryal* metatheatrically, to appreciate some of the ways in which this play investigates amateurism and private entertainment in relation to gender and space. Hanna Scolnicov has recently written, in *Woman's Theatrical Space* (1994), that "the very shape a play gives its theatrical space is indicative of its views on the nature of the relationship between the sexes and on the position of women in society" (6–7). Such is certainly the case with Baillie's comedy, which depicts a woman caught between what she calls "a reasonable woman's desire" (196) to direct her own future and cultural imperatives that require her to marry.[18] Nevertheless, for the first part of the play Agnes Withrington attempts to take charge of her destiny by creating, performing in, and directing an improvisational theatrical in the privacy of her uncle's home: the social and closeted spaces of a fashionable English house in Bath become the setting for amateur acting. Wanting to be certain that the man she marries is "sensible" (I.i.204), for much of *The Tryal* the "sun-burnt" Agnes (III.i.238) resembles the merrily assertive Beatrice of Shakespeare's comedy *Much Ado About Nothing*. Like her cousin, Mariane—who has become engaged without her uncle's consent— Agnes is portrayed as independent and strong-willed, qualities that both amuse and unsettle her uncle Anthony Withrington. Mariane observes to Agnes that, before she arrived on the scene, Mariane thought her uncle "severe and unreasonable, with his fiddle faddle fancies about delicacy and decorum; but since you came amongst us, Agnes, you have so coaxed him, and laughed at him, and played with him, that he has become almost as frolicksome as ourselves" (I.i.202).

The frequency and ease with which the two young women touch their uncle's body indicate the relaxed atmosphere over which Withrington presides, and show how the dynamic of this domestic space encourages the women to use their imaginations. Introduced by the stage directions as "hanging upon [Withrington's] arms, coaxing him in a playful manner as they advance towards the front of the Stage" (I.i.195), Agnes and Mariane are subsequently described as "clapping his shoulder" (I.i.196), "stroaking his hand gently" (I.i.199), resting an "arm on his shoulder" (I.i.200), "leaping round his neck" (I.i.201), and taking "him by the hands and begin[ning] to play with him" (I.i.238). For a time female laughter reigns as Agnes, using winks and gestures to control the movement of bodies in domestic space, directs her cousin Mariane and her maid, Betty, in an improvisation designed to expose the greed of Agnes's suitors and determine the true character of Harwood, the man whom Agnes wants to marry.

Given this jocular familiarity between uncle and nieces, one might expect that Agnes and Mariane could persuade Withrington temporarily to become an actor in their plot. But he will not participate, foreshadowing Fanny Price's staunch refusal in *Mansfield Park* to perform in a private production given by her cousins. The language with which Withrington refuses suggests that the nexus of amateurism, women, and private performance is central to the dramaturgy of *The Tryal*: "It would be very pleasant, truly," he says teasingly, "to see an old fellow, with a wig upon his bald pate, making one in a holy-day mummery with a couple of madcaps" (I.i.195). This comparison between Agnes and Mariane's proposed improvisation and "holy-day mummery" recalls that the origins of English amateur acting were in the Christian church, once the locus of theatrical activity in spite of its anxiety about theater's potential to lure audiences into identifying with and imitating characters represented on stage. Christianity's historical ambivalence toward English theater is embodied in Uncle Withrington's ambivalence toward his nieces' amateur acting. As *The Tryal* progresses, Withrington's seeming approval of amateurism gives way to his attempt to regain control of his domicile, which he fears is becoming, under Agnes's direction, the scene of what we might call "street theater." In act 3, Withrington says that his house seems foreign to him— like "a cabin in Kamschatka,[19] and common to a whole tribe"—because it has been infiltrated by entertainers, animals, and indigent children:

> In every corner of it I find some visitor, or showman, or milliner's apprentice, loitering about: my best books are cast upon footstools and window-seats, and my library is littered over with work-bags; dogs, cats, and kittens, take possession of every chair, and refuse to be disturbed: and the very beggar children go hopping before my door with their half-eaten scraps in their hands, as if it were an entry to a workhouse. (III.i.60)

Alarmed at the means by which Agnes and Mariane reveal the absurdity of their suitors' performed postures, Withrington expresses his anxiety about the security of his nieces' gender and class position by saying that "all this playing, and laughing, and hoydening about, is not gentlewomanlike; nay, I might say, is not maidenly. . . . A high-bred elegant woman is a creature which man approaches with awe and respect; but nobody would think of accosting you with such impressions, any more than if you were a couple of young *female tinkers*" (III.i.240; my emphasis). Indeed, although he is extremely fond of his nieces and seems at times to enjoy the exuberance of their high-spirited acting, Withrington continually criticizes their jolly improvisations by equating theatricality with foolery, witchery, and madness. It is therefore no surprise when he comes to complain that he "can't approve of every farce you please to play off in my family, nor to have my relations affronted, and driven from my house for your entertainment" (III.i.239), or when he declares, a few lines later, "I am tired of this" (240).

The "this" is Agnes's plot, which requires that Mariane pretend to be Agnes in order to "get the men to bow to us, and tremble" (240–41) and that Agnes and her servant Betty produce a feminist variation of *The Taming of the Shrew*.[20] By acting peevishly and staging several tantrums for the sole purpose of discerning how well Harwood can tolerate a woman who expresses herself passionately, Agnes investigates why female anger is so upsetting to many men. She senses that the veneer of tolerance worn by her suitors during the courtship ritual masks their disgruntledness at having to affect such a pose, that such seeming delight in the woman wooed will give way to a desire to control her person. Therefore, much of the fun for Agnes in staging this improvisation rests with exposing the real motives of her suitors, such as Sir Loftus Prettyman who, when treated to a dose of Mariane's affected indifference, vows, in a series of asides: "when she is once secured, I'll be revenged! I'll vex her! I'll drive the spirit out of her. . . . I'll tame her!" (IV.iii.271). Exposing the avaricious motives of her suitors is Agnes's ultimate aim.

Harwood has no difficulty passing Agnes's test. But the play does not allow the lovers to come together so easily, and it is this complication that raises some of the problems faced by women who would do theater in the privacy of their homes. A monologue in act 5 marks the turning point of the play, for it is at this juncture that Agnes abandons the trajectory of her original improvisation in order to devise another plot responsive to her uncle's concerns. Here is Withrington's speech:

> To be the disinterested choice of a worthy man is what every woman, who means to marry at all, would be ambitious of; and a point in regard to her marriage, which a woman of fortune would be unwilling to leave doubtful. But there are men whose passions are of such a violent, overbearing nature, that love in them may be considered as a disease of the mind; and the object of it claims no more perfection or pre-eminence among women, than chalk, lime, or oatmeal do amongst dainties, because some diseased stomachs do prefer them to all things. Such men as these we sometimes see attach themselves even to ugliness and infamy, in defiance of honour and decency. With such men as these, women of sense and refinement can never be happy; nay, to be willingly the object of their love is not respectable. (Pauses). But you don't care for all this, I suppose? It does well enough for an old uncle to perplex himself with these niceties: it is you yourself the dear man happens to love, and none of these naughty women I have been talking of, so all is very right. (V.ii.276–77)

On the one hand, this monologue reads as the expression of Withrington's concern for Agnes's welfare; but on the other it seems designed to make her incredulous that any man could actually desire her as his wife. He "withers" Agnes's spirits by insinuating that Harwood's apparent devotion to her may be something to shun rather than to admire, since "there are men whose passions are of such a violent, overbearing nature, that love in them may be considered as a disease of the mind." If Harwood is indeed the indiscriminately passionate man that Withrington implies, then the object of his love can be discounted. For such a man—in claiming from women "no more perfection or pre-eminence . . . than chalk, lime, or oatmeal may do amongst dainties"—can be assessed as having a "diseased stomach." This diseased appetite might cause a man to "attach" himself "even to ugliness and infamy," a choice of words that Agnes in all probability interprets as a reference to herself, accustomed as she is to having her physicality criticized. Although her uncle implies that Agnes is a woman of "sense and refinement," he goes on to say that if one "willingly" allows herself to be the object of such a diseased person, then she is "naughty." This is a statement the harshness of which Withrington apparently recognizes when he disingenuously trivializes his judgments as "niceties." You are still "respectable," he tries to convey to Agnes, after having implied just the opposite.

Agnes is stunned. The young woman who has earlier described herself as "light as an air-ball!" (III.i.238), in reference to the fun she derives from her private theater, now becomes quite somber and quiet, telling Withrington that she has "ventured farther than I ought" (V.i.278). She apologizes for her direction of the first plot, through which she has already achieved her goal of proving Harwood genuinely attracted to her character. Mariane, who enters the stage after Withrington's speech to find Agnes looking glum, immediately asserts that she is "very sure the plot is of [Withrington's] hatching, then, for I never saw Agnes with any thing of this kind in her head, wear such a spiritless face" (V.i.279). From this point on in the play Agnes "seems thoughtful" and speaks with "a grave and more dignified air" (V.i.277). By contrast—as if to symbolize his regaining control of the domestic space—her uncle borrows a gesture that we have come to associate with Agnes and Mariane when they were at their most confident: he "claps" Agnes on "her shoulder affectionately" (V.i.278).

At the beginning of *The Tryal*, in answer to Withrington's question about "who will fall in love with a little ordinary girl like thee," Agnes pointedly reminded him that "an old hunks of a father" once prevented his marrying the beautiful rich lady who was in love with him (I.i.197). Withrington comes dangerously close to exerting this kind of patriarchal control when he suggests the insufficiency of Agnes's first plot to determine Harwood's suitability. Indeed, in an apparent gesture toward Rousseau's *La Nouvelle Heloise* (1761)—in which Wolmar, the reigning patriarch at novel's end, devises a two-tiered trial to test the virtue of his wife, Julie, and her former lover, Saint-Preux—Withrington urges a second test that will determine whether Harwood elevates desire for virtue over his desire for Agnes's person. Agnes's original plot had been constructed, not to discover whether Harwood would choose virtue over the flawed woman in a quest after some feminine ideal, but rather to see how he would deal with imperfections, idiosyncrasies, and mood swings. In the scenes that follow, Agnes designs a new plot, but her contributions as an actor and director are curtailed. Instead, her cousin Royston takes centerstage, performing in an improvisation to which Agnes is but a silent witness, sequestered behind a screen. (In fact, at several points during this scene, Agnes chafes at her passive position, complaining about Royston's inability to understand what good acting is and his compulsion to explain to others what is intended as stage illusion.)

That it is a serious risk for Agnes to undertake this second plot is confirmed when the scene is later performed. Presented with a letter written by Agnes, Harwood is so undone by the implications of Agnes's impropriety that "his hand trembles" and he has trouble holding it. Subsequently "staggering back," "[he] throws himself into a chair . . . and covers his upper face with his hand" (V.ii.289–90). "See how his lips quiver," Royston exclaims, "and his bosom heaves! Let us unbutton him: I fear he is going into a fit." As Harwood starts to rise to leave the room, "he falls back again in a faint" (V.ii.290). The potential danger to Harwood's health casts a skeptical light on the merit of what in retrospect can be seen as Withrington's unnecessary interference in Agnes's private theatrical, even though Harwood proves himself to be vitally concerned that Agnes not behave immorally, thus passing the test and satisfying Withrington's concerns.

I want to suggest that Withrington's misgivings about Harwood do not derive simply from the former's uneasiness over the dramaturgy of Agnes's plot, which reveals the potential of private theatricals to destabilize domesticity. Withrington's doubt about Harwood's virtue may also mask his unease about the way in which Harwood "does" his gender. Described as wearing "a plain brownish coat" (I.i.204)—Baillie's sartorial signal that Harwood is destined for the physically plain Agnes (whom he nevertheless recognizes as "the most beautiful native character in the world" [I.ii.210])—Harwood the future lawyer is characterized in direct opposition to "your men of fashion" (I.ii.211), the pretentious Sir Loftus and his sidekick, Jack Opal. Harwood's idealism about his profession, his scholarliness, and his open enthusiasm pair him with Agnes as the "heartwood" of the play. Both are genuinely interested in extending themselves to help others, as Agnes's private staging suggests when she opens up Withrington's fashionable home to poverty-stricken children. Likewise, Harwood is praised for conceiving of the practice of law as more than "a dry treasuring up of facts in the memory," as (additionally) the profession of one "who pleads the cause of man before fellow-men," and who must therefore "know what is in the heart of man as well as what is in the book of records" (II.ii.228). When Agnes thanks Harwood for promising to marry her at play's end, she predicts that he "shall . . . exert your powers in the profession you have chosen: you shall be the weak one's stay, the poor man's advocate; you shall gain fair fame in recompense, and that will be our nobility" (V.ii.299). Throughout the play Harwood claims that he is looking for a real partner rather than an idealized paragon: "insipid constitutional good nature is a tiresome thing" (IV.i.253), he says to himself; "we ought not to expect a faultless woman" (IV.i.258), he confesses to his friend Colonel Hardy; "I can't bear your insipid passionless women: I would as soon live upon sweet curd all my life, as attach myself to one of them" (V.ii.288), he exclaims to Royston.

Yet though clearly the hero destined for Baillie's heroine, Harwood is also characterized as a man who often assumes an exaggeratedly expressive gesture and speech typically associated with femininity: he runs breathlessly onto the stage; he hangs around Agnes without apology; he blurts out his feelings. Furthermore, in act 4, Harwood offers to thread Agnes's needle, albeit "awkwardly" (IV.ii.66); and in the final act of the play, like many of the heroines in English Romantic drama who, when confronted with surprising news, sink to the ground, Harwood does something quite unusual for a male character in a play from this period: he swoons. Given Withrington's concerns about Agnes's femininity in the context of her original improvisation, Harwood's characterization seems to require that Uncle Withrington assert his role as patriarch of a fashionable home and propose a further test for the young lawyer, one designed to answer some of the questions that Withrington has about the degree to which Harwood's masculine identity can be regarded as secure, and one that requires Agnes to restrict her involvement in private theater.

The Private Theatrical in Fiction

With its focus on women and amateur acting, Joanna Baillie's *The Tryal* may be compared to several other works of fiction from this period that feature the private theatrical movement in order to debate its effect upon domestic stability. Because women powerfully influenced the dynamics of domestic space, fictional works from the British Romantic period that treated the private theatrical often focused their anxiety on women characters. The issue of women acting on any stage (whether public or private) has been throughout British history a source of deep concern for certain segments of the population, and the idea that closet spaces were becoming formally theatricalized during the late eighteenth century often aroused strong responses.

For instance, Richard Brinsley Peake's *Amateurs and Actors* (1818) links private theatricals to disorder and impropriety through a plot in which the two main female characters run amok. It is the lot of a retired manufacturer named Elderberry—"simple in wit and manners, and utterly unacquainted with Theatricals" (10)—to try to retrieve his ward, Mary Hardacre, from an elopement that uses a private performance as a strategy to override parental consent. Mary's lover, David Dulcet, has arranged to announce their marriage to his relatives immediately after he and Mary have participated in a private production of *Romeo and Juliet*, which will be attended by Dulcet's family. The plot also contains the conflict between a poor country actor, Wing, and his estranged wife, Mary Goneril, a "Strolling Tragedy Actress" (10), who has run off with a manager but finds herself hired to act Juliet on the same private stage with her former husband.

As the person who perceives Dulcet's house as "a receptacle for lunatics" (30), Elderberry is presented as a ridiculous figure for his ignorance about amateur acting. But amateur performances are also satirized with equal force, especially in the exchanges between O. P. Bustle, the manager of a provincial theater hired to supervise this private production, and Wing. "[W]e who know something of the matter," says Bustle, "must laugh at private performers. As Garrick observed, one easily sees, when the Amateurs are acting, that there is not an *Actor* among them" (17). This is a theme anticipated by Archibald Maclaren's musical drama, *The Private Theatre* (1809), which ties together private entertainment, domestic disorder, and moral corruption. Modewart chastises his brother for writing private plays by saying: "Let us have no more of your Pantomimical Funerals. Convert your private theatre into a public school, or useful work-shop. Mind your own business, and leave the trade of acting to those who make it their profession" (II.i.24).

But although private theaters made many uneasy because they brought acting into the home, the idea that amateurism could provide a corrective to professional stage practices was a theme also consistently sounded during this period. In the same essay cited above (1788), Richard Cumberland admitted that the aristocracy was usually better suited than the professional actor to perform a variety of theatrical roles, because in "all scenes of high life they are at home; noble sentiments are natural to them; low-parts they can play by instinct; and as for all the crafts of rakes, gamesters, and fine gentlemen, they can fill them to the life" (116). That the amateur can narrow the gap between actor and character in the service of greater realism and less artificiality ironically plays into the hands of anti-theatrical commentators, who worry precisely about this merging of actor with role. But this conflation is also one of the reasons amateurism (or "informalism") continued to be championed throughout the nineteenth century and into the twentieth, from the time of its institutional origin with the founding of the Pic Nic in 1802, "the first amateur dramatic society in high life" (Rosenfeld, "Jane Austen" 43). In 1917, for example, American pastor John Talbot Smith described what he identified as "the parish theatre" movement in language that celebrated amateur drama's radical simplicity. An amateur play is "the parent of the professional drama" because it "acts towards its offspring as country grandmothers often do, taking the worn-out creature back to the simplicity of the farm, lecturing it on its origin, reminding it of the simplicity which should be at the root of the healthy variety, and otherwise steadying its mind and its nerves" (7). Less colorfully, Bonamy Dobrée wrote in 1947 that he was "very anxious that the amateur stage should play its full part in the development of the drama" (26), for the "amateur very often beats the professional—not at his own game, but in doing something different" (27): "By this I mean that the amateur approaches any play he is going to take part in as something to be related to life; . . . the amateur is not bound by tradition; he has no grooves to get out of" (28). Late-twentieth-century theorists who look to performers unaffiliated with either academic or commercial programs for supposedly "purer" and simpler acting styles share with advocates of amateurism like Dobrée an admiration for theater forged in the workshops of daily life. Hollis Huston, for example, celebrates the street performer for creating "the simple stage" (1)—that is, a space in which "one performs according to a rule that is ours, that answers our agenda rather than someone else's" (7).

Eleven years before *The Tryal* was published, James Powell's farce about the rage for amateur acting, *Private Theatricals* (1787), also featured a plot in which the head of a household tries to control his family's and servants' enthusiasm for putting on private plays. But, unlike Baillie, Powell reserved for his leading female character a subversive moment at play's end. The actress playing Lady Grubb is allowed to advance "to the front of the Stage," where she asserts her love of private theater: "But if my audience

do but approve, I shall bless the day when I first commenc'd my PRIVATE
THEATRICALS" (II.viii.37).[21]

The manager of a private production of *Romeo and Juliet*, Lady Grubb
is shown to appreciate theater so intensely that her enthusiasm wars against
the domestic orderliness her husband has come to value. Nothing is as it
should be, Alderman Grubb worries at play's start: all "the fine leaden gods
on my lawn she [Lady Grubb] has thrown down to make room for her
own whim":

> instead of my Jupiter and Juno, here we have tragedy on one side, and comedy
> on the other, for all the world like an April day; look one way it is all clouds
> and tears, look the other it is all sun-shine and laughter. Then there was my
> grotto at the head of my canal, where I had placed my beautiful figure of a
> river god with a great tub under his arm, with the water spouting out of it,
> she has thrown down too; and a marble Shakspeare placed at top, and a Ben
> Jonson at the bottom. My hermitage likewise she has pulled to pieces and re-
> built, and now called Prospero's cave. (I.ii.6)

From Grubb's perspective, his wife's passion for theater has destroyed
his authority. Even his servants, like Betty the maid in *The Tryal* and the
"five . . . under-servants" in *Mansfield Park* (described as "idle and dissatisfied" [206] for having been introduced to theater), elude his control. The
kitchen servants have recently seemed to create a scene from "Bedlam": in
"one corner," Grubb recounts in a monologue, "stood a captive Zara rat-
tling a jack chain":

> In another a Juliet making her quietus, not with a bare bodkin; but a bare roll-
> ing pin. In another an Alexander brandishing a spit, and a pot lid, and in the
> middle stood the fat scullion holding a brass candlestick in one hand and rub-
> bing her greasy fist with the other! Exclaiming, "yet here's a spot! out damn'd
> spot! out I say, not all the water in the sea would cleanse this little hand." And
> d-m-e-! if I believe it would. Presently out burst from the closet a great lusty
> fellow with "Die all! die nobly! die like demi gods!" and kicks over a tea table
> with a set of your lady-ship's best Dresden china, which came to the ground
> with a hideous crash. (I.ii.11–12)

This cacophony strikes Lady Grubb differently, for she is passionately involved in acting and playwrighting, in decorating and managing her private theater. For her, domestic chaos is "such divine confusion" (II.ii.25).

The struggle for control of domestic space culminates in Grubb's determination to "stick up for the 'Rights of Man' once in my life." Citing

Blackstone's maxim "every man's house is his castle" (II.iii.28), Grubb brings the rehearsals to an end when he surprises his wife in an amorous scene with a professional actor named Buskin and catches their daughter about to elope with Villars, an amateur performer. It is left to Villars the amateur to condemn the "present rage for theatrical performances, [which] has grown to a ridiculous pitch," because this trend is "productive of much mischief to the morals of society, by admitting the loose and profligate (who are a scandal to the age) into the houses of virtue, whose reputation and honor they generally endanger" (II.vii.35). But then the dramaturgy undercuts his moralizing when Lady Grubb steps forward and addresses the audience directly about how "blessed" was the day when she first became involved in private theater.

This kind of moment is missing from *The Tryal*, which charts the process by which the owner of a fashionable home reasserts his control over domestic space, in his view rendered chaotic by amateur performance. As we have seen, Anthony Withrington resembles several other characters in the fiction of the private theatrical movement who function to suggest that amateur acting on private stages is potentially disruptive. Although not a consistently antitheatrical force like Austen's Sir Thomas Bertram in *Mansfield Park*, who is so upset by his children's experiment with private theater that he burns "every unbound copy of 'Lovers' Vows' in the house" (206) when he returns from the West Indies, still Withrington closes *The Tryal* with words that evoke Austen's description of how Sir Thomas "reinstates himself" upon his arrival at Mansfield Park: one of the tasks that Sir Thomas performs before he can resume "his seat as master of the house at dinner" is to oversee the dismantling of the little theater in the billiard room (206). Similarly reestablishing himself as the benevolent host of an orderly domicile, Withrington says to the company gathered onstage at the end of *The Tryal*: "Now, let us take our leave of plots and story-telling, if you please, and all go to my house to supper" (V.ii.299).

Baillie's Theory of Comedy

Read in the context of the amateur entertainment vogue, Baillie's first comedy emerges as an exploration of how some women sought to theatricalize domestic space in order to respond to "a reasonable woman's desire" to control the representation of women's social reality. Indeed, Baillie's eight comedies richly reward students of late-eighteenth- and early-nineteenth-century culture by attending to some of the more pressing social issues of the period. *The Election* (1802), which resembles Maria Edgeworth's novel *Castle Rackrent* (1800), focuses on the dilemma of the landed gentry (some of whom had titles but little money) in order to explore the struggle between Lord Baltimore and Charles Freeman to see who will be elected to represent the borough. This plot also debates the dilemma of how to educate young women, by weighing the importance of "refinement" against the acquisition of a variety of artistic and linguistic "skills."[22] In *The Second Marriage* (1802) Baillie confronts anxious responses to class struggle and social mobility[23] by showing how the persecution of a second wife by the family that has recently lost its beloved mother and mistress expresses an ideology of domestic insularity. The Seabrights' triumphant casting off of their new stepmother, Lady Sarah (a comic Lady Macbeth), raises questions about why this woman—whose most serious fault is her penchant for economizing—must be banished at play's end, when she has actually shown herself a virtuous wife by working earnestly to help her ambitious husband fulfill his dream of a baronet's title. *The Alienated Manor* (1836) brings together an estate improver, a German philosopher, and a black servant named Sancho to discuss jealousy through a plot that centers on women's boredom in marriage. The bluestockings' salon-like gatherings and the alarmed responses to their intellectualism are gently mocked in *The Match* (1836), when Latitia Vane's lady-in-waiting, Flounce, tells the butler she hopes that her mistress will "remain as she is, with her lovers, and her confidants, and her flatterers, and her concerts, and her parties, and all proper suitable things that a rich lady ought to have. . . . but if she takes it into her head that a lady of thirty should give up gay dressing, and apply to her learning, and become a book-fancier, and a blue-stocking virtuoso, what's to become of my perquisites? It would make your hair stand on end, to hear all the nonsense I have heard about them there books" (700).

Perhaps because Baillie's comedies address topics that would have interested some early-nineteenth-century playgoers through a subtle exploration of her characters' emotional trials, critics have generally had difficulty appreciating them. Baillie alluded to the unpopularity of her comic plays in her preface to the second edition of *Miscellaneous Plays* (1805) when she wrote that the comedy *The Country Inn* (1804) "has been generally disliked" (386). Seven years after publishing *The Tryal*, Baillie had come to realize that, to "those who are chiefly accustomed, in works of this kind, to admire quick turns of thought, pointed expression, witty repartée, and the ludicrous display of the transient passing follies and fashions of the world, this play will have but few attractions" (389).

Time has proved her thus far prophetic. In 1930 Allardyce Nicoll wrote that every one of Baillie's comedies "is stilted. Not a laugh rises from a single scene" (1:209). More recently, in 1974, Terence Tobin overlooked Agnes's dilemma to focus on the subplot—Mariane Withrington's secret engagement—and concluded that a lack of "complications" dooms *The Tryal*, a critique that echoes Margaret Carhart's over fifty years earlier (*Plays by Scots* 199–200). Tobin asserted that the "exclusion of all other elements but the dominant feeling is more suited to tragedy than comedy, which thrives on complications. These are absent in *The Tryal*. . . . This comedy is over-simplified and never achieves the portrayal of the desired emotion. The couple's love resembles that of arranged marriages which abound in novels of the period" (195–96).

As Tobin failed to notice, *The Tryal*'s complications arise from Baillie's characterization of Agnes, whom Alice Meynell summarized in 1922 as "hard to capture" (61). Yet Meynell is almost alone in appreciating Baillie for making "such pretty eighteenth-century sport of her theme (her hero keeping the fine sensibilities, expressed with impassioned elegance, of Steele's *Conscious Lovers*) that it is not easy to realize that she passed the middle of the nineteenth century, albeit in extreme old age. . . . It is the exceeding sweetness of the two good girls bent upon their frolic (which is also a romp) that makes the charm of this happy play. They exchange names upon the wildest impulse consistent with their Georgia manners" (59). But Thomas Lawrence, who proposed *The Tryal* for a private theatrical in 1803, is thus far the only reader of the play I have found to praise it for those very features that Baillie herself advocated in her theory of comedy. In a letter to his sister, Lawrence wrote that he was "for Miss Bailey's Comedy, 'The Trial,' one slightly spoken of by the world, but which I am sure, Mr. Homer would like for *its truly natural dialogue and character*" (cited in Rosenfeld, *Temples of Thespis* 154; my emphasis).[24]

Baillie articulated her theory of comedy at length in her "Introductory Discourse," the essay she attached to the volume of plays in which *The Tryal* appeared in 1798 and which—as I discussed in Chapter 3—suggests that domestic spaces are fruitful sources of theater and drama. Baillie's belief that it is comedy's "task to exhibit" people "engaged in the busy turmoil of ordinary life, . . . and engaged with those smaller *trials* of the mind by which men are most apt to be overcome" (11; my emphasis) caused her to prefer realistic situations that she could have encountered in her own life. In contrast to the "satirical, witty, sentimental, and, above all, busy or circumstantial Comedy," Baillie advocated what she called "Characteristic Comedy," a genre that represents "this motley world of men and women . . . under those circumstances of ordinary and familiar life most favorable to the discovery of the human heart" (12). This kind of play

> stands but little in need of busy plot, extraordinary incidents, witty repartée, or studied sentiments. It naturally produces for itself all that it requires. Characters, who are to speak for themselves, who are to be known by their own words and actions, not by the accounts that are given of them by others, cannot well be developed without considerable variety of judicious incident; a smile that is raised by some trait of undisguised nature, and a laugh that is provoked by some ludicrous effect of passion, or clashing of opposite characters, will be more pleasing to the generality of men than either the one or the other when occasioned by a play upon words, or a whimsical combination of ideas; and to behold the operation and effects of the different propensities and weaknesses of men, will naturally call up in the mind of the spectator moral reflections more applicable, and more impressive than all the high-sounding sentiments with which the graver scenes of Satirical and Sentimental Comedy are so frequently interlarded. (13)

Eschewing contrivance, artificiality, and self-conscious wit, Baillie's theory argues that the "most interesting and instructive class of Comedy" (12) derives from what we might today be inclined to call "situational" writing in which "even the bold and striking in character, should, to the best of the author's judgment, be kept in due subordination to nature" (14). Such dramas amuse and teach us in proportion to the degree that they present credible or "probable" events.[25]

But even as Baillie argued for a more subtle kind of dramatic writing—one focused on "the harmonious shades" of character—she wanted to avoid dwelling on "senseless minuteness" (13). Her entire dramatic project was shaped by her desire to exhibit the passions, to trace an emotion's "varieties and progress in the breast of man" (14). Nevertheless, Baillie criticized eccentric characterizations: "Above all, it is to be regretted that those adventitious distinctions among men, of age, fortune, rank, profession, and country, are so often brought forward in preference to the great original distinctions of nature" (15), because such an approach has "tempted our less skillful dramatists to exaggerate, and step, in further quest of the ludicrous, so much beyond the bounds of nature, that the very effect they are so anxious to produce is thereby destroyed, and all useful application of it entirely cut off, for we never apply to ourselves a false representation of nature" (14). It is in "ordinary life," Baillie emphasized throughout her theater theory, that "strong passions will foster themselves within the breast; and what are all the evils which vanity, folly, prejudice, or peculiarity of temper lead to, compared with those which such unquiet inmates produce?" (14). By seeking to justify a focus on "unquiet inmates" in domestic settings, Baillie's theory of comedy suggests that we should pay close attention to the drama and theater produced in closet spaces, a theatricality largely controlled by women confined to the private sphere.

Thirty-six years old when she published her first plays—which, in addition to *The Tryal*, included *Count Basil* and *De Monfort* (discussed in Chapter 4)—Baillie argued the need for a *mature* comedy, one that featured characters in "the middle stages of life; when they are too old for lovers or the confidents of lovers, and too young to be the fathers, uncles, and guardians, who are contrasted with them; but when they are still in full vigour of mind, eagerly engaged with the world, joining the activity of youth to the providence of age, and offer to our attention objects sufficiently interesting and instructive" (13). Because the character of Agnes Withrington is young, she may at first strike readers as the opposite of "reserved." But in fact, it is Agnes's very openness and impetuosity in the first part of *The Tryal* that fire this piece with energy. Baillie's biographer, Margaret Carhart, finds the characterization of Agnes "typical of the busy comedy that Miss Baillie criticized so sweepingly" (196). Yet Agnes is also nothing if not "thoughtful," and the complexity of her struggle to determine whether her beloved Harwood is morally the best match for her is at the heart of the play's plot. Although her uncle eventually succeeds in restraining Agnes's theatrical experiments, Baillie gives us a play in which the struggle of her heroine to control the rituals of courtship centers on her attempt to theatricalize domestic space according to her own design.

Though not generally regarded as a women's movement, the British private theatrical is significant for those scholars who are trying to fill in the picture of women's history in theater. In addition to affording a certain class of women increased opportunities for theatrical endeavor, the private theatrical movement anticipated subsequent developments that highlight the achievement of women in theater. For example, Madame Vestris's management of the Olympic theater in the 1830s—conceived as an alternative to the London patent stages—is a logical outgrowth of an eighteenth-century phenomenon in which a number of women had the experience of managing small theaters for the first time.[26] In praising Vestris's direction of the theater in the dedication letter he attached to *The Two Figaros* (1836), playwright James Robinson Planché wrote that "the model is not less instructive because it is made on so small a scale and preserved in the cabinet of a lady" (cited in Griffinhoof, 1830). Likewise, Frances Maria Kelly's "Little Theatre in Dean Street," which was built in the 1830s "as an extension to her private house" (Francis 156), resembles the private theaters of the previous era, in that Kelly planned to feature those fledgling performers whom she trained in the acting school, which she also moved to her house from the Strand.[27] Biographer Basil Francis describes Kelly's idea of this little theater as follows:

> she felt she needed a *model* theatre, one which would incorporate all the alterations and improvements she had in mind. The majority of the theatres in which she played were ill-designed, both before and behind the curtain; for years she had suffered from backstage arrangements that were grossly inadequate, and had been obliged to pick her way to the stage across piles of properties and scenery through tangles of ropes and counterweights and antique stage-machinery. What she had in mind was a "modern" Little Theatre, well-appointed, both from the view of the player and playgoer, with "modern" machinery, ample entrances and exits, comfortable dressing-rooms and above all a stage that would incorporate every new improvement that the mind of man could devise. (155)

Though Kelly's dream went unrealized (as the result of stage machinery so noisy that the actors could not be heard), her desire to create a space for actor training and performance within the bounds of her home reminds us once again to pay closer attention to the theatrical experiments originating within domestic settings, and in the closeted spaces in which many lived a large portion of their lives, for it is in these locations that fascinating theatrical experiments have been conceived and launched.

Even in the late twentieth century, when an astonishing array of theatrical venues is now available to women who work on commercial and academic stages, some of the more interesting theatrical experiments performed by women have paid homage to this domestic tradition. Hanna Scolnicov observes that "it is the new feminist playwrights [Maureen Duffy, Pam Gems, Caryl Churchill, Charlotte Keayley] who go back to the recognizable, mimetic spaces, to what for them is still the unresolved question of the home" (155). Performance artists have also brought renewed attention to those domestic environments in which so much of women's theatrical art has been produced and enacted. For example, Leslie Labowitz performed *Sproutime* (1980) in her home in Venice, California, for an audience "who were also her friends, [and who] entered her dark garage to discover racks of germinating seeds from floor to ceiling and Labowitz, nude, watering her plants" (Case, *Feminism and Theatre* 58). Judy Chicago's famous art exhibit, *Dinner Party*, which featured place settings in the form of clitorises alluding to the achievements of specific women in history, in certain ways recalls the noted private entertainment hosted by Madame Vigée-Lebrun in late-eighteenth-century France, at which friends arrived for a dinner party to discover the entire dining room decked out with the accoutrements of Grecian culture and the hostess and her daughters classically dressed.

Because the private theatrical movement celebrated those very spaces in which women had for centuries been making theater, a study of this late-eighteenth-century trend focuses our attention on several facts important to British women's theater history. It reminds us that a particular class of women have had a long history of theatricalizing closet space, which associations of the Romantic closet with antitheatricality, or the act of simply reading plays, fail to reveal. A focus on the private theatrical also helps us more readily appreciate the degree to which some plays from the Romantic period confront the issue of how women have sought to control domestic spaces, for both theatrical and nontheatrical purposes. Moreover, the act of opening up British Romantic closets in order to expose the variety of theatrical activities that actually took place there can deepen our understanding of how private spaces and domestic settings influenced public stages. In addition, studying a play like Baillie's *The Tryal* can motivate us to focus anew on the dramaturgy of other women playwrights from the Romantic period in order to learn more about how fictional writings complement and interrogate nonfictional discourse; to expand the contexts for discussing women's theories of the stage; and to revise conceptions of early-nineteenth-century British theater as a culture of exciting theatricality in which a wide array of spaces were explored for their dramatic and theatrical potential.

Appendix: Selected List of Texts Containing Women's Theater Theory Published in Great Britain (1790–1850)

JOANNA BAILLIE (1762–1851)
"Introductory Discourse" to the First Volume of *Plays on the Passions* (1798).

"Preface" to the Second Volume of *Plays on the Passions* (1802).

"Preface" to the Third Volume of *Plays on the Passions* (1812).

"Preface" to *Miscellaneous Plays* (1804).

"Preface" to *The Family Legend* (1810).

"Preface" to *The Bride* (1826).

"Preface" to *The Martyr* (1826).

"Preface" to *Dramas* (1836).

MARY BERRY (1763–1852)
A Comparative View of Social Life in England and France (1828–31).

Extracts of the Journals and Correspondence of Miss Berry, from 1783–1852. Ed. Lady Theresa Lewis (1865).

HANNAH COWLEY [PSEUDONYM "ANNA MATILDA"] (1743–1809)
"Advertisement" to *A Day in Turkey* (1792).

ELIZABETH (BERKELEY) CRAVEN (MARGRAVINE OF ANSPACH) (1750–1828)
Memoirs of the Margravine of Anspach. Written by Herself (1826).

FELICIA HEMANS (1793–1835)
Life of Mrs. Hemans, With Illustrations of Her Literary Character from her Private Correspondence. By Henry F. Chorley (1836).

ANN CATHERINE HOLBROOK (1780–1837)
The Dramatist: or, Memoirs of the Stage (1809).

ELIZABETH INCHBALD (1753–1821)
Critical Prefaces to John Bell's twenty-five volume series called *The British Theatre* (1806–9).

"To *The Artist.*" Vol. 2 of *The Artist*. Ed. Prince Hoare. 2 vols. (1809).

Memoirs of Mrs. Inchbald, Including her Familiar Correspondence with the Most Distinguished Persons of Her Time. By James Boaden. 2 vols. (1833).

ANNA JAMESON (1794–1860)
Characteristics of Women (1832).

A Commonplace Book of Thoughts, Memories, and Fancies, Original and Selected (1854). (This text is included because it discusses events of the early nineteenth century.)

DOROTHY JORDAN (1761–1816)
Interview between Helen Maria Williams and Jordan in *Public and Private Life of That Celebrated Actress, Miss Bland, otherwise Mrs. Ford, or Mrs. Jordan; Late Mistress of HRH the Duke of Clarence; now King William IV*. By a Confidential Friend of the Departed. London: J. Duncombe, n.d. (1832?).

HARRIET LEE (1757–1851)
"Advertisement" to *The Mysterious Marriage, or The Heirship of Roselva* (1798).

SOPHIA LEE (1750–1824)
"Preface" to *The Chapter of Accidents* (1796).

ANNE MATHEWS (1782–1869)
Anecdotes of Actors with Other Desultory Recollections (1844).

Tea-Table Talk: Ennobled Actresses and Other Miscellanies (1857). (This text is included because it discusses actors and stage life from the early nineteenth century.)

MARY RUSSELL MITFORD (1787–1855)
"Preface" to *Charles the First* (1834).

Recollections of a Literary Life: or, Books, Places and People (1852).

"Introduction" to the first volume of *The Dramatic Works of Mary*

Russell Mitford (1854). (The plays collected in this text were written during the 1820s.)

HANNAH MORE (1745–1833)
"General Preface" and "Preface to Tragedies," in *The Works of Hannah More* (1830).

MARY ROBINSON (1758–1800)
Memoirs of the Late Mrs. Robinson Written by Herself. Ed. Maria E. Robinson (1801).

SARAH SIDDONS (1755–1831)
"Remarks on the Character of Lady Macbeth" in volume 2 of Thomas Campbell's *Life of Mrs. Siddons* (1834).

The Reminiscences of Sarah Kemble Siddons (1831). Ed. William Van Lennep (1942).

EGLANTINE WALLACE (?D. 1803)
"Address to the Public," which precedes her play *The Whim* (1795).

MARY (DAVIES) WELLS [LEAH SUMBEL] (FL. 1781–1812)
Memoirs of the Life of Mrs. Sumbel Written by Herself. Including Her Correspondence with Mr. Reynolds the Dramatist (1811).

JANE WEST (1758–1852)
"Preface" to vol. 1 of *Poems and Plays* (1799).

HELEN MARIA WILLIAMS (1761?–1827)
Interviews between Williams and Dorothy Jordan in *Public and Private Life of that Celebrated Actress, Miss Bland, otherwise Mrs. Ford, or Mrs. Jordan; Late Mistress of HRH the Duke of Clarence; now King William IV*. By a Confidential Friend of the Departed. London: J. Duncombe, n.d. (1832?).

MARY JULIA YOUNG (?–1821)
Memoirs of Mrs. [Anna Maria] Crouch, Including a Retrospect of the Stage During the Years She Performed (1806).

Notes

Chapter 1

1. The middle- to upper-class label refers to the majority of writers discussed in this book. However, in the case of actresses, as Mary Jean Corbett observes, contemporary statistics "show that the vast majority of those who went on the stage in the first half of the nineteenth century were not middle class at all: . . . they performed in the theater simply because one or both of their parents had done so" (119).

2. For an article that troubles this distinction between "public and private spheres," see Lawrence E. Klein's "Gender and the Public/Private Distinction in the Eighteenth Century: Some Questions about Evidence and Analytic Procedure" (1995). Questioning scholars' reliance on the "domestic thesis" (97), which creates a binary between women/private/domestic and men/public/nondomestic, Klein demonstrates why "there is no one 'public/private' distinction to which interpretation can confidently secure itself" (99). In this project, I share Klein's belief that "a more precise account of gender in relation to publicity and privacy can be achieved by closer examination of both space and *language*" (102).

3. In attempting to answer why "English crowds, especially the OPs in 1809, behave so theatrically" (10), Marc Baer's study, *Theatre and Disorder in Late Georgian London* (1992), discusses how social and theatrical stages interface. For instance, Baer writes: "Given intense interest in the stage among all social groups in urban society—and this is perhaps nowhere more true than in London—it should come as no surprise that life imitated art" (11). He argues that theatricality "is, then, appropriation from the stage and, . . . from audience behaviour as well" (11). An article on the same subject that takes a similar approach to reading the theatricality of audience behavior in its political, social, and cultural contexts is Elaine Hadley's "The Old Price Wars: Melodramatizing the Public Sphere in Early Nineteenth-Century England" (1992).

4. My experience of recovering women's theater theory from the Romantic period mirrors that of The Folger Collective on Early Women Critics, who write in the introduction to their anthology (*Women Critics, 1660–1820*) that "the search for criticism by early women" resulted in exploring "writings in a wide spectrum of genres," a process that invites "us to expand the generic boundaries with which criticism has traditionally been identified and to explore the relationship between critical content and critical form" (xv).

5. I am grateful to Susan Lanser for permission to cite her unpublished remarks here.

6. The kind of review I have in mind is discussed in William A. Coles's article, "Magazine and Other Contributions by Mary Russell Mitford and Thomas

Noon Talfourd" (1959). Coles alerts us to Mitford's review of *Orestes* and the last three acts of *King John* at the Reading School in the Oct. 22, 1821, issue of the *Reading Mercury*.

7. William Godwin, *Memoirs of the Author of a Vindication of the Rights of Woman* (ed. Holmes, 1987), p. 255.

8. For a thorough and appreciative analysis of Anna Jameson's critical contributions, see Helen M. Buss's article, which discusses Jameson's creation of an "epistolary dijournal" in her *Winter Studies and Summer Rambles in Canada*. Buss helps us view Jameson's text not as "the 'fragments' of a journal' (9), the 'mere unconnected, incongruous heap' (10) that Jameson feared it might seem to readers who discount the 'flimsy thread of sentiment' that is her self." Rather, when her "method of storytelling [is] viewed through its gender consciousness and the contribution that makes to subject position," one can better appreciate how Jameson "establishes the 'sliding' subject position of her text" and "creates a narrative method that complicates the slippage from one subject stance to another" (48). This approach to reading Jameson's fragments and jottings, as shaped "by Jameson's consciousness of gender constructs" (48), is a useful way to appreciate her commonplace book as well (which is cited at several points in my text).

9. See Gilbert and Gubar, *The Madwoman in the Attic: The Woman Writer and the Nineteenth-Century Literary Imagination* (1979).

10. Other Romantic women translators or adaptors of foreign plays were: Elizabeth Inchbald; Elizabeth Craven; Anne Gittins Francis (1738–1800); Maria Geisweiler (fl. 1799); Elizabeth Gunning (fl. 1803); Hannah Brand (?–1821); Rose Lawrence (fl. 1799); Marie Thérèse DeCamp Kemble (1775–1836); Annabella Plumptre (fl. 1795–1812); Anne Plumptre (1760–1818); Agnes Stratford (fl. 1794–95). My source for this information is David Mann's article, "Checklist of Female Dramatists, 1660–1823" (1990).

11. This quotation is taken from the facsimile edition of Inchbald's *British Theatre* series (1990). As the same page numbers appear throughout the text, in order to avoid confusion I have not included them here.

12. This was a view forecast by a playwright of private theatricals, Elizabeth Craven, when discussing her translation, *The Fashionable Day* (1780). She summarized her theory of translation to her brother:

> The following beautiful little performance (for such I am sure it is in the original) appeared, first in a poetical fulldress in Italy, then in a prose undress in France. To-day she is introduced to England. She speaks English, it is true (at least, I hope she does), and her dress, unlike that of my countrywomen, is of English materials; but, in endeavouring to adorn her, I have adhered to forms and fashions of her own country, *because none other would so well become her*. (v–vi; my emphasis)

13. It is not my intention to discuss those historical factors which resulted in the late-eighteenth-century preoccupation with this dichotomy, but I will mention one. In pointing to the emergence of two English publications that used the closet/stage opposition as early as 1759—Edward Young's *Conjectures on Origi-*

nal Composition and Oliver Goldsmith's *An Enquiry into the Present State of Polite Learning*—Stephen A. Larrabee cites Allardyce Nicoll's assertion that "there seems not the slightest doubt that the main cause contributing to this development [the closet/stage split] was the unprecedented activity in the realm of translation—particularly of translation from the German—which extended from 1790 onwards" (282).

14. See Janet Ruth Heller's *Coleridge, Lamb, Hazlitt, and the Reader of Drama* (1990) for a "reevaluation of romantic drama criticism that puts [the closet critics'] writings in the context of literary history of ideas" (1). Heller wants us not to dismiss these critics as "isolated extremists" but to appreciate how their criticism evinces an "interest in their own reading public and [shows] their attempts to broaden the reader's imaginative and analytic powers" (4).

15. For further discussion of this significant piece of theater legislation and its effects on political freedom, see: Zygmunt Hubner's *Theater and Politics* (1992; orig. 1988), 38–40; and Vincent J. Liesenfeld's *The Licensing Act of 1737* (1984).

16. See Richardson's "Romanticism and the Colonization of the Feminine" (1988) for a discussion of how male Romantic poets "coveted conventionally 'feminine' qualities to the point of striving to incorporate them, figuratively cannibalizing their nearest female relatives of the time" (21).

17. William Galperin writes:

> Lamb's quarrel in his Shakespeare essay is less with the "artificial world" of the theater . . . than with the real world: with the world of "bodies"—black and white, male and female—the mere sight of which is sufficient to wrench "the reader" from his solitary stance of "meditation" into a corporality, and a visibility, by which any disagreement or difference with community is immediately collapsed. (*The Return of the Visible* 134)

For a discussion of "the problematic nature of the connection between body and mind" in "debates over romantic stage drama," see Julie Carlson's article "A New Stage for Romantic Drama" (1988) in which she argues:

> As romantic playwrights perceived, the stage's special relation to the body is the source at once of its greatest effectiveness and greatest danger. On the one hand, the stage's dependence on physical "reality" makes its investigations of even the most abstract subjects more accessible and engaging to its audience. . . . On the other hand, the stage's special relation to body is also its chief danger, since the body's appeal can block out the less palpable and immediate workings of mind. This has negative consequences both for the way characters are presented on stage, where the morality of their actions is determined by success, not motive, thereby endorsing an utilitarian ethic anathema to romantic "intention," and for the way minds are formed and reformed in the audience. Rather than elevating the mind by presenting the audience with visions of ideal perfection, too much appeal to the body fixes the mind in stationary images of sense and, by bypassing the imagination altogether, subverts the chief end of drama. (426)

Carlson's *In the Theatre of Romanticism* offers an excellent discussion of romantic antitheatricality, linking it to misogyny: "Romantic men seek to closet Shakespeare, then, in order to avoid the 'too-close pressing' reality of women in theatre" (29). Also see Steven Bruhm's discussion (1994) of the body/mind dichotomy and Romantic antitheatricality in reference to *The Cenci*:

> Shelley's reluctance to stage the play's violence indicates his sense of the ideal imagination's vulnerability, in that an observer can be easily manipulated or swayed by the staging of pain. Yet, like Byron and Coleridge, Shelley is also aware that a refusal to make tyranny visible carries with it its own political prices. . . . Thus, while Shelley on the one hand keeps violent excesses off stage, in the private, secret space of the imagination, he seems on the other to argue that secrecy and discretion are themselves agents of tyranny. Like Byron and Coleridge, Shelley makes problematic the holy space of the secret as the potential site of barbarism and cruelty. (86–87)

18. See Greg Kucich, " 'A Haunted Ruin': Romantic Drama, Renaissance Tradition, and the Critical Establishment" (1992).

19. An example of this tendency occurs as recently as Patrick Parrinder's 1991 study (revised from the 1977 version), *Authors and Authority: English and American Criticism, 1750–1990*, in which he features only the closet critics in his chapter on Romantic criticism.

Whereas anthologies and analyses of criticism and theater theory from the Romantic period still tend to represent the age by the essays of the closet critics and the theater criticism of Leigh Hunt, Walter Scott, and Thomas De Quincey—instead of, for instance, Joanna Baillie's "Introductory Discourse," Elizabeth Inchbald's scores of play prefaces, or Sarah Siddons's notes on performing Shakespeare—one of the few studies thus far to shift focus from the canonized male poets to other theoretical voices from the Romantic period is Frederick Burwick's *Illusion and the Drama: Critical Theory of the Enlightenment and Romantic Era* (1991). Burwick features theater theories by men only, but in addition to the English critics he also looks at key theorists in Germany and France and therefore attests to the importance of a renewed engagement with the dramatic theories of writers whose ideas have often been simplified in the service of the " 'history of ideas' approach" (1). Arguing that "the effort" of Enlightenment and Romantic dramatic criticism "to sort out the differences between delusion and illusion raised issues of ontology and freedom that twentieth-century theorists continue to address" (16), Burwick also highlights the metadramatic quality of Romantic play scripts when he observes that "the Romantics endeavored to transform the deliberations of philosophy and critical theory into the very substance and subject matter of dramatic representation" (303).

In addition to Burwick's revisionist reading of "the function of 'illusion' in eighteenth-century aesthetics and dramatic criticism" (1), Barry V. Daniels has given us a study of French Romantic theories of the drama (1983) that features a female theorist, Germaine de Stael (1766–1817). Daniels represents her *Influence of*

Literature on Society (1801) as forecasting themes that emerged in other theoretical texts throughout the French Romantic era.

20. As Philippa Tristram (1989) has observed, "what is and is not a closet" in the latter half of the eighteenth century is not always clear.

> In 1756 Isaac Ware seems to regard it as a walk-in cupboard— . . . a definition which Jane Austen is beginning to accept in the Regency, when these personal retreats came to be regarded as vulgar. Johnson gives a similar definition in his dictionary, but also describes it as 'a small room of privacy or retirement,' as it had been in medieval and Elizabethan houses. Richardson's own use of the term is elastic, at one extreme describing a housekeeper's store-cupboard or a walk-in wardrobe; at the other, Mr. B's library in Bedfordshire, with its outer door opening into the garden. . . . The pyschological significance of the room for Richardson is, however, clear enough: rooms are defined as closets when they are felt to enclose; they thus become *the definition of a woman's right to privacy*—that is, to her virginity—before marriage, and her liberty after it only to receive her husband as she wishes. Conversely, when the right to privacy is violated, the closet becomes a prison, not a sanctuary. (253–55; my emphasis)

21. In addition to the *OED*, my information for the items that one might find in an early modern closet derives from books published between the sixteenth and eighteenth centuries and from discussions of "the closet" in studies on drinking tea and eighteenth-century architecture. In *British Teapots and Tea Drinking, 1700–1850* (1992), for instance, Robin Emmerson observes:

> The Private Closet of Elizabeth, Duchess of Lauderdale, at Ham House in Surrey retains the "Tea table, carved and guilt," recorded there in an inventory of 1683, together with the matching chairs described as "Japaned backstools with cane bottomes." . . . Tea was kept by the duchess in a box in her private sanctum because it was an exotic and precious delicacy and extremely costly. (3)

See also Sarah Fyge Egerton's (1670–1723) ironic comments in her poem "The Liberty" (1703) in which she rues that her closet is not supposed to contain books but is, instead, with "Sweat-meets cram'd":

> A little China, to advance the Show,
> My prayer Book, and seven Champions, or so.
> My Pen if ever us'd imply'd must be,
> In lofty Themes of useful Housewifery,
> Transcribing old Receipts of Cookery:
> And what is necessary 'mongst the rest,
> Good Cures for Agues, and a cancer'd Breast . . .
> (cited in Uphaus and Foster 140)

The best study to date of "the early modern closet" is Alan Stewart's article, listed in the Works Cited, in which he argues that "the epistemology of the Early Modern closet—and by extension, our contemporary closets—demands an analysis that rejects the search for the secret subject in favor of an interrogation of secret spaces and relationships; that extends our knowledge of the closet beyond the binaries within which it currently obtains . . . ; and that proposes an alternative reading of the closet as a politically crucial transactive space" (77).

22. I owe this information to Tristram's reproduction in *Living Space in Fact and Fiction* (1989) of details of two closets (254) as well as her helpful discussion of closets in Richardson's and Austen's novels (253–59).

Reinforcing the connections between women and closet space, Donald Reiman writes that Felicia Hemans (1793–1835), one of the era's popular poets, "is reported to have read and memorized long sections of verse dramas such as Home's *Douglas* which she would act out in the privacy of her room or would recite to her mother" (*Records of a Woman* vi). Like a number of their eighteenth-century forebears, Jane Austen (1775–1817) and John Keats (among many Romantic writers) provide us with fictional images of women retreating to a closet space in order to rehearse responses to a particular problem; both Fanny Price in Austen's novel *Mansfield Park* (1814) and Auranthe in Keats's only full-length drama, *Otho the Great* (1819), practice strategies in their closet or apartment room for facing problems on the world's stage. I am thinking of Austen's description of Fanny Price's "nest of comforts" (174) and Auranthe's soliloquy in act 4, in which her apartment serves as "a workshop where she practices a variety of emotions . . . and also tries on several feminine guises familiar in Romantic drama" in order to determine how to persuade Albert to keep quiet about her treachery concerning Erminia (Burroughs, "Acting in the Closet" 134).

23. All citations from Baillie's prefaces are from the 1976 facsimile edition of her 1851 collected works (Georg Olms Verlag).

24. See, for example, O. Heywood's *Closet-Prayer: A Christian Duty or Treatise upon Mat[thew] VI.vi* (1671), in which the minister writes: *"God sees in secret,* Therefore Closet-Prayer is a solemn acknowledgement of God's omniscience and omnipresence: When you pray in a corner you testifie your faith in God's ubiquity, and look upon him as filling Heaven and Earth; and this God commands us to believe, yea would have us to lye under the sense hereof" (30).

25. In the introduction to their bibliography of drama by women who published prior to 1900, Gwenn Davis and Beverly A. Joyce (1992) write that closet drama is one of the three major forms of drama created by women and that it originated as "primarily an aristocratic pursuit. The works of Viscountess Falkland, the Countesses of Pembroke and Winchelsea, the Duchess of Newcastle, and Queen Elizabeth I established the genre and defined its characteristics for the less exalted writers who followed" (xi). Their list of other women who wrote closet dramas through the ages includes (in addition to Joanna Baillie): the Countess of Strathmore, Princess Troubetzkey, Katherine Bardley, Edith Cooper, Elizabeth (Barrett) Browning, George Eliot, Felicia Hemans, Emma Lazarus, Mary Russell Mitford, Frances Fuller Victor, and Constance Woolson, "to cite only a few" (xii).

In tracing the development of closet drama from Seneca to Christopher Fry in the twentieth century, Om Prakash Mathur (1978) mentions two women, Roswitha and the Countess of Pembroke, as practitioners of the genre (11).

26. Aside from the numerous journal articles and the rash of dissertations on the drama of the male English Romantic poets published by Universität Salzburg in the 1970s, a number of books on Romantic theater and drama written between 1966 and the present have helped literary critics and theater historians revise views of late eighteenth- and early nineteenth-century stages. Among these are: Richard Fletcher's *English Romantic Drama 1795–1843: A Critical History* (1966); Jerome McGann's *Fiery Dust: Byron's Poetic Development* (1968); Stuart Curran's *Shelley's Cenci: Scorpions Ringed with Fire* (1970); Joseph Donohue's *Dramatic Character in the English Romantic Age* (1970) and *Theatre in the Age of Kean* (1975); Kenneth Richards's and Peter Thomson's *Essays on Nineteenth Century British Theatre* (1971); Terry Otten's *The Deserted Stage: The Search for Dramatic Form in Nineteenth-Century England* (1972); Michael Booth's *Prefaces to English Nineteenth-Century Theatre* (1980); Erika Gottlieb's *Lost Angels of a Ruined Paradise: Themes of Cosmic Strife in Romantic Tragedy* (1981): Robertson Davies's *The Mirror of Nature* (1983); Richard Allen Cave's *The Romantic Theatre: An International Symposium* (1986); Jeffrey Cox's *In the Shadows of Romance: Romantic Tragic Drama in Germany, England, and France* (1987) and *Seven Gothic Dramas, 1789–1825* (1992); Martyn Corbett's *Byron and Tragedy* (1988); Alan Richardson's *A Mental Theatre: Poetic Drama and Consciousness in the Romantic Age* (1988); Shou-ren Wang's *The Theatre of the Mind* (1990); Richard Lansdown's *Byron's Historical Dramas* (1992); Daniel P. Watkins's *A Materialist Critique of English Romantic Drama* (1993); Julie Carlson's *In the Theatre of Romanticism: Coleridge, Nationalism, Women* (1994); Marjean D. Purinton's *Romantic Ideology Unmasked: The Mentally Constructed Tyrannies in Dramas of William Wordsworth, Lord Byron, Percy Shelley, and Joanna Baillie* (1994). Special Issues on Romantic drama have been published by *Studies in Romanticism* (27.3 and 31.3) and *The Wordsworth Circle* (23.2).

For helpful bibliographies on the primary and secondary sources in the field of Romantic drama and theater, see the following: James Donohue's extensive bibliography (with annotations) in *Dramatic Character in English Romantic Drama* (1970) and Charles J. Clancy's *A Selected Bibliography of English Romantic Drama* (1976).

27. Closet drama revisionism is an important and varied movement that focuses primarily on historical and metatheatrical issues in order to explore more fully the split between closet and stage. See the following: Murray Biggs's "Staging *The Borderers*: Dragging Romantic Drama Out of the Closet" (1988) and "Notes on Performing *Sardanapalus*" (1992); Steven Bruhm's third chapter ("Spectacular Pain: Politics and the Romantic Theatre") in *Gothic Bodies: The Politics of Pain in Romantic Fiction* (1994); Catherine Burroughs's "English Romantic Women Writers and Theatre Theory: Joanna Baillie's Prefaces to the *Plays on the Passions*" (1994) and " 'Out of the Pale of Social Kindred Cast': Conflicted Performance Styles in Joanna Baillie's *De Monfort*" (1995); Julie Carlson's *In the Theatre of Romanticism: Coleridge, Nationalism, Women* (1994); Julie Carlson's "A New Stage for Romantic Drama" (1988); Martyn Corbett's "Lugging Byron Out of the Library" (1992); Jeffrey N. Cox's "Ideology and Genre in the British Antirevolutionary Drama of the 1790s" (1991) and his introduction to his edition of *Seven Gothic Dramas: 1789–1825* (1992); Michael Evenden's "Inter-mediate Stages:

Reconsidering the Body in 'Closet Drama'" (1993); Terence Hoagwood's "Prolegomenon for a Theory of Romantic Drama" (1992); Mary Jacobus's "'That Great Stage Where Senators Perform': *Macbeth* and the Politics of Romantic Theatre" (1989); Greg Kucich's "'A Haunted Ruin': Romantic Drama, Renaissance Tradition, and the Critical Establishment" (1992); Anne K. Mellor's "Joanna Baillie and the Counter-Public Sphere" (1994); Reeve Parker's "Reading Wordsworth's Power: Narrative and Usurpation in *The Borderers*" (1987) and "*Osorio*'s Dark Employments: Tricking Out Coleridgean Tragedy" (1994); Marjean D. Purinton's *Romantic Ideology Unmasked: The Mentally Constructed Tyrannies in Dramas of William Wordsworth, Lord Byron, Percy Shelley, and Joanna Baillie* (1994); Daniel Watkins's *A Materialist Critique of English Romantic Drama* (1993); and Thomas Whitaker's "Reading the Unreadable, Acting the Unactable" (1988).

A number of critics have called for the staging of these closet plays. In 1992 Martyn Corbett wrote, on the occasion of Yale University's performance of *Sardanapalus*:

> It is extraordinary then that today, when academic literary studies are so sophisticated and developed and there is unprecedented scope for "intellectual" or "art" theater, this substantial corpus of drama is still neglected or dismissed with little more than a passing comment from literary critics and historians and is entirely overlooked by theater managements, even by those enlightened subsidized companies which have done so much to regenerate theater in Britain since the Second World War. This baneful tradition has left nineteenth-century poetic drama unregarded, unperformed and unread. ("Lugging Byron" 362)

Richard Allen Cave writes about English productions of *Faust*, *Don Carlos*, and *Maria Stuart*, also performed in the late 1980s (see *The Keats-Shelley Review* 3 [1988]). Yale University has performed *The Borderers* (1987) and *Sardanapalus* (1990) in recent years, under the direction of Murray Biggs. Shelley's *The Cenci* was given a concert reading at Cambridge University in 1993 (Reeve Parker produced; David Farr directed), and in 1995, at the NASSR conference, Willing Suspension Productions of Boston University presented *The Borderers*.

In his review of Daniel P. Watkins's *A Materialist Critique of English Romantic Drama* (1993), William Jewett questions the motives behind the closet drama revival, asserting that it "looks more often like Kenneth Branagh attempting to credential himself by performing a galvanic resuscitation" (312). Because "large claims are now routinely staked on what was once considered very unstable ground" (309), Jewett wonders if "the prevalence of hyperbole" might "not signal an awareness that no effort to rehabilitate romantic drama can hope to share in the unassimilable shock-value of the texts themselves" (310).

28. See Alan Sinfield's discussion of particular postwar plays—such as John Osborne's *A Patriot for Me* (1965)—as "closet dramas," or plays about homosexual experience. Sky Gilbert uses the term "closet plays" to refer to dramas that are "afraid to present real gay characters" (58).

29. The term "closet drama" is not defined in the *OED*, although it lists

plenty of definitions of "closet." For additional definitions of "closet drama" see the following: (1) Martin Harrison's, in *Theatre* (1993), which connects the term to contemporary definitions of "closet":

> In this context, *closet* (from OF [old French] clos, from the stem of L. [Latin] *clore*, from *claudere*, "to close or shut") refers to "a small, private room, often used for meetings and interviews," a sense it has had since [the fourteenth century]. Its other, less grand senses of "cupboard, storage recess," and its common later use in the term *water closet* (which now gives *closet drama* a comic ring), are later developments from [the seventeenth century]. Plays which fall into the category of closet drama are those intended for private reading rather than public *production*. The genre starts with Seneca and includes many plays written by poets, especially in [the nineteenth century]. There is something odd about the concept of private, unacted plays. Currently, closet drama is an obsolete *genre*, though who knows what is happening behind closed doors? Closet, used in this sense, is found most commonly in the term "closet homosexual": one who has not yet "come out" (of the closet). (56)

(2) Phyllis Hartnoll's and Peter Found's, in *The Concise Oxford Companion to the Theatre* (1992), which also defines closet drama in relation to translation: "The term 'closet drama' also includes translations of plays, usually classics in their own countries, intended for reading and not for acting" (94).

(3) Jonnie Patricia Mobley's, in *NTC's Dictionary of Theatre and Drama Terms* (1992), which refers readers to the "chamber play," that is, "[a] play written to be performed or merely read aloud, in a room rather than onstage, and for an audience of friends rather than for paying customers" (23).

30. For recent discussions of performativity, see the collection of essays edited by Andrew Parker and Eve Kosofsky Sedgwick (*Performativity and Performance*, 1995). I appreciate Steven Bruhm's sharing with me his ideas about the relationship between the concepts of "performance" and "performativity" in the context of this study.

31. For book-length publications that feature Romanticism and gender issues, see Mary Poovey's *The Proper Lady and the Woman Writer: Ideology as Style in the Works of Mary Wollstonecraft, Mary Shelley, and Jane Austen* (1984); Anne K. Mellor's *Romanticism and Feminism* (1988) and *Romanticism and Gender* (1993); Leslie Rabine's *The Romantic Heroine: Text, History, Ideology* (1985); Marlon Ross's *The Contours of Masculine Desire: Romanticism and the Rise of Women's Poetry* (1989); Meena Alexander's *Women in Romanticism* (1989); Susan Levin's *Dorothy Wordsworth and Romanticism* (1987); Diane Long Hoeveler's *Romantic Androgyny: The Women Within* (1990); Julie Ellison's *Delicate Subjects: Romanticism, Gender, and the Ethics of Understanding* (1990); Jane Aaron's *A Double Singleness: Gender and the Writings of Charles and Mary Lamb* (1991); Moira Ferguson's *Colonialism and Gender Relations from Mary Wollstonecraft to Jamaica Kincaid* (1993); Mary Favret's *Romantic Correspondence: Women, Politics, and the Fiction of Letters* (1993); Judith Page's *Wordsworth and the Cultivation of Women* (1994); Carol Shiner Wilson's and Joel Haefner's *Re-Visioning Romanticism: British Women Writers, 1776–1837* (1994);

Paula Feldman's and Theresa Kelley's *Romantic Women Writers: Voices and Counter-voices* (1995).

For discussions of early women critics, see Mellor's "A Criticism of Their Own: Romantic Women Literary Critics" (1995), in which she argues that Baillie and other women writers of the Romantic period "upheld an aesthetic theory different from but as coherent as those developed by Coleridge, William Wordsworth, Hazlitt, Keats, Percy Shelley and their male peers" (29) in which they "celebrated not the achievements of genius nor the spontaneous overflow of powerful feelings but rather the workings of the rational mind, a mind relocated—in a gesture of revolutionary social implications—in the female as well as the male body" (31). See also Ellen Argyros's " 'Intruding Herself into the Chair of Criticism': Elizabeth Griffith and *The Morality of Shakespeare's Drama Illustrated*" (1988), which argues that in reading female critics from earlier periods "we need to reassess the very criteria by which we judge literary criticism" (289), and Susan Green's "A Cultural Reading of Charlotte Lennox's *Shakespear Illustrated*" (1995), which posits that "Lennox's approach to Shakespeare, like the processes of abjection, exists on a borderline where subject and object are not yet separated" (231). More recently, Elizabeth Bohls has published a study of Romantic women writers who, through their comments on landscape, "broke out of masculine tutelage to make unrecognized contributions during the formative period of modern aesthetic thought" (3).

Studies of women writing for and/or about English Romantic theater include: Joseph A. Grau's "Fanny Burney and the Theatre" (1981); Joyce E. East's "Mrs. Hannah Cowley, Playwright" (1988); Alan Richardson's "*Proserpine* and *Midas*: Gender, Genre, and Mythic Revisionism in Mary Shelley's Dramas" (1993); and Ellen Donkin's *Getting into the Act: Women Playwrights in London, 1776–1829* (1995).

For a study that features German Romantic women associated with late-eighteenth- and early-nineteenth-century theater, see Katharine R. Goodman and Edith Waldstein's edited volume, *In the Shadow of Olympus: German Women Writers around 1800* (1992), which contains an essay on Charlotte von Stein's matinees. There is also a discussion of Caroline Schlegel-Schelling as "an original thinker in her own right and major contributor to romantic ethics and aesthetics" (Friedrichsmeyer 116).

A recent article (1996) by J. S. Bratton focuses on Romantic theater artists Jane Scott and Elizabeth Macauley in order to make the following plea/prediction on behalf of women from this period of theater history: "New insights into the physical, material, and often nonverbal vitality of the theatre and new histories of sexuality and gendered work will, I hope, offer not only a new estimate of the worth of these women but also an entirely revised reading of the nineteenth-century roots of modern performance" (72).

In addition, Elaine Aston offers a brief analysis of two contemporary plays that "perform feminist re-inscriptions of Romanticism" (143)—Liz Lochhead's *Blood and Ice* and April de Angelis's *Breathless*—in her chapter, "Performing Romantic Criticism: Case Study and Conclusion" in *An Introduction to Feminism and Theatre* (1995).

Since the 1980s, feminists in theater have used a range of critical tools from a variety of fields to deepen their own analyses of existing texts (see Gayle Austin's *Feminist Theories for Dramatic Criticism* [1990]), as well as to make visible the assumptions that inform traditional disciplines and areas of study. In the process, they have opened up the canon to new plays, genres, and methods of performance, direction, and design. The publications in this burgeoning field are too numerous to list, but Susan M. Steadman provides a helpful overview in her annotated bibliography, *Dramatic Re-Visions* (1991). I offer but a selection of titles here: Helene Keyssar's *Feminist Theatre* (1984); Elizabeth J. Natalle's *Feminist Theatre: A Study in Persuasion* (1985); Jill Dolan's *The Feminist Spectator as Critic* (1988); Lynda Hart's *Making a Spectacle: Feminist Essays on Contemporary Women's Drama* (1989); Sue-Ellen Case's *Performing Feminisms: Feminist Critical Theory and Practice* (1990); Janet Brown's *Taking Center Stage: Feminism in Contemporary U.S. Drama* (1991); Sue-Ellen Case and Janelle Reinelt's *The Performance of Power: Theatrical Discourse and Politics* (1991); Laurence Senelick's *Gender in Performance: The Presentation of Difference in the Performing Arts* (1992); the section on feminism in Janelle G. Reinelt and Joseph R. Roach's *Critical Theory and Performance* (1992); Lizbeth Goodman's *Contemporary Feminist Theatres: To Each Her Own* (1993); Elaine Aston's *An Introduction to Feminism and Theatre* (1995).

Sue-Ellen Case offers reasons for why "theatre studies has come 'later' to the feminist critique than work in other genres" (2):

> Primary among them is the status theatre studies inhabits in the university at large. Theatre departments are relatively new to the university. Prior to their founding, the study of theatre was located within English departments. This location meant that the study of theatre was regarded primarily as the analysis of playtexts, isolating them from practice, and employing the devices common to literary studies. When theatre departments were founded, their primary focus was and still is, in training practitioners. As the study of theatre within theatre departments developed, it was dominated by the history of theatre, rather than its criticism. Theatre criticism still resides primarily in English departments, where it focuses on Renaissance studies, with only marginal attention to contemporary theatre. Thus, current critical strategies applied to contemporary texts and practices, such as those of feminist theory, inhabit a severely marginal position in both theatre and English departments. (2)

See also Nancy S. Reinhardt's 1981 discussion of why "women's studies in theatre criticism . . . and theatre history" was only then "just beginning" (25), in which she offers several reasons for "the apparent discrepancy between feminist film and feminist theatre criticism, why theatre scholarship has essentially been so conservative in contrast to many innovative feminist film studies" (26).

32. In a similar vein, William C. Snyder uses the Romantic categories of the sublime, the beautiful, and the picturesque to discuss how the domesticated landscape is depicted by English Romantic women writers in ways distinguishable from male writers. Jon Klancher uses similar categories to discuss how women theorists of the period, including Joanna Baillie, extended the boundaries of the domestic, drawing attention to its political contours:

> By displacing tragedy from the realm of the state to the domestic spheres of civil society, Baillie also tried to make the latter, gender-defined arena a basis

for criticizing the public world, where, in traditional tragedy, the "tragic passions" had been made to appear transhistorical rather than specifically masculine and contextually linked to the larger "tyranny" of England's own *ancien regime*. In this way, Baillie's theory of tragedy was less an attempt to privatize and domesticate formerly public and political controversy than an effort to rethink the mode of dramatic representation as a discourse capable of making explicit the political restaging of private life. ("British Theory and Criticism" 113)

This observation evokes Donna Landry's in her discussion of the poetry of the late-eighteenth-century poet and playwright Ann Yearsley: "in the final phase of her career," Yearsley "thus simultaneously attempts to domesticate the political by 'bringing it home' and to generate, in a more visionary, utopian, and incompletely articulated sense, a radical democratic politics in which domestic relations, hitherto marginal, are at the center" (171).

33. For a discussion of the difficulty of determining what constitutes a "play" or "drama" when talking about women writers, see also Gwenn Davis and Beverly A. Joyce's introduction to their very helpful *Drama by Women to 1900: A Bibliography of American and British Writers* (1992), which includes—in addition to plays performed and closeted—listings of translations, pageants, tableaux, and charades, prologues, epilogues, and interludes. Davis and Joyce's argument is that "[o]nly the broadest definitions of form and of time frame can accommodate women's dramatic writings" (viii).

34. See chapter 3 of Case's *Feminism and Theatre* (1988) for a further discussion of this "form."

35. For approaches to feminist theater history, I have drawn upon several influential analyses. In 1989 Susan Bassnett wrote:

> We need some comprehensive work on women's theatre history. We need to go back into the archives, to look again at what was happening in Europe from the end of the Roman Empire onwards. We need to stop thinking about the "exceptions" such as Hrostvitha or Aphra Behn, and look seriously at the contexts in which those women were writing and the tradition out of which they wrote, accepting that the small list of names we have could be very much longer.
>
> We need to reconsider the importance we have attached as theatre historians to the text-based theatre in the light of the role of women in alternative theatre. . . . We need a lot more work on analysis of reviews of female performers, to examine in depth some of the implications of the discourse of male critics regarding the work of women. We need to look at theatre in context, to examine the social, economic, and political implications of women's work in particular. We need to ask a lot of questions about accepted notions of cultural history and revise many of them. (112)

In the same year Tracy C. Davis raised three important questions for those interested in employing "a feminist methodology in theatre history": (1) How does the ideology of the dominant culture affect women's status? (2) How do social, class, and economic factors affect privilege? (3) How is the status quo maintained or challenged in artistic media? Davis concludes her essay ("Questions for a Feminist Methodology in Theatre History") by writing: "The eclectic nature of theatre (and hence of theatre history) is complemented by the pluralistic approach of feminist history, which constantly seeks to question the traditions by which knowledge becomes accredited, often rejecting both the traditions and the knowledge thus generated" (76). This commentary can be applied to the epistemological frameworks that have traditionally structured the fields of theater theory, theater criticism, and dramatic criticism.

In 1993 Charlotte Canning described the "act of theorizing a feminist history" as "caught between several sets of conflicts and contradictions":

> between a distrust of the patriarchal biases and assumptions of theatre historiography and the need to theorize and implement a feminist theatre historiography, between the imperative to recuperate women's theatre work erased by history and the responsibility to critique that work, between the historical moment under examination and the current moment in history, and between the feminist investment in essentialism and the feminist use of poststructuralist theory. (529)

Advocating a negotiation between consciousness-raising, New Women's History, and "feminist theatre historiography that draws on post-structuralism" (534), Canning proposes an approach to talking about the experiences of women in theater that neglects neither the contributions of the first phase of feminist scholarship nor the critiques of that scholarship leveled by the second phase of feminist theorists.

36. See also Judith Pascoe's forthcoming analysis of how female writers of the Romantic period—specifically Mary Robinson—drew on the theatricality of Georgian culture to complicate divisions between public and private spheres and to discuss their gendered position on social stages (*Romantic Theatricality: Gender, Poetry, and Spectatorship*, Cornell University Press).

37. This quotation is from page 27 of Ann Catherine Holbrook's *The Dramatist* (1809). I thank Kathleen Anderson for bringing this text to my attention.

38. Christina Hoff Sommers uses this term in *Who Stole Feminism?: How Women Have Betrayed Women* (1994). In her view, "gender feminists" are those social constructionists (primarily academics) whom Sommers targets as being out of touch with the complaints and concerns of mainstream, middle-class women.

Chapter 2

1. See the sketch entitled "Ingleby and Miss Biffin" in Mathews, *Anecdotes of Actors with Other Desultory Recollections* (1844), 238–40.

2. This quotation is from Wollstonecraft's *An Historical and Moral View of the French Revolution* (1993; 387).

3. For an important essay on the issue of critical theory and gender, see Mary Jacobus's "Is There a Woman in This Text?" (1982; rpt. 1986). She writes that it is "no part of my purpose to indict 'theory' as such—on the contrary; still less to imply, as some feminist critics have tended to do, that theory is of itself 'male,' a dangerous abstraction which denies the specificity of female experience and serves chiefly to promote men in the academy."

> Instead I want to offer some thoughts about the relation between women and theory—about the deflection of gender harassment (aggression against the class of women) or sexual harassment (aggression against the bodies of women) onto the 'body' of the text. The result might be called textual harassment, the specular appropriation of woman, or even her elimination altogether. It's not just that women figure conveniently for acts of narcissistic self-completion on the part of some male theorists, or that the shutting up of a female 'victim' can open up theoretical discourse. It's also a matter of the adversarial relation between rival theorists which often seems to underlie a triangle such as the one in Fish's anecdote. This triangle characteristically invokes its third (female) term only in the interests of the original rivalry and works finally to get rid of the woman, leaving theorist and theorist face to face. (85–86)

See also Jill Dolan's essay, "In Defense of the Discourse: Materialist Feminism, Postmodernism, Poststructuralism . . . and Theory" (1989; rpt. 1993), in which she offers a "personal defense of theory in discourse" by asserting that "I work in theory to save [my life]. Theory allows me to articulate my differences from a feminism I first learned as monolithic. Theory enables me to see that there is no tenable position for me in the totalizing strategies of radical feminism and that I can align myself profitably elsewhere" (95).

In addition, a very helpful overview of the topic, with special emphasis on the eighteenth century (especially Eliza Haywood), is provided by Kristina Straub in "Women, Gender and Criticism" (1989).

4. All citations from Baillie in this chapter are from *The Dramatic and Poetical Works (1851)*, 1976 facsimile edition.

5. For helpful summaries of the positions of these writers, see Marvin Carlson's *Theories of Theatre* (1993) and Edwin Duerr's *The Length and Depth of Acting* (1962).

6. See Susan Wolfson's article on Mary Lamb's 1807 preface to *Tales from Shakespear* (1990), in which she views Lamb's plots as precursors to "modern feminist explanations—especially those concerned to recognize in Shakespeare's plays an important stage for many of our culture's most deeply embedded attitudes about the roles men and women are given to play" (35).

7. Citations from Inchbald are from the 1990 facsimile edition listed in Works Cited. I do not cite page numbers because they are reproduced throughout the facsimile text.

8. For this information, see David D. Mann, "Checklist of Female Dramatists, 1660–1823" (1990).

9. For an excellent discussion of the statistics on women playwrights in England between 1660 and 1800, see Stanton's article, "'This New-Found Path Attempting': Women Dramatists in England, 1660–1800" (1991), which also provides helpful tables on women's play production (including a list of all plays by women and the dates of their production).

10. While playwrighting could be lucrative for women—Joanna Baillie, for example, made three hundred pounds for her second volume of *Plays on the Passions in 1802* (Carhart 18)—popular female actors also stood to make a lot of money. A. Aspinall (1951) has called my attention to the fact that Dorothy Jordan estimated having made over £100,000 before fleeing her creditors for France (xiii).

11. Scholars have recently begun to investigate the reception of English actresses who worked on the stage prior to 1900. Kristina Straub writes about "the politics of spectatorship" in relation to actors during the eighteenth century, and Elizabeth Howe has shown how a focus on actresses' sexual behavior (on and off the stage) in London theaters between 1660 and 1700 served both to reinforce gender stereotypes and to uncover new ways of reading female roles. Sandra Richards's history of the English actress includes a chapter on Sarah Siddons, the greatest celebrity actor of the late eighteenth century. Tracy C. Davis investigates the social identity of the Victorian actress as "working woman," and Thomas Postlewait has written specifically about the genre of theatrical memoir in relation to the actress of the Late Victorian and Modern eras.

12. In their biographical entry on Mellon, Highfil, Burnim, and Langhans, *Biographical Dictionary*, write that "a man named Mitford" published these memoirs (10:178).

13. Likewise, the short biographical sketch of Julia Glover (1779–1850)—who acted in such successful plays as Hannah More's *Percy* (1777) and Samuel Taylor Coleridge's *Remorse* (1813)—also concludes with a moral, a directive to young actresses to adopt Glover's work ethic: "She is very attentive to her business, always perfect, was never known to disppoint an audience but twice, then only from accident, and is a very early riser; points, which we beg to recommend to the serious consideration of young ladies who think themselves far above the top of the histrionic tree. . . ." (N.B.: There are no page numbers in the text cited.)

14. Inchbald refers to the phenomenon of "green-room marriages" as the expected outcome for certain actresses playing certain roles, another example of how female actors' offstage and onstage identities were conflated. In her remarks on Gay's *The Beggar's Opera*, Inchbald writes: "Polly Peachum is endowed with such superior charms, from the unoffending qualities she possesses, that when she was first represented, every actress who performed the part made her fortune by marriage;—and Miss Fenton, the original Polly, so fascinated the Duke of Bolton, that he elevated her to the highest rank of a female subject, by making her his wife" (no page numbers appear).

However, the greenroom marriage could spark venomous portrayals of the Romantic actress and result in outbursts such as the following, which refers to Elizabeth Farren, who became the countess of Derby. In the *Memoirs of the Present Countess of Derby*, the pseudonymous Petronious Arbiter reminds readers of the British actor's servile history in order to place Farren's ascendency to the peerage in a diminished light: "the Performers of the Theatre Royal, Drury Lane, are THEIR MAJESTIES' SERVANTS; and . . . all Players are, by several statutes, declared Vagabonds and excommunicates, of course not entitled to Christian burial" (25).

15. Divulging the private details of the female actor's sexual history under the guise of actually instructing the public in morality, many celebrity memoirs from the British Romantic period aimed to titillate their readers by assessing women's anatomy. Elizabeth Farren, for instance, is described by her memoirist as poorly suited for breeches roles because "she has no prominence either before or behind — all is a straight line from head to foot; and for her legs, they are shaped like a sugar loaf" (Arbiter 17). Even Farren's defender in the corrective to her life summarizes her physicality fairly critically: "Her figure is tall, but not sufficiently muscular; were it a little more embonpoint, it would be one of the finest the Theatre can boast" (Anonymous, *The Testimony of Truth to Exalted Merit*, 23). Two of the bluntest articulations of what was physically desirable in the woman who acts occur in the biographical sketch of Julia Glover and in Frances Anne Kemble's memoirs: "Why do women ever grow old"? moans the narrator of the former; and in the latter, Kemble records Elizabeth Inchbald's stammer as she vehemently rejected a female actor who read for one of her plays: "No, no, no; I-I-I won't have that s-s-s-stick of a girl! D-d-d-do give me a-a-a-girl with *bumps!*" (cited in Kemble, *Records of a Girlhood* 213).

Inchbald was preoccupied with breast size, especially her own. Her "Description of Me," which her biographer James Boaden included in her memoirs, demonstrates the degree to which she and other female actors absorbed a standard of femininity in which the breast was to be prominent. Reducing "Me" to the physical categories by which women were constantly assessed on stage — age, height, figure, shape, skin — Inchbald directs her least flattering remarks to the subject of her "Bosom," writing: "None; or so diminuitive, that it's like a needle in a bottle of hay" (Boaden, *Memoirs of Mrs. Inchbald* 1:176).

16. Appleton's 1974 biography of Vestris contains the information that the 1830 edition of Vestris's memoirs was "based on [John] Duncombe's [1826] account, supplemented by a few additional scandals" (217). For further biographical information on Vestris, see Pearce (1923) and Waitzkin (1933).

17. In his *The Life of Mrs. Jordan* (1831), James Boaden identifies Arthur Griffinhoof as the pseudonymous author of the Vestris memoir. "I presume this terrible appellation was suggested to the manager by the proprietor of the Monthly Review, *Ralph Griffiths* . . ." (2:129).

18. Peter Wagner's *Eros Revived* (1988) has called my attention to this term. For an excellent discussion of Victorian actresses and erotica of the nineteenth century, see Tracy C. Davis's *Actresses as Working Women* (1991).

19. Janet Todd writes that Mary Anne Radcliffe was "identified in a contemporary biographical dictionary as 'one of the Wollstonecraft school'" (*Dictionary* 264). For further information on Radcliffe, see Coral Ann Howells's introduction to the 1972 edition of Radcliffe's gothic novel *Manfrone* (1809), especially her description of the theatrical techniques and dramatic effects that Radcliffe incorporates into her narrative (vii–ix).

20. This essay is called "Mrs. Jordan and the Times" and appears in vol. 2 of *The Theatrical Inquisitor: or Literary Mirror*, written by "Cerberus" (1813).

21. Those who viewed theater as an institution for the instruction of moral virtue were often opposed to the onslaught of imported German tragedies. In her "Preface to the Plays" (1799), Jane West describes some of the reasons for these objections:

> The dreadful tendency of the German dramas has been pointed out by several able writers; but by none with more justness than by an anonymous essayist in the Gentleman's Magazine for last January, who properly notices, among other faults, the highly indecorous levity with which they introduce the name of that awful Being, who ought never to be alluded to but with the most profound reverence, to inforce some important serious truth. Offensive familiarity becomes impiety, when we recollect that the author of all purity and truth is frequently appealed to, to justify violations of his own precepts, and to invalidate the authority of his revealed will. If we would see the effect of these audacious blasphemies against our Maker, these libels upon all governments, these pasquinades upon the moral virtues, these denunciations of every Christian excellence, these institutes of every vice, look at the continent of Europe. The avidity with which they have been read, and the celebrity enjoyed by their authors, may be considered as certain omens which foreboded the dreadful calamities of the present times. (xi–xii)

22. It was not only the direct and unapologetic stares of female actors that were problematic for the culture. Other "fronts" intruded. Drawings from this period of theatrical history show female actors wearing white, gauzy nightgown-like dresses cut to reveal high, erect breasts that seem on the verge of tumbling out of bodices. Male actors often have their hands near or on these "fronts." Female costume was certainly a factor in encouraging audiences to equate femaleness with sexual availability, and thus the wearing of particular kinds of contemporary clothing (which actresses often supplied themselves) caused many to confuse "the public woman" with the private one. Actress's clothes, which were but a variation on the costumes worn in social theaters and on the street, contributed to the sexually charged atmosphere that actual play scripts from this period do not often reveal, and it was this heightened reality to which Styles and other conservative theater reformists objected.

For drawings of female costume and the sexualization by male actors of women's bodies on the stage, see the facsimile edition (1990) of Inchbald's play prefaces to *The British Theatre*, which contains a picture of a scene from each of the plays under discussion. The plate from John Hughes's *The Siege of Damascus* is especially suggestive, as it depicts a brawny male hand grabbing the high-breasted heroine just below her left breast, itself emphasized by the white empire-waisted dress and her arms thrown high in the air. See also Paula R. Backscheider's brief discussion of the presentation of women's breasts in gothic drama (1993; 193).

23. See Cecilia Macheski's "Herself as Heroine: Portraits as Autobiography for Elizabeth Inchbald" (1991).

24. Highfill, Burnim, and Langhams write that Abington's "influence over Miss Phillips gradually diminished" and she "then quickly developed an irresistable comic style of her own which kept her in public favor for exactly 20 years" (4:83).

Yet one of the features often missing in analyses of women actors is how a female tradition of acting gets handed down over time and the degree to which one actress remains an influence over another. My comment on Abington's influence is purely speculative. But I include it in my text to indicate that an actress can develop her own style without forgetting her debt to her acting teachers, in this case a powerful woman actor of the eighteenth century.

25. Mathews both edited the memoirs of her husband, the celebrated comedian Charles Mathews, and narrated stories from his own life and their life together. At the time Mathews wrote her *Anecdotes of Actors* (1844) there were 150 "printed volumes of autobiography," this according to Sandra Richards, who cites Margaret Cornwell Baron-Wilson's *Our Actresses* (1844) as her source (268).

26. For further analysis of this particular evening, see Ellen Donkin's "Mrs. Siddons Looks Back in Anger: Feminist Historiography for Eighteenth-Century British Theater" (1992). Feminist performance historians are starting to contribute fascinating information about how female actors counter the reading of "Woman" in play scripts (especially those that are male-authored), interpreting them before an audience in ways that confound expectations and open a space for the dramatization of "female subjectivity" (Donkin, "Siddons" 285). In the essay cited above Donkin writes: "The feminist theater historian must identify material like this [such as Donkin's discussion of Siddons's performance in October 1784] as a form of politically unconscious theater history and begin the work of extricating the female performer from the ideological apparatus in which she worked" (287). See also the work of Carol J. Carlisle on Victorian actor Helen Faucit's interpretation of Lady Macbeth (1977) and Gay Gibson Cima's *Performing Women* (1993), in which she discusses how female actors from the modern period used different acting styles to critique the position of women on and off the stage. For an analysis of how contemporary British female actors have performed political interventions in the representation of women onstage, see Carol Rutter's interviews in *Clamorous Voices: Shakespeare's Women Today* (1989). Patti Gillespie has written about how the female actor can perform cultural critique: "As a fictional character, then, a woman is free to decide, to take action, and even to attack contemporary practices with little reason to fear the renunciation or retribution of the audience upon her personally. Able to present a view of 'reality' with no need personally to explain it logically or defend it rationally, even a timid woman may become bold enough to function actively as persuader" (289). Penny Gay's *As She Likes It: Shakespeare's Unruly Women* (1984) traces the Royal Shakespeare Company's performances of five comedies over several decades to demonstrate how a "determined actress (or actor) can disrupt" reviewers' fantasies about "the perfect heterosexual marriage in a self-regulating community" by "investing all the textualities of the production (speeches, costume, body language, how she inhabits the stage space and how she relates to the other performers) with her own individual energy; in a sense, by fighting for her role, as the embodiment of a *particular* woman enclosed in a narrative that pretends to be universal" (4).

27. Elizabeth Berkeley Craven takes a similar tone in her memoirs (published in 1826), assessing her career in private theater as "a *negative*. . . ." "I have been," she writes, "like other women, flattered with the brilliancy of my talents, my figure,

and all those things, to which my successes in the world are attributed; but these only raised malice and envy against me . . ." (1:202).

28. Siddons's most extended piece of writing, the *Reminiscences*, reveals a good deal about the offstage experiences of late-eighteenth-century actresses as they navigated public and private space. Siddons describes the following events: the demands of childcare and studying for a role (8); Siddons's amazement when Samuel Johnson told her that the actress Hannah Pritchard " 'never read any part of [*Macbeth*], except her own part' " (14), especially because character study had been for Siddons, since the age of twenty at least, a consuming passion; her encounter with a near riot in a salon of bluestockings, when the hostess made her the unwitting centerpiece for their talk theater (15–16); the storming of her own home by a Scottish lady who claimed to be too ill to go to the theater " 'so I am come to look at you here' " (21); and her fainting at a performance at which a London audience booed her for allegedly refusing to appear at a benefit and being insensitive to other actors (29–32).

Siddons's *Reminiscences* are forecast by the tone of Leah Wells Sumbel's *Memoirs* (1811), which deglamorizes the life of an actress by telling forthrightly about her problems with a verbally and physically abusive husband. An example of Sumbel's bluntness appears in the following passage: "He [my husband] was so extremely jealous, that when he went with me to the theatre, I dare not, for my life, look any where but on the stage; and that not for any length of time, or the consequences would be, I should be immediately knocked down, which I underwent more than once" (1:201).

29. For one of the few studies that describes pre–twentieth-century women as theorists of acting, see Malpede's *Women in Theatre: Compassion and Hope* (1983). A chapter that brings together the commentary on acting by Frances Anne Kemble is especially relevant to my study, as are Malpede's introductory remarks:

> Fanny Kemble wrote a great deal about her stage life and about the nature of acting itself. In so doing, she made a significant contribution to the body of acting theory written by women which, as I become more and more acquainted with it, seems more and more to suggest an approach to acting that has been uniquely shaped by female sensibilities. The fact that much of this theory appears in the midst of autobiographies or journal entries (as well as in essays) in no way compromises its importance as original work of the mind. (17)

30. By emphasizing Siddons's preoccupation (in her notes) with performing Lady Macbeth as "feminine" I do not mean to discount recent suggestions by Backscheider (1993), Donkin (1992), and Julie Carlson (1994) that her performances of Lady Macbeth—and her self-presentation in portraits—convey a "masculine" persona as well.

31. The notes by G. J. Bell on Siddons's performance of Lady Macbeth were (according to Brander Matthews) first printed in the journal *Nineteenth Century* (1878); the essay on Siddons as Queen Katharine, Mrs. Beverley, and Lady Randolph appeared in *Macmillan's Magazine* (April 1882). Both were reprinted "in the

first volume of 'Papers, Literary, Scientific, &c.' by Fleeming Jenkin . . . [e]dited by Sidney Colvin and J. A. Ewing, F.R.S. London, and New York: Longmans, Green and Co., 1887" (Matthews, cited in Jenkin III). The Dramatic Museum of Columbia University reprinted them in 1915. This is the text I am citing in this chapter. See Julie Carlson's discussion of Bell's notes on Siddons's performances in *In the Theater of Romanticism* (165–66), as well as her fascinating account of the threat to Romantic men that Siddons's performances of Lady Macbeth posed.

32. Note how differently Siddons's niece, Frances Anne Kemble, reads this section. In her *Notes upon Some of Shakespeare's Plays*, Kemble takes exception to Siddons's suggestion that Lady Macbeth is conscience-stricken and remorseful as the play progresses. Finding her to possess "more of the essentially manly nature" than Macbeth (57), Kemble's reading condemns the character rather than seeking to explore (by attempting to inhabit) Lady Macbeth's "mind."

33. In Siddons's "Remarks," she implies that her process of studying character evolved over the years especially as a result of playing the difficult role of Lady Macbeth:

> It was my custom to study my characters at night, when all the domestic cares and business of the day were over. On the night preceding that in which I was to appear in this part for the first time, I shut myself up, as usual, when all the family were retired, and commenced my study of *Lady Macbeth*. As the character is very short, I thought I should soon accomplish it. Being then only twenty years of age, I believed, as many others do believe, that little more was necessary than to get the words into my head; for the necessity of discrimination, and the development of character, at that time of my life, had scarcely entered into my imagination. ("Remarks," cited in Campbell 1:134)

34. In discussing the "aesthetic geography" of Romantic women writers, Haefner emphasizes "the conversation," which for a number of women writers "fuses expressivism and affectivism because it successfully negotiates the perils of gender and genius: that is, woman's art based on woman's skills (conversational abilities) will slip by cultural censors/critics" (268).

35. It is interesting to note that Frances Maria Kelly herself wondered why Lamb took such pains to conceal her identity, even to the point of including a footnote to the essay that sought further to erase Kelly from the picture (Holman 73). In a letter to Charles Kent written in her old age (1875), Kelly puzzled about this obfuscation: "I have never been able thoroughly to appreciate the extraordinary skill with which he [Lamb] has, in the construction of his story, desired so to mystify and characterize the events, as to keep me out of sight, and render it utterly impossible for any one to guess at me as the original heroine." In the lengthy section that follows this complaint, Kelly details her actual history in order to counter Lamb's misrepresentation: "[I]f I am to be, as it seems, considered and announced the bona fide heroine of the tale, I frankly declare, that I infinitely prefer the position and feelings of 'little Fanny Kelly' to those of Miss Barbara. The question is, how truly, and to what extent, it even 'shadows' the early life of Frances Maria Kelly" (cited in Holman 75).

36. The passages I am citing here appear at the end of an "extra-illustrated" book that is at the Huntington Library, not to be confused with other editions bearing the same title, which (of those I've seen) — in *non*-extra-illustrated form — omit the Williams–Jordan interviews.

37. Mary A. Favret uses theatrical analogy to discuss the kinds of gatherings to which I here refer, viewing as "private theatricals" (278) Helen Maria Williams's orchestration of meetings in her Paris home. Favret writes that Williams "plays director . . . , managing both actors and audience from her unique position both outside (politically) and inside (emotionally) the scenes she depicts" (285). "The home, a woman's space, can then serve as political theater, where relationships and feelings perform lead roles" (290).

38. For further information about this intellectual circle, see R. B. Johnson's "Introduction" (1926); Myers (1990); Schnorrenberg (1990).

39. Jill Dolan explains the feminist critique of mimesis as follows: "the form's attempt to recreate reality through psychological identification processes that objectify women renders it unable to frame subject positions that differ from representation's white, middle-class, heterosexual, male ideal spectator" ("Personal, Political, Polemical" 48).

40. For another stunning articulation of how men and women should treat each other in marriage, see Hester Chapone's "Matrimonial Creed," included in her address "To Samuel Richardson" (1791), which itself contains memorable phrases such as "make matches of souls" (194) and "no person can be justly said to love who does not prefer the happiness of the object beloved to their own" (195).

Chapter 3

1. Writing of Helen Maria Williams's "self-conscious declarations" about "her lack of political intent" in *Letters Written in France in the Summer of 1790*, Matthew Bray reminds us that the self-effacing statements which appeared in prefatory remarks "were virtually clichés required of women writers in order to avoid charges of impropriety" (1).

2. This passage is from Charlotte Smith's dedicatory letter to Thomas Harris, which precedes her comedy *What Is She?* (1799).

3. This information is provided by Dale Spender in her section on the Lees in *Mothers of the Novel* (1986; 232).

4. In *The Empty Space* (1968), Peter Brook writes that the aim of his theatrical art is "immediate theatre" (see his chapter 4).

5. Inchbald's vocabulary is similar to Byron's when she remarks on Addison's *Cato*:

> The joy or sorrow which an author is certain to experience upon every new production, is far more powerful in the heart of the dramatist, than in that of any other writer. The sound of clamorous plaudits raises his spirits to a kind of ecstacy; whilst hisses and groans, from a dissatisfied audience, strike on the ear like a personal insult, avowing loud and public contempt

for that, in which he has been labouring to show his skill. ("Remarks on *Cato*")

(For explanation for the lack of pagination see note 14 below.)

6. For recent discussions of Byron's concept of "mental theatre," see Gatton (1987); Corbett (1988); Richardson (*A Mental Theater* 1988); Kubiak (1991); Special Issue of *Studies in Romanticism* 31.3 (1992); Purinton (1994); Crochunis (1995); and Moody (1996).

7. Frances Burney, for example, did not allow illness to keep her from navigating literally between closet and stage when she attended what was (in the opinion of participants and audiences) a disastrous production of her play *Edwy and Elgiva* (1795) at Drury Lane. "I sat, snug & retired & wrapt up in a Bonnet & immense Pelice," she wrote in a letter that describes this frustrating occasion (dated April 5, 1795, which appears in Hemlow's edition of Burney's journals and letters [3:99]). (For a sense of the reception of *Edwy and Elgiva*, see Appendix A above. For the text of *Edwy and Elgiva*, see Miriam Benkowitz's 1957 edition).

8. In Case's introductory essay to *Performing Feminisms* (1990), she provides an analysis of how the topic of positionality has been discussed by feminist theater historians in recent years:

> Positionality addresses the position from which the feminist critic writes. How does she situate, or delimit, or begin to inscribe her "project" or set of "strategies" upon the theoretical terrain of agency? For she, herself, inscribes a certain kind of agency in "approaching" her own combination of theory and theatre. Materialist analysis has taught how the critic inscribes her own gendered socio-economic and sexual compound, either self-consciously, or by formation of her critical apparatus. In earlier feminist criticism, the device for locating the voice was often an introductory testimonial, such as, "I am a white, heterosexual, middle-class academic." Although there may be political contexts in which such a statement remains effective, its theoretical assumptions, in regard to writing, overlook certain key issues. In the generality and stability of such identifications, a certain essentialism appears that has been corrected by later, more materialist strategies of positionality. (6–7)

9. Occasionally one finds a male playwright using this dichotomy between innocence and experience in his prefaces. William Hayley's 1811 preface to his *Three Plays* is forthrightly confessional. In telling the story of Garrick's rejection of his first play, he writes that he was "deeply chagrined, that I had suffered Garrick artfully to draw me forth from privacy, which I loved; and to make me the dupe of his adulation," and he casts himself as an adviser to the naive playwright, chastened by his negative experiences: "I have given this long and frank history of my earliest tragedy in the hope that the occurrences relating to it may prove a useful lesson to young ingenuous dramatic writers, and put them on their guard against the various perils of sanguine expectation" (xxxii).

10. For a discussion of Mitford's experience with the banning of *Charles the First* (and a reading of the play in its political context), see Kenneth Johnston and

Joseph Nicoles's "Transitory Actions, Men Betrayed: The French Revolution in the English Revolution in Romantic Drama" (1992).

11. Although Mitford does not identify Bennoch by name in her introduction, she makes it clear that she is speaking of him when she writes: "For the publication of these volumes, the excellent friend *to whom they are inscribed* is solely accountable" (1:v; my emphasis).

12. Overt defiance of the Licenser (or Examiner) of Plays in a preface from this period is quite rare, especially in one composed by a woman. More often than not, one sees an almost fatalistic acceptance of the Licenser's decisions, as occurs in Jane West's (1758–1852) preface to her poems and plays (1799) in which, citing rejections by both Covent Garden and Drury Lane, she confesses that she "does not complain of ill-treatment in either instance" because her "knowledge of stage effect is too limited to allow her to question the propriety of this decision" (1:v).

Because acquiescence to the decisions made by the theater industry was commonplace in published prefaces and advertisements, it is all the more noteworthy to see Lady Eglantine Wallace (?d. 1803) clearly thumbing her nose at the Licenser in her preface to *The Whim* (1795), called "Address to the Public." (N.B.: Wallace's name appears alternately as Eglantine and Eglinton. In her list of women dramatists in England, 1660–1800, Judith Phillips Stanton spells Wallace's first name as "Eglinton" ["This New-Found Path" 352].) In this astonishing preface, Wallace tells her readership that her "harmless COMEDY," written to raise money for the poor, has been rejected on the grounds that it is politically dangerous. Then, launching into a scathing challenge of the Licenser's "hand of power . . . outstretched to blast all my Fairy dreams, of thus feeding the hungry—and relieving the sick" (3), Wallace questions his reasons for pulling her play in the eleventh hour: "Whatever motives the *Licencer* may have, for giving a preference to particular people, he has no right to affix odium to the reputation of any individual, by such unjust and injurious remarks. From reading the Comedy, it may easily be conceived, that other motives, independent [*sic*] of the sentiments and merits of it, influenced his decision" (4). Wallace will not be whisked so embarrassingly offstage without challenging the person responsible, and in fighting back she tells her readers that not only has she written to the marquis of Salisbury in an effort to have the Licenser overruled, but she is attaching her letter to the preface so that her case may be vindicated on the public stage. Using phrases such as "I glory" and "I exult," Wallace defends her actions by drawing on the fact of the recent French Revolution to argue that censorship led to that country's chaos, and she frames her closing remarks with a theme common in eighteenth-century theater theory by referring to the theater as a significant forum for the education of moral English adults: "The Stage is the only school which overgrown boys and girls can go to, and did the Licencer permit more satire, more sentiment, and less ribaldry, *outre* pantomime, and folly, to appear under his auspices, it would be doing the State more service, than thus taking the alarm at *The Whim* of renewing the Saturnalia Feast" (14). Wallace's preface is exceptional for the directness and vehemence with which its female author challenges the institutional structures of London theaters.

See also Martin Archer Shee's "Preface" to the tragedy *Alasco* (1824), probably the most lengthy articulation of wounded pride in relation to the Licenser's rejection. Shee even has his name printed on the title page in conjunction with the phrase: "Excluded from the Stage, by the Authority of the Lord Chamberlain."

13. As Katharine Rogers writes, Inchbald's life story contains many instances when she was defiant of male managers and playwrights who would challenge her authority as well as statements that this very boldness could, as P. M. Zall notes in reference to the challenge from Colman, make her " 'extremely unhappy' " (272). As a result of that incident, Inchbald subsequently declined a position on the staff of the new *Quarterly Review* and gave up preface writing altogether (Zall 272).

14. This interchange between Colman and Inchbald appears in the facsimile edition (1990) of Inchbald's prefatory remarks and contains no page numbers to distinguish it. As I have stated in previous notes in other chapters, because the numbers are reproduced throughout the text, I have not included them here.

15. See "The Cool World of Samuel Taylor Coleridge: Elizabeth Inchbald; or, Sex and Sensibility" (270–73).

16. For a helpful feminist analysis of Inchbald's prefaces, see Anna Lott's "Sexual Politics in Elizabeth Inchbald" (1994).

17. Marlon B. Ross has provided a context for studying Baillie's *Plays on the Passions* in his extensive analysis of women Romantic poets, calling this series of plays "perhaps the most ambitious poetic project taken on by a woman in the early nineteenth century" (258). See also Stuart Curran (1988), who has observed that Baillie's plays "exerted the most direct practical and theoretical force on serious drama written in the Romantic period" (186). Other recent discussions of Baillie include Zall (1982); Noble (1983); Brewer (1991 and 1995); Ranger (1991); McKerrow (1992); Watkins (1993); Cox (1992); Burroughs (1994 and 1995); Page (1994); Purinton (1994); Yudin (1994); Mellor (1994); and Donkin (1995).

Baillie's letters are in the process of being collected and annotated by Judith Bailey Slagle, in *The Collected Letters of Joanna Baillie*.

18. I am aware that some critics extend these dates to 1836. This is because, while the three volumes in the series of plays were published in 1798, 1802, and 1812, Baillie continued to write plays that she considered part of this project, collecting them together in a volume with other "non-passion" plays published in 1836. (See her note to the preface attached to the first volume of her three-volume *Dramas* [1836], 312.) These were not the first plays Baillie had composed. Her first play was called *Arnold*, but it does not survive. Catherine Jane Hamilton writes that, although Baillie worked for three months on this play, it was "flung into the waste-paper basket, or used as curl-papers by [Baillie] and her sister" (1:117).

19. Marvin Carlson's *Theories of the Theatre* (1984) has called my attention to the following relevant works that preceded Baillie's *Plays on the Passions* (aside from Ben Jonson's "theory of humours"). John Dennis's *Usefulness of the Stage to the Happiness of Mankind* (1698)—in Carlson's words—"suggests that drama works in such a way as to stimulate the passions while not denying the reason" (125). Aaron Hill's *Essay on the Art of Acting* (1746) "considers all dramatic passion essentially reducible to ten emotions: joy, grief, fear, anger, pity, scorn, hatred, jealousy, wonder, and love" (139). Samuel Foote's *Treatise on the Passions* (1747) uses language that anticipates Baillie's in her "Introductory Discourse" when he writes that his aim is "to trace the Rise and Progress of the Passions, together with the Effects on the

Organs of our Bodies" (cited in Marvin Carlson 139). Compare Baillie's words: "To trace them [the passions] in their rise and progress in the heart, seems but rarely to have been the object of any dramatist" (10).

In addition, Edwin Duerr's survey of theories of acting mentions James Burgh's anonymously published book on elocution called *The Art of Speaking: containing I. An Essay: in which are given Rules for expressing properly the principal Passions and Humours* (1761), which contains an "Index of Passions, or 'Humours'" thirteen pages long (250).

Note also that Margaret Carhart, in her 1923 critical biography of Baillie, writes that the "idea did not originate with her, for in 1781 at the Haymarket Theatre had appeared *The School of Shakespeare, or Humours and Passions*," which dramatized scenes from different plays that each represented a particular emotion, such as vanity, cruelty, ambition, revenge, cowardice, etc. (191).

20. See Baillie's comments in her "Preface to the Second Edition of *Miscellaneous Plays*" (1805): "It has been, and still is, my strongest desire to add a few pieces to the stock of what may be called our national or permanently acting plays, however unequal soever my abilities may be to the object of my ambition" (387). Later in the same preface she confesses how strongly this desire affected her when she actually went to see plays performed on the stage:

> I have seldom seen any piece, not appearing to me to possess great merit (for such things I have seen), succeed upon the stage, without feeling inclined to say to myself, "don't despise this: very probably in attempting, even upon no higher grounds, such success as the present, and giving to it also the whole bent of your thoughts, you would find yourself miserably disappointed." (387)

For an excellent discussion of Baillie's attempts to get her plays staged—and some of the reasons for their poor reception—see Ellen Donkin's chapter on Baillie in *Getting into the Act* (1995).

21. This concept of "sympathetic curiosity" seems to have stemmed from Baillie's own conduct, described in Thomas Sadler's sermon on her death as the product of "a great and noble spirit, [who] could not be hemmed in by any party or sectarian limits. She held as a dear treasure the results of her own free and diligent search after revealed truth, and she respected the faithful convictions of others in proportion as she valued her own" (Sadler 22). See Anne K. Mellor's discussion of this concept in terms of the recent feminist work on epistemology ("Joanna Baillie" 561; "A Criticism of Their Own" 44).

22. Note that Baillie does not consider the audience of "the drama" to be "the lowest classes of the labouring people, who are the broad foundation of society, which can never be generally moved without endangering every thing that is constructed upon it, and who are our potent and formidable ballad-readers." Instead, her plays "reach to the classes next in order to them, and who will always have over them no inconsiderable influence" (14). For discussions of the issue of class in Baillie's work, see Carhart (203–4) and Watkins (1993).

23. Mary Yudin makes a similar point when she writes that "Baillie's impact on theater, while not always acknowledged, was lasting. . . . in the third volume of

A Series of Plays, Baillie decries the size and staging techniques of the contemporary theater world. She calls for smaller, more intimate theaters and softer, more realistic lighting—trends which would gain favor in the latter third of the century" (13). In a footnote to this passage, Yudin draws parallels between Baillie's discourse on small stages and the " 'little theater' movement advocated by Antoine, Grahm and others" (16, n. 11). Baillie's focus on smaller stages was echoed in the British literature that advocated theatrical reform, especially in the 1830s. Frederick Guest Tomlins wrote in support of the theatrical changes recommended by the 1832 *Report from the Select Committee on Dramatic Literature*, emphasizing first and foremost the reduction of the theatrical arena in order to counter the huge auditoria of the patent theaters, which made nuanced acting difficult and permitted boisterous crowd behavior:

> Let us imagine Mr. Macready instated in a small theatre; well constructed for hearing and seeing the finest intonations of voice, and the most delicate expressions of the countenance; at a moderate rent, with no other aid but that of a well-selected company and talented authors; discarding all the expenses of an immense orchestra, complicated machinery, extravagant scenery, and a mob of supernumeraries; performing only the regular high passionate drama; avoiding all competition with musical exhibitions and pageantry; trusting to the power of dramatic art over the imagination and the passions. Let us suppose his theatre well situated; plainfully, but tastefully adorned; its business simple, and regularly conducted (as it must be under his control); capable of containing about one hundred and fifty pounds, at admissions of three shillings and five shillings; beginning and concluding at suitable hours; and, above all, confining itself strictly and unswervingly to the high regular drama. (29)

24. In the context of his discussion of other Gothic playwrights, Paul Ranger notes Baillie's interest in lighting techniques:

> Unlike her contemporaries, Baillie gave no directions about the facial reactions necessary for portraying De Monfort. Her expectation that Kemble would take the role would make these superfluous. However, she did realise the necessity for the actor's face to be clearly visible to the audience, a point which few gothic playwrights, setting many scenes in melancholy gloom, seemed to consider. . . . Other than in their use of flaming brands, few playwrights had attempted to exploit the use of localised lighting in their creation of a dark scene of horror. (100)

In an unpublished essay, Maureen Dowd discusses how Baillie's use of the magic lantern show, which "came into prominence in France in the 1780s and 1790s" (3), as a metaphor "graphically illustrates her theories of stage architectonics, yet it also rhetorically situates her plays as 'tragedies' untainted by contemporary taste for spectacular and sensational melodrama associated with magic lantern shows" (4). Dowd uses these observations about Baillie's interest in the stage techniques of her era to argue the following: "Baillie's fascination with gothic melodrama, her exploitation of spectacular battle scenes and processions, and her experiments with 'musical dramas' blur the generic boundaries she so forcefully establishes in her prefaces and cater to popular tastes associated with the dangerous excesses of feeling common in magic lantern shows which replicated spectral and revolutionary phantasmagorias" (1). I appreciate Maureen Dowd's permission to cite her work here. See also Bertrand Evans's discussion of Baillie's emphasis on lighting (205–6).

25. The motives for advocating a move from the stage to the closet (and by extension, for appreciating theater in domestic settings) vary depending on the writer. Elizabeth Craven's approach to celebrating private space differs from Hannah More's, who used gender to frame her complaint about the immorality of the London patent theaters. Craven's rationale for putting on plays within the privacy of one's home is constructed in terms of class, as she criticizes the performance of English "manners" performed on the stage. In a series of elaborately produced private theater pieces that Craven wrote and adapted—*The Statue Feast* (1782), *The Yorkshire Ghost* (1794), *Puss in Boots* (1803), and *Love in a Convent* (1805), among others—she may be said to have staged her theory of theater in domestic space. Comparing English plays unfavorably with French fare in her autobiography—"all that was not dignified and noble would [in French plays] have been rejected; and the *parterre* would have laughed to see a humpback and distorted legs [as in *Richard III*] on the person of one who was to excite terror and pity" (*Memoirs* 1:234)—Craven expressed a strong distaste for the imperfectly formed, the unbounded, the weird. Her preference for staging neoclassical plays in private settings is tied to her desire to move away from the commonplaces of public life and into the safe haven of the carefully controlled English aristocratic country house.

26. For further information on Baillie's religious views and responses to them by her contemporaries, see her *A View of the General Tenour of the New Testament Regarding the Nature and Dignity of Jesus Christ* (1831) as well as her prefaces to *The Martyr* and *The Bride*. See also the Bishop of Salisbury's 78-page essay, *Remarks on the General Tenour of the New Testament, Regarding the Nature and Dignity of Jesus Christ: Addressed to Mrs. Joanna Baillie* (1831).

27. Shortly after her death Baillie became almost immediately distinguished as a writer of Scottish songs. Charles Rogers's six-volume *The Modern Scottish Minstrel; or, The Songs of Scotland of the Past Half Century* (1855) includes a short essay on Baillie's life and several of her musical lyrics. The essay praises Baillie as "well entitled to the place assigned her as one of the first of modern dramatists" (1:130) before concluding that the "songs of Joanna Baillie immediately [upon her death] obtained an honourable place in the minstrelsy of her native kingdom" (1:131).

28. This citation is from *A Room of One's Own* (1929). In response to Woolf's comment, I want to point out that Mary McKerrow's comparison of Baillie with Mary Brunton appears in one of the few articles I've found published in the latter half of the twentieth century that discusses Baillie's influence on other writers. William D. Brewer's essay on Baillie and Byron (1995) is another.

29. Praise for Baillie was widespread during the Romantic period. Mary McKerrow notes the following passage in Walter Scott's introduction to the third

canto of *Marmion* (1808), in which the footnote identifies "the bold Enchantress" as Joanna Baillie and refers to two of the three plays in her first volume of the *Plays on the Passions* (1798):

". . . Restore the ancient tragic line,
And emulate the notes that rung
From the wild harp which silent hung
By silver Avon's holy shore
Till twice an hundred years rolled o'er;
When she, *the bold Enchantress*, came
With fearless hand and heart on flame,
From the pale willow snatched the treasure,
And swept it with a kindred measure,
Till Avon's swans, while rung the grove
With Monfort's hate and Basil's love,
Awakening at the inspired strain,
Deemed *their own Shakespeare* lived again."
(90–91; my emphasis)

"To Joanna Baillie," a poem by William Sotheby, evokes similar tributes paid her by Scott, William Wordsworth, and Lord Byron: "Sister of Shakespeare!": "artless Nature's simple child / [Who] [c]an strike the chords that breathe sublimity." (I am grateful to Paula Feldman for bringing this poem to my attention.)

30. Other Victorian assessments of Baillie's work include Frederick Rowton's introduction to an anthology of women poets in which he wrote that "we certainly have no female Shakespeare" though "Poetesses . . . resemble him: Joanna Baillie is often like him" (xlix). Portraying Baillie according to the Victorian ideology of femininity, he asserts that "there is nothing phosphorescent or stage-firelike in Mrs. Baillie's poetry: it is the calm, soft, refreshing, wholesome sunshine of a clear spring morning." "We never meet with noise or bustle in her works: she is not at all of the steam-engine class of poets: everything is calm, unconscious, and serene" (288). Yet Rowton recognizes Baillie as an originator, as "not merely a powerful and successful dramatist, but a great literary reformer: if not the *very* first, at least *amongst* the first, of those who once again placed our poetry under the dominion of nature." Rowton observes that Baillie "preceded and heralded the school of Wordsworth," and he is quite forceful in asserting that the success of *Henriquez* and *The Separation* on the stage "clearly shows that with performers sedulously bent on carrying out the author's design, and willing to sacrifice momentary applause for ultimate appreciation, Mrs. Baillie's Plays would be as forcible in action as they are striking on perusal" (296).

31. In 1947 Bertrand Evans wrote in his study of Gothic drama that the "plays of Joanna Baillie clearly need revaluation. . . . Miss Baillie seems not to have received her rightful place in the history of English drama. . . . When both the quantity and quality of her contributions are considered, Joanna Baillie must be placed among the foremost Gothic dramatists" (200). (This praise for Baillie's achieve-

ment in Gothic drama would be echoed in the early 1990s, first by Paul Ranger and then Jeffrey N. Cox.)

32. This letter is to "Mrs. Phillips" and dated May 8, 1800.

33. See de Lauretis's *Technologies of Gender* (1987); Rabine's "A Feminist Politics of Non-Identity" (1988); and Sedgwick's *Epistemology of the Closet* (1990).

34. Marvin Carlson's *Theories of the Theatre* (1984) has directed my attention to this passage (140).

35. Studying the play prefaces written by women in Romanticism is made a bit easier by the 1990 reprinting of Elizabeth Inchbald's *Remarks for the British Theatre (1806–09)* prepared by Cecilia Macheski, as well as the anthology edited by Robert W. Uphaus and Gretchen M. Foster, *The "Other" Eighteenth Century: English Women of Letters 1660–1800* (1991), in which an edited version of Baillie's "Introductory Discourse" appears. The anthology *Women Critics 1660–1820* (edited by the Folger Collective on Early Women Critics) also includes several Baillie prefaces, as well as a number by Elizabeth Inchbald, Hannah More, and Hannah Parkhouse Cowley. See also the 1976 facsimile edition of Baillie's 1851 collected works and the 1977 facsimile edition of the three volumes of *Plays on the Passions* listed in Works Cited. Several of Baillie's plays—*Count Basil, The Trial,* and *De Monfort*—and her "Introductory discourse" were recently published by Woodstock Books in the "series of facsimile reprints chosen and introduced by Jonathan Wordsworth" (1990). Jeffrey Cox's collection of seven Gothic dramas includes an edition of *De Monfort* that aims to give "the fullest account of the play's historical life as both a printed work and a performed theatrical piece" (83). (See also Feldman and Mellor's anthologies listed in Works Cited.) Duncan Wu's *Romanticism: An Anthology* (1994) puzzlingly slights Baillie's work by including only a few paragraphs from her "Introductory Discourse."

36. See Pauline Kiernan's *Shakespeare's Theory of Drama* (1996), in which she explores "what might lie *behind* all this evident concern in the plays and poems with drama and aesthetics" (1). Through analyses of *Venus and Adonis,* the sonnets, *The Rape of Lucrece,* and a range of the plays, Kiernan posits a "dramatic theory" that "can be discerned in Shakespearean drama" (4).

Chapter 4

1. See Gloria Flaherty's article "Empathy and Distance" (1990) for a discussion of the distinction between these acting styles. For a fuller discussion of the Romantic debate about acting, see the following: Lily Campbell's "The Rise of a Theory of Stage Presentation in England during the Eighteenth Century" (1917); Alan S. Downer's "Nature to Advantage Dressed: Eighteenth-Century Acting" (1943) and "Players and Painted Stage: Nineteenth-Century Acting" (1946); William Angus's "Actors and Audiences in Eighteenth-Century London" (1944); Earl N. Wasserman's "The Sympathetic Imagination in Eighteenth-Century Theories of Acting" (1947); Carol J. Carlisle's "Edmund Kean on the Art of Acting" (1968); Gloria Flaherty's "Empathy and Distance: Romantic Theories of Acting

Reconsidered" (1990); Bryan Forbes's *That Despicable Race: A History of the British Acting Tradition* (1980); Joseph R. Roach's *The Player's Passion: Studies in the Science of Acting* (1985); Monica Murray's "English Theater Costume and the Zeitgeist of the Eighteenth Century" (1989); Marvin Rosenberg's "Macbeth and Lady Macbeth in the Eighteenth and Nineteenth Centuries" (1982); Edwin Duerr's *The Length and Depth of Acting* (1962); Thomas Crochunis's "Byronic Heroes and Acting: The Embodiment of Mental Theatre" (1995).

2. For further information on *tableaux vivants*, see Kirsten Gram Holmstrom's 1967 study.

3. For an excellent discussion of Keanian acting, and "why he (and not Cooke, for example)" has been "historicized in the twentieth century as the paradigm shifter" (950) from neoclassical to "Romantic" acting, see Tracy C. Davis's essay, " 'Reading Shakespeare by Flashes of Lightning': Challenging the Foundations of Romantic Acting Theory" (1995). She persuasively argues that "Coleridge's famous comment [on Kean's acting style] is a backhand remark on the degeneration of Kean's abilities—not the supremacy of his technique" (944).

4. For a reading of Engel's text in the context of acting theory and a discussion of the way in which acting "not only mirrors but partakes in and contributes to the historical process of civilization and thus fulfills important social functions" (23), see Erika Fischer-Lichte's "Theatre and the Civilizing Process: An Approach to the History of Acting" (1989). See also Edwin Duerr's discussion of Henry Siddons's adaptation of Engel's *Ideen zu einer Mimik* (272). Holmstrom writes that "Engel's book was of immense importance for the acting of the future" and that "it set the pattern for books on acting technique and theory right up to our own times" (86).

5. Matthew Baillie's popularity is attested to by the appearance of his biography in 1825. James Wardrop, Esq., observes that between 1795 and 1825 "no individual held a more exalted station in the medical profession than Dr. Baillie" (3). For further discussion of Matthew Baillie's life and career, see the following: *The Works of Matthew Baillie, M.D.* (1825); *The Gold-Headed Cane* (1968, orig. 1827, which contains a brief biographical sketch of Baillie); *The Influence of Matthew Baillie's Morbid Anatomy* (1973). Note that Joanna Baillie dedicated her second volume of *Plays on the Passions* (1812) to Matthew Baillie, and her biographer, Margaret Carhart, has observed that Baillie's plays "contain many indications of medical knowledge, which she undoubtedly acquired from her brother" (88).

6. Mary Berry did not think it indecorous to pursue the notable woman into the privacy of her closet, nor did she worry about the problem of how to preserve the facts of a woman celebrity's private experience without ransacking the closet of her reputation. In response to Baillie, Berry wrote: "if women treat of *human* nature and *human* life in *history* and not in fiction . . . human nature and human life are often indelicate; and if such passages in them are treated always with the gravity and reprobation they deserve, it is all a sensible woman can do, and (not writing for children) all she can think necessary" (*Extracts* 3:371). In reference to Lady Rachel Russell (whose letters Berry edited and to which she added "copious biographical notes" [Lewis xxii]), Berry observed that the problem when creating

narratives about women was how to locate information about a woman's private life in the first place:

> The biographers of those who have been distinguished in the active paths of life, who have directed the councils or fought the battles of nations, have, perhaps, an easier task than those who engage to satisfy the curiosity sometimes excited by persons whose situation, circumstances, or sex, have confined them to private life. To the biographers of public characters the pages of history, and the archives of the state, furnish many of the documents required; while those of private individuals have to collect every particular from accidental materials, from combining and comparing letters, and otherwise insignificant papers, never intended to convey any part of the information sought in them. (*Extracts* 1:xxii)

Berry's remarks about narrating the stories of women's lives are applicable to the search for female-authored theater theory: one indeed has "to collect every particular from accidental materials," "combining and comparing letters, and otherwise insignificant papers, never intended to convey any part of the information sought in them." This is certainly the case in confronting the issue of how women playwrights theorized female character as correctives to the representation of actresses in celebrity memoirs discussed in Chapter 2.

7. See Agnes Withrington in *The Tryal* (analyzed Chapter 5) and Miss Martin in *The Country Inn* (1804), both of whom gesture toward feminist positions by arguing for marriages on their own terms: "Can one give to another what he is not possessed of himself?" Miss Martin exclaims in frustration to Lady Goodbody, who is trying to marry her off. "Can a woman receive any additional respectability because some drivelling, insignificant man, whom all the world despises, has put a wedding-ring upon her finger?—ha! ha! ha!" (428).

8. In contrast to their collective portrayal in their prefaces of themselves as playwrights, when women theorized the construction of female characters in these same documents, they often envisioned women who possessed sufficient strength to consistently challenge cultural authority. For instance, in the preface she wrote to Henry Jones's male-centered interpretation of the story of the Earl of Essex (1753), Inchbald faults Jones for failing to introduce "even a female character . . . from fiction," and in the case of the queen, for not paying much attention to the drama inherent in her historical role. In Inchbald's view, *The Earl of Essex* neglects the feminine contours of Queen Elizabeth's responses in favor of scenes between Rutland and Nottingham. The fact that Elizabeth's love for the earl is "expressed by indirect means, [and] has often the greatest hold upon the attention and sympathy of the spectator" implies that "many an auditor and reader will feel more interest in the restrained affection of Elizabeth for her paramour, than in the unbridled fondness of Rutland for her husband.—The scene, where the queen bestows the ring, as a pledge of her kindest regard for his safety, is peculiarly affecting, because the strength of her passion is there discoverable, under a demeanour properly dignified" ("Remarks on *The Earl of Essex*"). (All citations from Inchbald are from the

1990 facsimile edition listed in Works Cited. As the pages repeat, I do not list page numbers here).

Inchbald's concern that the subtle expressions required of women by standards of gender be featured onstage was shared by other women playwrights of the era. Some saw clearly, as James Boaden complained, that the female parts of contemporary playwrights were "comparatively unimportant—the writers appeared to have lived, all of them, in chambers, and studied nothing female above their bedmakers. They knew nothing that constituted the feminine feelings. They guessed only at the *mental distinction* that for ever exists between man and his helpmate— their young women had no character at all; and their *old* uniformly a bad one" (*The Life of Mrs. Jordan* 2:68).

Paula R. Backscheider has recently observed that the heroines of Sophia Lee and Hannah Cowley (1743–1809) provide "illuminating" contrasts with the female characters in other Gothic plays written by men: they are "active, even complex forces; their dilemmas and sufferings compete successfully with their male protagonists' ambitions for attention" (202). In her preface to *The Chapter of Accidents* (1780), for example, Sophia Lee calls attention to the occasion on which she "first conceived the design of introducing into the drama a female heart, capable of frailty, yet shuddering at vice" (iv).

9. See Judith Butler, "Performative Acts and Gender Constitution" (1988).

10. Baillie sought to deny the German influence on her plays in the preface to her second edition of *Miscellaneous Plays* (1805), probably because of their contemporary association with immorality:

> A play, with the scene laid in Germany, and opening with a noisy meeting of midnight robbers over their wine, will, I believe, suggest to my readers certain sources from which he will suppose my ideas have certainly been taken. Will he give me perfect credit when I assure him, at the time this play was written, I had not only never read any German plays, but was even ignorant that such things as German plays of any reputation existed? (389)

11. In a footnote attached to the 1851 edition of her collected works Baillie wrote: "Should this play [*De Monfort*] ever again be acted, perhaps it would be better that the curtain should drop here [V.iv]; since here the story may be considered as completed, and what comes after, prolongs the piece too much when our interest for the fate is at an end" (101). Baillie's footnote to the 1851 text also indicates her self-consciousness about Jane De Monfort's biases. She writes:

> The last three lines of the last speech are not intended to give the reader a true character of *De Monfort* [Baillie means the character and not the play], whom I have endeavoured to represent throughout the play as, notwithstanding his other good qualities, proud, suspicious, and susceptible of envy, but only to express the partial sentiments of an affectionate sister, naturally more inclined to praise him from the misfortune into which he had fallen. (104n)

Paul Ranger writes that Baillie "enthusiastically expressed her satisfaction with Kean's interpretation," which, when the play was restaged in 1821, prompted her to restructure "the final act of the play, which, she felt, made it 'better fitted for exhibition.' The principal change involved leaving De Monfort alone with the corpse at the end of the play so that, having made his final speech, Kean threw himself to the ground as the curtain fell" (103).

12. In the case of *De Monfort*, I am using Jeffrey Cox's edition to give readers a better sense of the play in the performance (83). Cox's text is "that of the first edition [1798], with cuts made for the Larpent performance version [1800] being indicated by double quotation marks and material added in the Larpent version marked by square brackets" (*Seven Gothic Dramas* 232). Of *De Monfort*, Cox writes that, because "Baillie tended to alter the play as she republished it over the years, often including changes made in performance, . . . we do not . . . have a simple tension between an authorial version of the play intended for the closet and a performance version adapted by actors for the stage" (82).

For my discussion of *Basil*, I am using Baillie's 1851 edition rather than *Count Basil*, the title she used when she first published the play in 1798. In choosing the 1851 edition, I am guided by Baillie's footnote at the end of act 1 (in the 1851 version) in which she tells us that the slight plot variation between the first and third versions—Basil's having sighted Victoria several years before the play begins—was not what Baillie originally planned: "My first idea when I wrote this play," she says, "was to represent Basil as having seen Victoria for the first time in the procession,"

> that I might show more perfectly the passion from its first beginning, and also its sudden power over the mind; but I was induced, from the criticism of one whose judgment I very much respect, to alter it, and represent him as having formerly seen and loved her. The first Review that took notice of this work objected to Basil's having seen her before as a defect; and, as we are all easily determined to follow our own opinion, I have, upon after-consideration, given the play in this edition [*third*], as far as this is concerned, exactly in its original state. (22n)

My text for *The Tryal*, spelled as *The Trial* in the 1851 edition, is the 1990 Woodstock edition. For further references to poems, plays, and prose by Baillie, I am using the 1976 facsimile edition of her collected works (published in 1851).

13. See Evans (1947), Donohue (1970), Ranger (1991), and Cox (1992) for discussions of Baillie and the Gothic tradition.

14. I thank Steven Bruhm for reminding me of the relevance of this reference, especially Sedgwick's chapter 5 in her *Between Men: English Literature and Male Homosocial Desire* (1985).

15. See Purinton's comments on the two mask scenes in *De Monfort* and *Basil*, which, in her reading, enact "a recapitulation of an ideology demanding male and female spheres of activity" (151).

16. Another study is required to investigate the extent to which women in Romantic theater protested the culture's tendency to read character through cos-

tume (and, in the case of female actors, to confuse the adorned body of the performer with the behavior of the wearer—especially as women actors often wore their own clothes and jewelry on London stages). Baillie's dueling dress codes in *De Monfort* set the stage for such an inquiry. For a helpful article, which includes a discussion about Siddons's interest in drapery costume (132–34), see Lily Campbell's "A History of Costuming" (1968), listed in Works Cited.

17. In her remarks on *De Monfort*, Elizabeth Inchbald observed the similarities between Jane De Monfort and Siddons: "On Jane De Monfort she [Baillie] has bestowed some of her very best poetic descriptions; and, from the young Page's first account of the 'queenly' stranger, has given such a striking resemblance of both the person and mien of Mrs. Siddons, that it would almost raise a suspicion she was, at the time of the writing, designed for the representation of this noble female."

18. In addition to the scene from *The Election* cited above, see II.ii in *The Tryal*, in which Miss Eston "takes up a book, then looks at herself in the glass, then takes up the book again," according to the stage direction. Then she says, "(yawning): 'Tis all about the imagination, and the understanding, and I don't know what—I dare say it is good enough to read of a Sunday. (Yawns, and lays it down.) O la! I wish they would come" (I.ii.233).

19. See Alice C. Meynell's remarks on Mirando, written in 1922:

Of the preceding tragedy [*Basil*] I will say merely that one may detect in it a fancy of Antiquity, as the eighteenth century dressed it, which is wonderfully pleasing: a little boy, Mirando, vexes the capricious heroine by naming her lovers; he creeps into her arms and begins to trouble her free heart, making guesses for sugar-plums. The reader likes to think that by a candid allegory, fit for Sir Joshua Reynolds's painting of a gold-headed boy and a brown-eyed maid, Miss Joanna Baillie had given the name of Mirando to none other than Love himself, Cupid the bee. (58–59)

20. M. Norton compares *Basil* unfavorably with another Shakespearian drama, when he writes: "No one would place 'Basil,' for all its simplicity in the same category as *Antony and Cleopatra*; any more than he would suggest that 'Ethwald,' retelling at great length and with certain modifications the Macbeth story, compares favorably with its Elizabethan prototype" (136).

21. See Charles Mills Gayley, *The Classic Myths in English Literature and Art* (1939), 30.

22. Frances Anne Kemble was also effusive in her praise of *Count Basil*, writing, in a letter dated 1831, the following:

Yesterday, I read for the first time Joanna Baillie's "Count Basil." I am not sure that the love she describes does not affect me more even than Shakespeare's delineation of the passion in "Romeo and Juliet." There is a nerveless despondence about it that seems to me more intolerable than all the vivid palpitating anguish of the tragedy of Verona; it is like dying of slow poison, or malarial fever, compared with being shot or stabbed or even bleeding to death, which

is life pouring out from one, instead of drying up in one's brains. I think the
lines beginning—
"I have seen the last look of her heavenly eyes,"
some of the most poignantly pathetic I know. (342)

See also the exchange between Tickler and North in vol. 2 of John Wilson's
Noctes Ambrosianae:

Tickler: . . . I do not know whether my gallantry binds me, but I prefer much
of the female to the male poetry of the day.
North: O thou Polygamist!
Tickler: There is Joanna Baillie. Is there not more genius, passion, poetry, in
the tragedy of Count Basil, than in any book of Wordsworth?
North: Ten times. (102)

23. This quotation appears in the facsimile edition of Inchbald's *Remarks for
the British Theatre (1806–1809)* (1990). The same page numbers appear in each preface, so I do not include them here.

Chapter 5

1. This quotation is from the facsimile edition (Georg Olms Verlag, 1976) of
Baillie's 1851 collected works. All further references to Baillie's poetry, prose, and
dramas—with the exception of *The Tryal* (see note 19 below)—are from this edition. In the case of the dramas, I cite them by act, scene, and page number.
2. Baillie composed this verse for Mary Berry's private play *The Fashionable
Friends* (1800, private theatrical; 1802, published), which, although conceived as a
private theatrical, also received a public showing against Berry's wishes. According
to the editor of Berry's letters and journals, Lady Theresa Lewis, a "month after
Miss Berry returned from France, she had the mortification of finding that the play
which had been acted in private with such flattering success the preceding year at
Strawberry Hill, did not receive the sanction of the public voice. It was brought
out at Drury Lane with a cast of parts, comprising names which must have greatly
conduced to its success, and the cause of its failure cannot be attributed to a want
of ability on the part of the performers" (cited in *Extracts of the Journals and Correspondence of Miss Berry* 2:194).
3. A partial list of those women who participated in late-eighteenth-century
private theatricals (through a combination of acting, writing, and organizing) includes: Joanna Baillie, Mary Berry, Frances Burney, Marianne Chambers, Elizabeth
Knipe Cobbold, Elizabeth Berkeley Craven (the Margravine of Anspach), Mary
Champion Crespigny, Elizabeth Farren, Catherine Galindo, Elizabeth Inchbald,
Frances Anne Kemble, Harriot Mellon, Eliza O'Neill, Amelia Opie, Sarah Siddons,
Mariana Starke, and Peg Woffington.
The introduction by Gwenn Davis and Beverly A. Joyce to *Drama by Women*

to 1900 (1992) observes that private theatricals, "like closet drama, had aristocratic origins, but became a general pursuit" (xii). Davis and Joyce's list of women who created private theatricals between the seventeenth and nineteenth centuries includes: Queen Henrietta Maria, Elizabeth Craven, Lady Georgiana (Russell) Peel, Lady Victoria Russell, Lady Bell, Lady Cadogan, Gabrielle De Nottbeck, Florence Gailey, Jean Ingraham, Frances Peard, and Winnie Rover (xii).

4. Marvin Carlson notes that as late as 1833 in England a private theater was erected at the castle of Chatsworth (56).

5. These canonical works included plays by women writers, among them Susanna Centlivre, Hannah Cowley, and Elizabeth Inchbald. For a list of the most popular plays performed on the eighteenth-century private stage, see Sybil Rosenfeld, *Temples of Thespis* (1978), 169–70.

6. My information for this history is collected from the following sources: Charles Kendal Bushe's *The Private Theatre of Kilkenny* (1825), composed mostly of the information on playbills, along with the prologue and epilogue spoken to each play and reviews of performances; Tom Moore's review of that volume in the *Edinburgh Review* (1827), which after stating "There is no subject that we would sooner recommend to a male or female author, in distress for a topic, than a History of the Private Theatres of Europe" (368) situates British private theatricals in the context of private theaters in ancient Greece, Renaissance Italy, and modern Russia and France; Sybil Rosenfeld's *Temples of Thespis: Some Private Theatres and Theatricals in England and Wales, 1700–1820* (1978), which includes two helpful appendices drawn from her survey of records pertaining to "120 places in which private theatricals were held" (7): one listing the performance of private theatricals by year and the other identifying those English plays "first performed at private theatricals" (180); and Marvin Carlson's chapter called "The Jewel in the Casket," in *Places of Performance* (1989). Nina Auerbach's *Private Theatricals: The Lives of the Victorians* (1990), while promisingly titled, focuses not on the private theatrical phenomenon but rather uses the term to discuss "the source of Victorian fears of performance," which she argues "lay in the histrionic artifice of ordinary life" (114).

7. Further information about these players is provided by Suzanne R. Westfall's *Patrons and Performance* (1990).

8. See Karl Toepfer's fascinating account of this phenomenon, including erotic marionette theater, in chapter 2 of his *Theatre, Aristocracy, and Pornocracy: The Orgy Calculus* (1991).

9. See Case's chapter 4 of *Feminism and Theatre* (1988) for a discussion of this trend, led by theater groups such as Lavendar Cellar Theatre, Medusa's Revenge, and Red Dyke Theatre.

10. For more information on von Stein and her theatrical activities, see Katherine R. Goodman, "The Sign Speaks" (1992).

11. This quotation is from the preface to the Countess of Hardwicke's play, *The Court of Oberon, or The Three Wishes*, in which the writer explains why it took so long for the play to "see the light." (The play was written in the late seventeenth century.) On the occasion of Princess Victoria's intent to patronize "a Bazaar, for the succour of the distressed Irish," it was "suggested that among the contributions made by Ladies of their Fancy works for the profit of the Bazaar, this [play] might

also find a place. — Yet it could scarcely have been ventured upon without the condescending permission of Her Royal Highness the Duchess of Kent, to dedicate this little work to Her Royal Highness the Princess Victoria."

12. Elizabeth Berkeley Craven's original dramas are listed in Broadley and Melville's Introduction to her memoirs (1826), republished under the title *The Beautiful Lady Craven* (1914).

13. The French edition of Craven's memoirs (1828) was republished in 1991 by Mercure de France in an edition annotated by Jean-Pierre Guicciardi (with an introduction).

14. Although it is common to find professional actors participating in private theatricals, they often express a combination of amusement and frustration about the experience. Elizabeth Inchbald wrote in a letter that to "my extreme sorrow I am at present under the dread of being a party in a private theatrical myself."

> I was surprised into a promise, and now go every morning to attend rehearsals; still I foresee many impediments, which I will as far as in my power increase. One is, the drama on which they have fixed has a supper in it, and I have represented that the hurry of clearing away the table, which is a part of the comic incidents of the piece, will probably break the wine bottles and throw the hot dishes against the beautiful hangings and furniture of the room. This observation gave Mr. Monk Lewis, M.P., (who is one of the performers,) an opportunity of saying an excellent thing to the lady of the house, who, alarmed at my remark, immediately cried out she would not have a *real* supper, but that every thing should be *counterfeit*. On which she rang for her butler, and ordered him to go and bespeak a couple of wooden fowls, a wooden tongue, wooden jellies, and so forth. "Nay," cried Monk Lewis, "if your ladyship gives a wooden supper, the audience will say all your actors are STICKS." (cited in Boaden, *Memoirs* 2:56)

In 1831, Frances Anne Kemble discussed her participation in Francis Leveson's adaptation of Victor Hugo's *Hernani* at Bridgewater House as follows: "I have consented to this, not knowing well how to refuse, yet for one or two reasons I almost think I had better not have done so. I expect to be excessively amused by it, but it will take up a terrible deal of my time, for I am sure they will need rehearsals without end" (*Records of a Girlhood* 365).

15. Observing that the "amateur theatricals at Barborne in effect initiated Frances Burney into the performance of womanhood," Gillian Russell writes that "the amateur theatricals of the minor gentry . . . not only enacted and defined family relationships but also educated the younger generation in the gendered roles which they would perform as adults" (131).

16. For further discussion of women, theatrical contamination, and private life, see Joseph Litvak's first chapter, "The Infection of Acting: Theatricals and Theatricality in *Mansfield Park*," in *Caught in the Act: Theatricality in the Nineteenth-Century English Novel* (1992). His discussion of the commentaries on theater by Thomas Gisborne, Hannah More, Elizabeth Inchbald, and William Hazlitt is especially relevant to my argument here.

17. This pervasiveness is recognized by Sybil Rosenfeld in "Jane Austen and Private Theatricals" (1962), who writes: "there were apprentices' theatricals, military and naval theatricals, children's and school theatricals and small theatres in which amateurs could try out their histrionic abilities for a modest fee" (42).

18. My text for *The Tryal* is the 1990 reprint of Baillie's 1798 *Series of Plays* published by Woodstock Books. (N.B.: the 1851 edition of this play spells *The Tryal* as *The Trial*.)

19. Kamchatka is a peninsula of northeast Russia between the Bering Sea and the Sea of Okhotsk (Stamp 224).

20. Margaret Carhart has observed that "Harwood's railing against Agnes is an echo of the tone of Petruchio in *The Taming of the Shrew*, and Agnes' description of her suitors recalls the similar scene in *The Merchant of Venice*" (73).

21. For a brief discussion of this play, see Smith and Lawhon, *Plays about the Theatre in England, 1737–1800* (1979), 135–37.

22. See also Mrs. Overall's letter in Baillie's *The Match*, at which Emma smiles but which the indecisive Latitia defends: "Education of every kind has, till lately, proceeded upon a wrong principle. Every body taught the same things, without regard to talent or capacity. Should not a boy's instruction be adapted to his genius?" (I.ii.688).

23. See Daniel P. Watkins's discussion of class issues in Baillie's *De Monfort*, in *A Materialist Critique of English Romantic Drama* (1993).

24. Rosenfeld also cites a letter written by Harriet Cavendish concerning the same private theater, which indicates that another Baillie play, *Count Basil*, was also under consideration. Like *The Tryal*, however, it went unperformed (158).

25. For a discussion of this emphasis on the "probable" or "credible" by Romantic women writers, see Anne K. Mellor, "A Criticism of Their Own" (1995).

26. See, for example, chapter 5 of Sandra Richards's *The Rise of the English Actress* (1993), in which she writes of Madame Vestris:

> Her greatest contribution to the status of actors was the introduction of salaries paid in advance, a practice wholly against the grain of what was considered thrifty management. The move was instrumental in generating a reconsideration of professional rights among all players. It culminated in the British Actors' Association and its present system of insisting that two weeks' salary per company member be held by Equity as insurance against managerial breaches. (104)

27. For more information about Kelly's acting career, her theater, and her acting school, see Holman (1935) and Francis (1950).

Works Cited

Aaron, Jane. *A Double Singleness: Gender and the Writings of Charles and Mary Lamb*. Oxford: Clarendon Press, 1991.

Alexander, Meena. *Women in Romanticism*. Handmills, Basingstoke, Hampshire: Macmillan Education, 1989.

Angus, William. "Actors and Audiences in Eighteenth-Century London." In *Studies in Speech and Drama in Honor of Alexander M. Drummond*, 123–38. Ithaca, N.Y.: Cornell University Press, 1944.

Anonymous [James Ridgway]. *Memoirs of Mrs. Billington*. London: James Ridgway, 1792.

Anonymous. "Mrs. Jordan and the Times." In Vol. 2 of *The Theatrical Inquisitor: or Literary Mirror*. By Cerberus. London: William Molineaux, 1813.

———. "An Original Biographical Sketch of Mrs. Glover." *The Country Squire*. By Charles Dance. London: Chapman and Hall, 1837.

———. "Preface." *The Court of Oberon, or The Three Wishes*. By the Countess of Hardwicke. London, 1831.

———. *Public and Private Life of that Celebrated Actress, Miss Bland, otherwise Mrs. Ford, or Mrs. Jordan; Late Mistress of HRH the Duke of Clarence; now King William IV*. By a Confidential Friend of the Departed. London: J. Duncombe, n.d. (1832?)

———. *The Secret History of the Green-Room*. Vol. 1. London: J. Owen, 1795.

———. *Secret Memoirs of Harriot Pumpkin*. London: J. Cahuac, n.d.

———. *The Testimony of Truth to Exalted Merit; or, A Biographical Sketch of the Right Honourable the Countess of Derby in Refutation of a False and Scandalous Libel*. 4th ed. London: George Cawthorn, 1797.

———. "To the Editor of the *European Magazine*. Plan for a Fashionable Rosciad; and some account of Mr. Fector's Private Theatre at Dover." *The European Magazine, and London Review* 14 (1788): 66–67.

Appleton, William W. *Madame Vestris and the London Stage*. New York and London: Columbia University Press, 1974.

Arbiter, Petronius. *Memoirs of the Present Countess of Derby*. London: Symonds, n.d. [1797].

Ardener, Shirley. "Ground Rules and Social Maps for Women: An Introduction." In *Women and Space: Ground Rules and Social Maps*, ed. Shirley Ardener, 1–30. London: Croom Helm; New York: St. Martin's Press, 1981.

Argyros, Ellen. " 'Intruding Herself into the Chair of Criticism': Elizabeth Griffith and *The Morality of Shakespeare's Drama Illustrated*." In *Eighteenth-Century Women and the Arts*, ed. Frederick M. Keener and Susan E. Lorsch, 283–89. New York: Greenwood Press, 1988.

Aspinall, A. "Introduction." In *Mrs. Jordan and Her Family, being the Unpublished*

Correspondence of Mrs. Jordan and the Duke of Clarence, later William IV, ed. A. Aspinall, ix–xxvii. London: Arthur Baker Ltd., 1951.

Aston, Elaine. *An Introduction to Feminism and Theatre*. New York and London: Routledge, 1995.

Auerbach, Nina. *Private Theatricals: The Lives of the Victorians*. Cambridge, Mass.: Harvard University Press, 1990.

Austen, Jane. *Mansfield Park*. Ed. Tony Tanner. London: Penguin Books, 1985 (orig. 1814).

Austin, Gayle. *Feminist Theories for Dramatic Criticism*. Ann Arbor: University of Michigan Press, 1990.

Backscheider, Paula R. *Spectacular Politics: Theatrical Power and Mass Culture in Early Modern England*. Baltimore and London: The Johns Hopkins University Press, 1993.

Baer, Marc. *Theatre and Disorder in Late Georgian London*. Oxford: Clarendon Press, 1992.

Baillie, Joanna. *The Dramatic and Poetical Works (1851)*. Hildesheim and New York: Georg Olms Verlag, 1976. Facsimile edition.

———. *A Series of Plays*. Oxford: Woodstock Books, 1990.

———. *Series of Plays (1798–1812)*. Ed. D. H. Reiman. New York: Garland Press, 1977. Facsimile edition.

———. *The Tryal. A Series of Plays*, 195–299. Oxford: Woodstock Books, 1990.

———. *A View of the General Tenour of the New Testament Regarding the Nature and Dignity of Jesus Christ*. London, 1831.

Baillie, Matthew. *The Morbid Anatomy of Some of the Most Important Parts of the Human Body*. Albany, N.Y.: Barber and Southwick, 1795 (orig. 1793).

———. *The Works of Matthew Baillie, M.D., to Which is Prefixed an Account of His Life, Collected from Authentic Sources*. 2 vols. Ed. James Wardrop. London: Longman, Hurst, Rees, Orme, Brown and Green, 1825.

Barish, Jonas. *The Antitheatrical Prejudice*. Berkeley and Los Angeles: University of California Press, 1981.

Barker-Benfield, G. J. *The Culture of Sensibility: Sex and Society in Eighteenth-Century Britain*. Chicago: University of Chicago Press, 1992.

Baron-Wilson, Mrs. [Margaret] Cornwell. *Memoirs of Harriot, Duchess of St. Albans*. 2 vols. London: Henry Colburn, 1839.

Basnett, Susan. "Struggling with the Past: Women's Theatre in Search of a History." *New Theatre Quarterly* 5 (1989): 107–12.

Beer, Gillian. "Re-Presenting Women: Re-Presenting the Past." *The Feminist Reader: Essays in Gender and the Politics of Literary Criticism*, ed. Catherine Belsey and Jane Moore, 63–80. Cambridge: Blackwell, 1989.

Bell, Susan Groag, and Marilyn Yalom. "Introduction." In *Revealing Lives: Autobiography, Biography, and Gender*, ed. Susan Groag Bell and Marilyn Yalom, 1–11. Albany: SUNY Press, 1990.

Berger, Harry, Jr. *Imaginary Audition: Shakespeare on Stage and Page*. Berkeley and Oxford: University of California Press, 1989.

Berry, Mary. *A Comparative View of Social Life in England and France*. 2 vols. London: Longman, Rees, Orme, Brown and Green, 1828.

———. *Extracts of the Journals and Correspondence of Miss Berry, from 1783–1852.* 3 vols. Ed. Lady Theresa Lewis. London: Longmans, Green, and Co., 1866.

———. *The Fashionable Friends.* London: J. Ridgway, 1802.

Biggs, Murray. "Notes on Performing *Sardanapalus. Studies in Romanticism* 31.3 (1992): 373–85.

———. "Staging *The Borderers*: Dragging Romantic Drama Out of the Closet." *Studies in Romanticism* 27.3 (1988): 411–17.

———, ed. Special Issue: Byron's *Sardanapalus. Studies in Romanticism* 31.3 (1992).

Bishop of Salisbury. *Remarks on the General Tenour of the New Testament, Regarding the Nature and Dignity of Jesus Christ: Addressed to Mrs. Joanna Baillie.* Salisbury: W. B. Brodie and Co., 1831.

Blair, Juliet. "Private Parts in Public Places: The Case of Actresses." In *Women and Space: Ground Rules and Social Maps*, ed. Shirley Ardener, 200–21. London: Croom Helm; New York: St. Martin's Press, 1981.

Boaden, James. *The Life of Mrs. Jordan.* 2 vols. London: Edward Bull, 1831.

———. *Memoirs of Mrs. Inchbald.* 2 vols. London: Richard Bentley, 1833.

Bohls, Elizabeth. *Women Travel Writers and the Language of Aesthetics, 1716–1818.* Cambridge: Cambridge University Press, 1995.

Booth, Michael. "Introduction." *English Plays of the Nineteenth Century*, 1:1–28. 5 vols. Ed. Michael Booth. Oxford: Oxford University Press, 1969.

———, ed. *Prefaces to English Nineteenth-Century Theatre.* Manchester: Manchester University Press, 1980.

Boswell, James. "On the Profession of a Player." *The London Magazine* 39 (1770).

Bratton, J. S. "Miss Scott and Miss Macauley: 'Genius Comes in All Disguises.'" *Theatre Survey* 37.1 (1996): 59–73.

Braudy, Leo. *The Frenzy of Renown: Fame and Its History.* New York and Oxford: Oxford University Press, 1986.

Bray, Matthew. "Helen Maria Williams and Edmund Burke: Radical Critique and Complicity." *Eighteenth-Century Life* 16.2 (1992): 1–24.

Brewer, William D. "Joanna Baillie and Lord Byron." *Keats-Shelley Journal* 44 (1995): 165–81.

———. "The Prefaces of Joanna Baillie and William Wordsworth." *The Friend: Comments on Romanticism* 1.2 (1991): 34–47.

Brook, Peter. *The Empty Space.* New York: Atheneum, 1968.

———. *The Shifting Point, 1946–1987.* New York: Harper and Row, 1987.

Brooks, Peter. *Body Work: Objects of Desire in Modern Narrative.* Cambridge and London: Harvard University Press, 1993.

Brown, Cedric C. *John Milton's Aristocratic Entertainments.* Cambridge: Cambridge University Press, 1985.

Brown, Janet. *Taking Center Stage: Feminism in Contemporary U.S. Drama. Methuen,* N.J., and London: The Scarecrow Press, 1991.

Bruhm, Steven. *Gothic Bodies: The Politics of Pain in Romantic Fiction.* Philadelphia: University of Pennsylvania Press, 1994.

Burack, Cynthia. *The Problem of the Passions: Feminism, Psychoanalysis, and Social Theory.* New York and London: New York University Press, 1994.

Burke, Edmund. *Reflections on the Revolution in France*. London: Penguin Books, 1968 (orig. 1790).

Burney, Frances. *Edwy and Elgiva*. Ed. Miriam J. Benkovitz. Saratoga Springs, N.Y.: Skidmore College, 1957.

——. *Evelina*. Oxford: Oxford University Press, 1968 (orig. 1778).

——. Vol. 3 of *The Journals and Letters of Fanny Burney (Madame D'Arblay)*. Ed. Joyce Hemlow, with Patricia Boutilier and Althea Douglas. 12 vols. Oxford: Clarendon Press, 1973.

Burrell, Sophia. "Dedication." *Maximian*. London: Luke Hanfard, 1800.

Burroughs, Catherine B. "Acting in the Closet: A Feminist Performance of Hazlitt's *Liber Amoris* and Keats' *Otho the Great*." *European Romantic Review* 2.2 (1992): 125–44.

——. "English Romantic Women Writers and Theatre Theory: Joanna Baillie's Prefaces to the *Plays on the Passions*." In *Re-Visioning Romanticism: British Women Writers, 1776-1837*, ed. Carol Shiner Wilson and Joel Haefner, 274–96. Philadelphia: University of Pennsylvania Press, 1994.

——. " 'Out of the Pale of Social Kindred Cast': Conflicted Performance Styles in Joanna Baillie's *De Monfort*." In *Romantic Women Writers: Voices and Counter-voices*, ed. Paula R. Feldman and Theresa M. Kelley, 223–35. Hanover, N.H.: University Press of New England, 1995.

Burwick, Frederick. *Illusion and the Drama: Critical Theory of the Enlightenment and Romantic Era*. University Park: Pennsylvania State University Press, 1991.

Bushe, Charles Kendal. *The Private Theatre of Kilkenny, with Introductory Observations on Other Private Theatres in Ireland, Before it was Opened*. N.p., 1825.

Buss, Helen M. "Anna Jameson's *Winter Studies and Summer Rambles in Canada* as Epistolary Dijournal." In *Essays on Life Writing: From Genre to Critical Practice*, ed. Marlene Kadar, 42–60. Toronto: University of Toronto Press, 1992.

Butler, Judith. *Bodies That Matter: On the Discursive Limits of 'Sex'*. New York and London: Routledge, 1993.

——. "Gender Trouble, Feminist Theory, and Psychoanalytic Discourse." In *Feminism/Postmodernism*, ed. Linda J. Nicholson, 324–40. New York: Routledge, 1990.

——. "Imitation and Gender Insubordination." In *Inside/Out: Lesbian Theories, Gay Theories*, ed. Diana Fuss, 13–31. New York: Routledge, 1991.

——. "Performative Acts and Gender Constitution: An Essay in Phenomenology and Feminist Theory." *Theatre Journal* 40.4 (1988): 519–31.

Byron, George Gordon, Lord. "Preface to *Marino Faliero, Doge of Venice*." In *The Poetical Works of Byron*, ed. Robert F. Gleckner, 497–99. Boston: Houghton Mifflin, 1975.

Campbell, Lily. "A History of Costuming on the English Stage between 1660 and 1823." *Collected Papers of Lily B. Campbell*, 103–39. New York: Russell and Russell, 1968. Reprinted from *University of Wisconsin Studies in Language and Literature* 2 (1918).

——. "The Rise of a Theory of Stage Presentation in England during the Eighteenth Century." *PMLA* 32.2 (1917): 163–200.

Campbell, Thomas. *Life of Mrs. Siddons*. 2 vols. London: Effingham Wilson, 1834.

Canning, Charlotte. "Constructing Experience: Theorizing a Feminist Theatre History." *Theatre Journal* 45 (1993): 529–40.

Carhart, Margaret. *The Life and Work of Joanna Baillie*. New Haven: Yale University Press, 1923.

Carlisle, Carol J. "Edmund Kean on the Art of Acting." *Theatre Notebook* 12.3 (1968): 119–20.

———. "Helen Faucit's Lady Macbeth." *Shakespeare Studies* (1977), 205–34.

Carlson, Julie. "A New Stage for Romantic Drama." *Studies in Romanticism* 27.3 (1988): 419–27.

———. *In the Theatre of Romanticism: Coleridge, Nationalism, Women*. Cambridge: Cambridge University Press, 1994.

Carlson, Marvin. *Places of Performance: The Semiotics of Theatre Architecture*. Ithaca and London: Cornell University Press, 1989.

———. *Theories of the Theatre: A Historical and Critical Survey, from the Greeks to the Present*. Ithaca and London: Cornell University Press, 1984; rpt. 1993.

Carswell, Donald. "Joanna Baillie." *Scott and His Circle*, 271–96. Garden City, N.Y.: Doubleday, Doran, and Co., 1930.

Case, Sue-Ellen. *Feminism and Theatre*. New York: Methuen, 1988.

———. "Introduction." In *Performing Feminisms: Feminist Critical Theory and Theatre*, ed. Sue-Ellen Case, 1–13. Baltimore and London: The Johns Hopkins University Press, 1990.

———. "Toward a Butch–Femme Aesthetic." In *Making a Spectacle: Feminist Essays on Contemporary Women's Theatre*, ed. Lynda Hart, 282–99. Ann Arbor: University of Michigan Press, 1989.

Case, Sue-Ellen, and Janelle Reinelt, eds. "Introduction." *The Performance of Power: Theatrical Discourse and Politics*, ix–xix. Iowa City: University of Iowa Press, 1991.

Castle, Terry. *Masquerade and Civilization: The Carnivalesque in Eighteenth-Century English Culture and Fiction*. Stanford, Calif.: Stanford University Press, 1986.

Cave, Richard Allen. "Romantic Drama in Performance: Goethe and Schiller." *The Keats-Shelley Review* 3 (1988): 108–20.

———, ed. *The Romantic Theatre: An International Symposium*. Totowa, N.J.: Barnes and Noble Books, 1986.

Chambers, Marianne. *Ourselves*. London: J. Barker, 1811.

Chapone, Hester. "Matrimonial Creed." In *Bluestocking Letters*, ed. R. B. Johnson, 195–202. London: John Lane The Bodley Head, 1926.

Chorley, Henry F. Vol. 1 of *Life of Mrs. Hemans*. 2 vols. London: Saunders and Otley, 1836.

Cima, Gay Gibson. *Performing Women: Female Characters, Male Playwrights, and the Modern Stage*. Ithaca and London: Cornell University Press, 1993.

Clancy, Charles J. *A Selected Bibliography of English Romantic Drama*. Norwood, Pa.: Norwood Editions, 1976.

Cole, David. *Acting as Reading: The Place of the Reading Process in the Actor's Work*. Ann Arbor: University of Michigan Press, 1992.

Coles, William A. "Magazine and Other Contributions by Mary Russell Mitford and Thomas Noon Talfourd." *Studies in Bibliography*, ed. Fredson Bowers, 12 (1959): 218–26.

Colley, Linda. *Britons: The Forging of a Nation, 1707–1837*. New Haven and London: Yale University Press, 1992.

Corbett, Martyn. *Byron and Tragedy*. New York: St. Martin's Press, 1988.

———. "Lugging Byron Out of the Library." *Studies in Romanticism* 31.3 (1992): 361–72.

Corbett, Mary Jean. *Representing Femininity: Middle-Class Subjectivity in Victorian and Edwardian Women's Autobiographies*. New York and Oxford: Oxford University Press, 1992.

Cowley, Hannah. "Advertisement to *A Day in Turkey*." Vol. 1 of *The Works of Mrs. Cowley: Dramas and Poems*. 3 vols. London: Wilkie and Robinson, 1813.

Cox, Jeffrey N. "Ideology and Genre in the British Antirevolutionary Drama of the 1790s." *ELH* 58 (1991): 579–610.

———. *In the Shadows of Romance: Romantic Tragic Drama in Germany England, and France*. Athens: Ohio University Press, 1987.

———. "Review of *Illusion and Drama: Critical Theory of the Enlightenment and Romantic Era*. By Frederick Burwick." *European Romantic Review* 4.1 (1993): 91–96.

Cox, Jeffrey N., ed., with an introduction. *Seven Gothic Dramas, 1789–1825*. Athens: Ohio University Press, 1992.

Craven, Elizabeth Berkeley. *The Beautiful Lady Craven: The Original Memoirs of Elizabeth Baronness Craven afterwards Margravine of Anspach and Bayreuth and Princess Berkeley of the Holy Roman Empire (1750–1828)*. 2 vols. London: John Lane The Bodley Head, 1914 (orig. 1826).

———. "Dedication" to *The Fashionable Day*. London: G. Kearsley, 1780.

———. *Memoires*. Edition presentée and annotée par Jean-Pierre Guicciardi. Paris: Mercure de France, 1991.

———. Vol. 1 of *Memoirs of the Margravine of Anspach, Written By Herself*. 2 vols. London: Henry Colburn, 1826.

Crochunis, Thomas. "Byronic Heroes and Acting: The Embodiment of Mental Theater." In *New Essays on Lord Byron*, ed. William D. Brewer, 57–73. Dallas: Contemporary Research Press, 1995.

Cumberland, Richard. "Remarks upon the Present Taste for Acting Private Plays." *The European Magazine, and London Review* 14 (1788): 115–18.

Curran, Stuart. "Romantic Poetry: The I Altered." In *Romanticism and Feminism*, ed. Anne K. Mellor, 185–207. Bloomington: Indiana University Press, 1988.

———. *Shelley's Cenci: Scorpions Ringed with Fire*. Princeton, N.J.: Princeton University Press, 1970.

Daniels, Barry V. *Revolution in the Theatre: French Romantic Theories of the Drama*. Westport, Conn.: Greenwood Press, 1983.

Davies, Robertson. *The Mirror of Nature*. Toronto: University of Toronto Press, 1983.

Davis, Gwenn, and Beverly A. Joyce. "Introduction." In *Drama by Women to 1900: A Bibliography of American and British Writers*, comp. Gwenn Davis and

Beverly A. Joyce, vii–xxi. Toronto and Buffalo: University of Toronto Press, 1992.

Davis, Tracy C. *Actresses as Working Women: Their Social Identity in Victorian Culture*. London and New York: Routledge, 1991.

———. "Introduction: Private Woman in the Public Realm." Special Section: Feminists Theorize the Past. *Theatre Survey: The Journal for Society for Theatre Research* 35.1 (1994): 65–71.

———. "Questions for a Feminist Methodology in Theatre History." In *Interpreting the Theatrical Past: Essays in the Historiography of Performance*, ed. Thomas Postlewait and Bruce McConachie, 59–81. Iowa City: University of Iowa Press, 1989.

———. " 'Reading Shakespeare by Flashes of Lightning': Challenging the Foundations of Romantic Acting Theory." *ELH* 62 (1995): 933–54.

De Lauretis, Teresa. *Technologies of Gender: Essays in Theory, Film, and Fiction*. Bloomington: Indiana University Press, 1987.

Diamond, Elin. "Brechtian Theory/Feminist Theory: Toward a Gestic Feminist Criticism." *The Drama Review* 32.1 (1988): 82–94.

Dobrée, Bonamy. *The Amateur and the Theatre*. London: The Hogarth Press, 1947.

Dolan, Jill. *The Feminist Spectator as Critic*. Ann Arbor: UMI Research Press, 1988.

———. "Geographies of Learning: Theatre Studies, Performance, and the 'Performative.' " *Theatre Journal* 45 (1993): 417–41.

———. "In Defense of the Discourse: Materialist Feminism, Postmodernism, Poststructuralism . . . and Theory." In *Presence and Desire: Essays on Gender, Sexuality, and Performance*, 85–97. Ann Arbor: University of Michigan Press, 1993.

———. "Personal, Political, Polemical: Feminist Approaches to Politics and Theater." In *Presence and Desire: Essays on Gender, Sexuality, and Performance*, 43–68. Ann Arbor: University of Michigan Press, 1993.

Donkin, Ellen. *Getting into the Act: Women Playwrights in London, 1776–1829*. London and New York: Routledge, 1995.

———. "Mrs. Siddons Looks Back in Anger: Feminist Historiography for Eighteenth-Century British Theater." In *Critical Theory and Performance*, ed. Janelle G. Reinelt and Joseph R. Roach, 276–90. Ann Arbor: University of Michigan Press, 1992.

Donkin, Ellen, and Susan Clement, eds. "Editors' Introduction." In *Upstaging Big Daddy: Directing Theater as if Gender and Race Matter*, 1–9. Ann Arbor: University of Michigan Press, 1993.

Donohue, Joseph. *Dramatic Character in the English Romantic Age*. Princeton, N.J.: Princeton University Press, 1970.

———. *Theatre in the Age of Kean*. Totowa, N.J.: Rowman and Littlefield, 1975.

Dorr, Priscilla. "Joanna Baillie." In *An Encyclopedia of British Women Writers*, ed. Paul and June Schlueter, 15–21. New York: Garland Press, 1988.

Dowd, Maureen. "Joanna Baillie's 'Extensive Design' as Cultural Performance." Unpublished essay.

Downer, Alan S. "Nature to Advantage Dressed: Eighteenth-Century Acting." *PMLA* 58.4 (1943): 1002–37.

———. "Players and Painted Stage: Nineteenth-Century Acting." *PMLA* 61.2 (1946): 522–76.

Duerr, Edwin. *The Length and Depth of Acting*. New York: Holt, Rinehart, and Winston, 1962.

Eagleton, Terry. *The Ideology of the Aesthetic*. London: Basil Blackwell, 1990.

———. *The Significance of Theory*. Oxford and Cambridge, Mass.: Blackwell Publishers, 1990.

East, Joyce E. "Mrs. Hannah Cowley, Playwright." In *Eighteenth-Century Women and the Arts*, ed. Frederick M. Keener and Susan E. Lorsch, 67–75. Westport, Conn.: Greenwood Press, 1988.

Ellison, Julie. *Delicate Subjects: Romanticism, Gender, and the Ethics of Understanding*. Ithaca, N.Y.: Cornell University Press, 1990.

Emmerson, Robin. *British Teapots and Tea Drinking, 1700–1850*. London: HMSO, 1992.

Evans, Bertrand. "Joanna Baillie and Gothic Drama." In *Gothic Drama from Walpole to Shelley*, 200–15. Berkeley and Los Angeles: University of California Press, 1947.

Evenden, Michael. "Inter-mediate Stages: Reconsidering the Body in 'Closet Drama.'" In *Reading the Social Body*, ed. Catherine B. Burroughs and Jeffrey David Ehrenreich, 244–69. Iowa City: University of Iowa Press, 1993.

Eyre, E. J. "Prologue." In *Ourselves*, by Marianne Chambers. London: J. Barker, 1811.

Ezell, Margaret. *Writing Women's Literary History*. Baltimore and London: The Johns Hopkins University Press, 1993.

Favret, Mary A. *Romantic Correspondence: Women, Politics, and the Fiction of Letters*. Cambridge: Cambridge University Press, 1993.

———. "Spectatrice as Spectacle: Helen Maria Williams at Home in the Revolution." *Studies in Romanticism* 32.2 (1993): 273–95.

Feldman, Paula R., ed. *British Romantic Poetry by Women, 1770–1840*. Baltimore and London: The Johns Hopkins University Press, forthcoming.

Feldman, Paula R., and Theresa M. Kelley, eds. *Romantic Women Writers: Voices and Counter Voices*. Hanover, N.H.: University Press of New England, 1995.

Ferguson, Moira. *Colonialism and Gender from Mary Wollstonecraft to Jamaica Kincaid: East Carribean Connections*. New York: Columbia University Press, 1993.

Fischer-Lichte, Erika. "Theatre and the Civilizing Process: An Approach to the History of Acting." *Interpreting the Theatrical Past: Essays in the Historiography of Performance*, ed. Thomas Postlewait and Bruce A. McConachie, 19–36. Iowa City: University of Iowa Press, 1989.

Flaherty, Gloria. "Empathy and Distance: Romantic Theories of Acting Reconsidered." *Theatre Research International* 15.2 (1990): 125–41.

Fletcher, Anthony. *Gender, Sex, and Subordination in England 1500–1800*. New Haven and London: Yale University Press, 1995.

Fletcher, Richard M. *English Romantic Drama, 1795–1843: A Critical History*. New York: Exposition Press, 1966.

The Folger Collective on Early Women Critics. "Introduction." In *Women Critics, 1660–1820*, ed. The Folger Collective on Early Women Critics, xiii–xxv. Bloomington: Indiana University Press, 1995.

Forbes, Bryan. *That Despicable Race: A History of the British Acting Tradition*. London: Elm Tree Books, 1980.

Fowles, Jib. *Star Struck: Celebrity Performers and the American Public*. Washington and London: Smithsonian Institution Press, 1992.

Francis, Basil. *Fanny Kelly of Drury Lane*. London: Rockliff Publishing Corporation, 1950.

Friedrichsmeyer, Sara. "Caroline Schegel-Schelling: 'A Good Woman and No Heroine.'" In *In the Shadows of Olympus: German Women Writers around 1800*, ed. Katharine R. Goodman and Edith Waldstein, 115–36. Albany: SUNY Press, 1992.

Galperin, William H. *The Return of the Visible in British Romanticism*. Baltimore and London: The Johns Hopkins University Press, 1993.

————. "The Theatre at Mansfield Park: From Classic to Romantic Once More." *Eighteenth-Century Life* 16.3 (1992): 247–71.

Gardner, Vivien, and Sarah Rutherford, eds. *The New Woman and Her Sisters: Feminism and the Theatre, 1850–1914*. Ann Arbor: University of Michigan Press, 1992.

Gatton, John Spalding. "'Put into Scenery': Theatrical Space in Byron's Closet Historical Dramas." In *The Theatrical Space*, 139–49. Cambridge: Cambridge University Press, 1987.

Gaull, Marilyn. "Romantic Theater." *Wordsworth Circle* 14.4 (1983): 255–63.

Gay, Penny. *As She Likes It: Shakespeare's Unruly Women*. London and New York: Routledge, 1994.

Gayley, Charles Mills. *The Classic Myths in English Literature and Art*. Toronto: Xerox College Publishing, 1939.

Gelman, David. "Homoeroticism in the Ranks." *Newsweek*, July 26, 1993, 28–29.

Gilbert, Sandra, and Susan Gubar. *The Madwoman in the Attic: The Woman Writer and the Nineteenth-Century Literary Imagination*. New Haven and London: Yale University Press, 1979.

Gilbert, Sky. "Closet Plays: An Exclusive Dramaturgy at Work." *Canadian Theatre Review* 59 (1989): 55–58.

Gillespie, Patti. "Feminist Theatre: A Rhetorical Phenomenon." *The Quarterly Journal of Speech* 64 (1978): 284–94.

Godwin, William. *Memoirs of the Author of the Rights of Woman*. Ed. Richard Holmes. New York: Viking Penguin, 1987 (orig. 1798).

Goodman, Katharine R. "The Sign Speaks: Charlotte von Stein's Matinees." In *In the Shadows of Olympus: German Women Writers around 1800*, ed. Katharine R. Goodman and Edith Waldstein. Albany: SUNY Press, 1992.

Goodman, Katharine R., and Edith Waldstein, eds. *In the Shadows of Olympus: German Women Writers around 1800*. Albany: SUNY Press, 1992.

Goodman, Lizbeth. *Contemporary Feminist Theatres: To Each Her Own*. London and New York: Routledge, 1993.

Gottlieb, Erika. *Lost Angels of a Ruined Paradise: Themes of Cosmic Strife in Romantic Tragedy*. Victoria, B. C.: Sono Nis Press, 1981.

Grau, Joseph A. "Fanny Burney and the Theatre." In *Fanny Burney: An Annotated Bibliography*, 149–60. New York and London: Garland Publishing, 1981.

Green, Susan. "A Cultural Reading of Charlotte Lennox's *Shakespeare Illustrated*.

Cultural Readings of Restoration and Eighteenth-Century Theatre. Ed. J. Douglas Canfield and Deborah C. Payne, 228–57. Athens: University of Georgia Press, 1995.

Griffinhoof, Arthur (pseud). *Memoirs of the Life of Madame Vestris*. Privately printed, 1830.

Gutierrez, Nancy A. "Valuing *Mariam*: Genre Study and Feminist Analysis." *Tulsa Studies in Women's Literature* 10.2 (1991): 233–51.

Hadley, Elaine. "The Old Price Wars: Melodramatizing the Public Sphere in Early Nineteenth-Century England." *PMLA* 107.3 (1992): 524–37.

Haefner, Joel. "The Romantic Scene(s) of Writing." In *Re-Visioning Romanticism: British Women Writers, 1776–1837*, ed. Carol Shiner Wilson and Joel Haefner, 256–73. Philadelphia: University of Pennsylvania Press, 1994.

Hale, Sarah Josepha. *Woman's Record; or, Sketches of all Distinguished Women, from Creation to A.D. 1854*. New York: Harper and Brothers, 1855.

Hamilton, Catherine Jane. "Joanna Baillie." Vol. 1 of *Women Writers: Their Works and Ways*, 110–31. 2 vols. London and New York: Ward, Lock, Bowden, and Co., 1892–93.

Harrison, Martin. "Closet Drama." *Theatre*, 56. Manchester: Carcanet Press, 1993.

Hart, Lynda, ed. "Introduction: Performing Feminism." In *Making a Spectacle: Feminist Essays on Contemporary Women's Theatre*, ed. Lynda Hart, 1–21. Ann Arbor: University of Michigan Press, 1989.

Hartnoll, Phyllis, and Peter Found. *The Concise Oxford Companion to the Theatre*. Oxford: Oxford University Press, 1992.

Hayley, William. *Three Plays with a Preface, including Dramaturgic Observations, of the Late Lieutenant-General Burgoyne*. London: William Mason, 1811.

Heller, Janet Ruth. *Coleridge, Lamb, Hazlitt, and the Reader of Drama*. Columbia and London: University of Missouri Press, 1990.

Heywood, O. *Closet Prayer: A Christian Duty or Treatise upon Mat[thew] VI*. London: Parkhurst, 1671.

Highfill, Philip H., Jr., Kalman A. Burnim, and Edward A. Langhans. *A Biographical Dictionary of Actors, Actresses, Musicians, Dancers, Managers, and Other Stage Personnel in London, 1660–1800*. 16 vols. Carbondale and Edwardsville: Southern Illinois University Press, 1973–93.

Hoagwood, Terence Allan. "Prologemenon for a Theory of Romantic Drama." *Wordsworth Circle* 23.2 (1992): 49–64.

Hoagwood, Terence A., and Daniel P. Watkins, eds. Special Issue: Romantic Drama: Historical and Critical Essays. *Wordsworth Circle* 23.2 (1992).

Hoeveler, Diane Long. *Romantic Androgyny: The Women Within*. University Park: Pennsylvania State University Press, 1990.

Holbrook, Ann Catherine. *The Dramatist; or, Memoirs of the Stage. With the Life of the Authoress, Prefixed, and Interspersed with, A Variety of Anecdotes, Humorous and Pathetic*. Birmingham, Eng.: Martin and Hunter, 1809.

Hollander, Anne. *Seeing Through Clothes*. New York: Viking Press, 1978.

Holman, L. E. *Lamb's 'Barbara S——': The Life of Frances Maria Kelly, Actress*. London: Methuen and Co., 1935.

Holmes, Richard, ed. *Memoirs of the Author of the Rights of Woman*. By William Godwin. New York: Viking Penguin, 1987 (orig. 1798).

Holmstrom, Kirsten Gram. *Monodrama, Attitudes, Tableaux Vivants: Studies on Some Trends in Theatrical Fashion, 1770–1815*. Uppsala: Almquist and Wiksells Boktryckeri, 1967.

Hornby, Richard. *The End of Acting: A Radical View*. New York: Applause Books, 1992.

Howe, Elizabeth. *The First English Actresses: Women and Drama, 1660–1700*. Cambridge: Cambridge University Press, 1992.

Howells, Coral Ann. "Introduction." In vol. 1 of *Manfrone or The One-Handed Monk*, by Mary-Anne Radcliffe, iii–x. 2 vols. New York: Arno Press, 1972.

Hubner, Zygmunt. *Theater and Politics*. Ed. and trans. Jadwiga Kosicka. Evanston, Ill.: Northwestern University Press, 1992 (orig. 1988).

Hughes, Anne. "To the Reader." *Moral Dramas, Intended for Private Representation*. London: William Lane, 1790.

Hunt, Leigh. "Duchess of St. Albans, and Marriages from the Stage." In Vol. 2 of *Men, Women, and Books: A Selection of Sketches, Essays, and Critical Memoirs*. 2 vols. New York: Harper and Brothers, 1847.

Hunter, J. Paul. "The World as Stage and Closet." In *British Theatre and the Other Arts, 1660–1800*, ed. Shirley Strum Kenny, 271–87. London and Toronto: Associated University Presses, 1984.

Huston, Hollis. *The Actor's Instrument: Body, Theory, Stage*. Ann Arbor: University of Michigan Press, 1992.

Inchbald, Elizabeth. *Remarks for the British Theatre (1806–09). By Elizabeth Inchbald*. Introduced by Cecilia Macheski. Delmar, N.Y.: Scholars' Facsimiles and Reprints, 1990.

Insch, A. G. "Joanna Baillie's *De Monfort* in Relation to Her Theory of Tragedy." *Durham University Journal* 23 (1961): 114–20.

Jacobus, Mary. "Is There a Woman in This Text?" *Reading Woman: Essays in Feminist Criticism*, 83–109. New York: Columbia University Press, 1986 (orig. 1982).

———. "'That Great Stage Where Senators Perform': *Macbeth* and the Politics of Romantic Theatre." *Romanticism, Writing, and Sexual Difference: Essays on The Prelude*. New York: Oxford University Press, 1989 (orig. 1983).

Jameson, Anna. *Characteristics of Women: Moral, Poetical, and Historical*. New York: Saunders and Otley, 1837 (orig. 1832).

———. *A Commonplace Book of Thoughts, Memories, and Fancies. Original and Selected*. London: Longman, Brown, Green, and Longmans, 1854.

———. Vol. 1 of *Winter Studies and Summer Rambles in Canada*. 2 vols. London: Saunders and Otley, 1838.

Jenkin, Fleeming. *Mrs. Siddons as Lady Macbeth and Queen Katharine*. New York: Dramatic Museum of Columbia University, 1915.

Jermyn, Laetitia. "A Memoir of Mrs. Elizabeth [Knipe] Cobbold." *Poems by Mrs. Elizabeth Cobbold. With a Memoir of the Author*. Ipswich: J. Row, 1825.

Jewett, William. "Review of *A Materialist Critique of English Romantic Drama*, by Daniel P. Watkins." *Studies in Romanticism* 34 (1995): 309–15.

Johnson, Reginald Brimley. "Introduction." *Bluestocking Letters*, 1–18. London: John Lane The Bodley Head, 1926.

Johnston, Kenneth, and Joseph Nicoles. "Transitory Actions, Men Betrayed: The

French Revolution in the English Revolution in Romantic Drama." *Words-worth Circle* 23.2 (1992): 76–96.

Jones, Charles Inigo. *Memoirs of Miss O'Neill.* London: D. Cox, 1816.

Keats, John. *Otho the Great: The Complete Poems of John Keats.* Ed. Jack Stillinger, 378–451. Cambridge, Mass.: The Belknap Press of Harvard University, 1978.

Kemble, Frances Anne. *Notes upon Some of Shakespeare's Plays.* London: Richard Bentley and Son, 1882.

———. *On the Stage.* New York: Dramatic Museum of Columbia University, 1926 (orig. 1863).

———. *Records of a Girlhood.* New York: Henry Holt and Company, 1879.

Keyssar, Helene. *Feminist Theatre.* New York: St. Martin's Press, 1984.

Kiernan, Pauline. *Shakespeare's Theory of Drama.* Cambridge: Cambridge University Press, 1996.

Kintz, Linda. *The Subject's Tragedy: Political Poetics, Feminist Theory, and Drama.* Ann Arbor: University of Michigan Press, 1992.

Klancher, Jon. "British Theory and Criticism: 3. Romantic Period and Early Nineteenth Century." In *The Johns Hopkins Guide to Literary Theory and Criticism*, ed. Michael Groden and Martin Kreiswirth, 112–15. Baltimore: The Johns Hopkins University Press, 1994.

———. "English Romanticism and Cultural Production." In *The New Historicism*, ed. Aram Veeser. New York: Routledge, 1989.

Klein, Lawrence E. "Gender and the Public/Private Distinction in the Eighteenth Century: Some Questions about Evidence and Analytic Procedure." *Eighteenth-Century Studies* 29.1 (1995): 97–109.

Krueger, Christine L. *The Reader's Repentance: Women Preachers, Women Writers, and Nineteenth-Century Social Discourse.* Chicago and London: University of Chicago Press, 1992.

Kubiak, Anthony. *Stages of Terror: Terrorism, Ideology, and Coercion as Theatre History.* Bloomington: Indiana University Press, 1991.

Kucich, Greg. "'A Haunted Ruin': Romantic Drama, Renaissance Tradition, and the Critical Establishment." *The Wordsworth Circle* 23.2 (1992): 64–76.

Kunitz, Stanley J., ed. *British Authors of the Nineteenth Century.* New York: The H. W. Wilson Co., 1936.

Lamb, Charles. "Barbara S———." *The Complete Works and Letters of Charles Lamb*, 180–84. New York: The Modern Library, 1935.

———. "On the Tragedies of Shakespeare." In vol. 1 of *The Works of Charles and Mary Lamb*, ed. E. V. Lucas, 97–111. New York: AMS Press, 1968 (orig. 1903).

Landes, Joan. *Women and the Public Sphere in the Age of the French Revolution.* Ithaca and London: Cornell University Press, 1988.

Landry, Donna. *The Muses of Resistance: Laboring-Class Women's Poetry in Britain, 1739–1796.* Cambridge: Cambridge University Press, 1990.

Lansdown, Richard. *Byron's Historical Dramas.* Oxford: Clarendon Press, 1992.

Lanser, Susan S. "Women Critics—and the Difference They Make: Response to Early Women Critics Session, 1991, MLA." Unpublished manuscript.

Lanser, Susan Sniader, and Evelyn Torton Beck. "[Why] Are There No Great Women Critics?: And What Difference Does It Make?" In *The Prism of Sex:*

Essays in the Sociology of Knowledge, ed. Julia A. Sherman and Evelyn Torton Beck, 79–91. Madison: University of Wisconsin Press, 1979.

Larrabee, Stephen A. "The 'Closet' and the 'Stage' in 1759." *Modern Language Notes* 56 (1941): 282–84.

Lee, Harriet. *The Mysterious Marriage*. Dublin: Wogan, Byrne, Jones, Rice, Kelly, and Folingsby, 1798.

———. *The New Peerage: or, Our Eyes May Deceive Us*. London: G. G. J. and J. Robinson, 1787.

Lee, Sophia. "Preface." *The Chapter of Accidents*. Vol. 24 of *Bell's British Theatre*, iii–vi. London: George Cawthorn, 1796.

Levin, Susan. *Dorothy Wordsworth and Romanticism*. New Brunswick, N.J.: Rutgers University Press, 1987.

Lewis, Lady Theresa. "Introduction." In vol. 1 of *Extracts of the Journals and Correspondence of Miss Berry, From the Years 1783–1852*, ed. Lady Theresa Lewis. 6 vols. London: Longmans, Green, and Co., 1865.

Liesenfield, Vincent J. *The Licensing Act of 1737*. Madison: University of Wisconsin Press, 1984.

Litvak, Joseph. *Caught in the Act: Theatricality in the Nineteenth-Century English Novel*. Berkeley and Los Angeles: University of California Press, 1992.

Lott, Anna. "Sexual Politics in Elizabeth Inchbald." *SEL* 34(1994): 635–48.

Macarthy, Eugene. *A Letter to the King and Queen on the Question Now at Issue Between the 'Major' and 'Minor' Theatres*. London: Effingham Wilson, Royal Exchange, 1832.

Macaulay, Catharine. "Preface." *Letters on Education, with Observations on Religious and Metaphysical Subjects*, i–viii. London: C. Dilly, 1790 (rpt. Garland 1974).

Macheski, Cecilia. "Herself as Heroine: Portraits as Autobiography for Elizabeth Inchbald." *Curtain Calls: British and American Women and the Theater, 1660–1820*. Ed. Mary Anne Schofield and Cecilia Macheski, 34–47. Athens: Ohio University Press, 1991.

———. "Introduction." In *Remarks for the British Theatre (1806–09). By Elizabeth Inchbald*, 7–12. Delmar, N.Y.: Scholars' Facsimiles and Reprints, 1990.

Maclaren, Archibald. *The Private Theatre: or, the Highland Funeral*. London: A. Macpherson, 1809.

MacMichael, William. *The Gold-Headed Cane*. London: The Royal College of Physicians, 1968 (orig. 1827).

Malpede, Karen. *Women in Theatre: Compassion and Hope*. New York: Limelight Editions, 1983.

Mann, David D. "Checklist of Female Dramatists, 1660–1823." *Restoration and Eighteenth-Century Theatre Research* 5.1 (1990): 30–62.

Massey, Doreen. *Space, Place, and Gender*. Minneapolis: University of Minnesota Press, 1994.

Mathews, Anne. *Anecdotes of Actors with Other Desultory Recollections*. 2 vols. London: T. C. Newby, 1844.

———. *Memoirs of Charles Mathews, Comedian*. 4 vols. London: Richard Bentley, 1839.

Mathur, Om Prakash. *The Closet Drama of the Romantic Revival*. Salzburg: Universität Salzburg, 1978.

McGann, Jerome. *Fiery Dust: Byron's Poetic Development*. Chicago: University of Chicago Press, 1968.

———. *The Romantic Ideology: A Critical Investigation*. Chicago: University of Chicago Press, 1983.

McKerrow, Mary. "Joanna Baillie and Mary Brunton: Women of the Manse." In *Living by the Pen: Early British Women Writers*, ed. Dale Spender, 160–74. New York: Teachers College Press, 1992.

Meisel, Martin. *Realizations: Narrative, Pictorial, and Theatrical Arts in Nineteenth-Century England*. Princeton, N.J.: Princeton University Press, 1983.

Mellor, Anne K. "A Criticism of Their Own: Romantic Women Literary Critics." In *Questioning Romanticism*, ed. John Beer, 29–48. Baltimore: The Johns Hopkins University Press, 1995.

———. "Joanna Baillie and the Counter-Public Sphere." *Studies in Romanticism* 33 (1994): 559–67.

———. *Romanticism and Gender*. New York and London: Routledge, 1993.

———, ed. *Romanticism and Feminism*. Bloomington: Indiana University Press, 1988.

Mellor, Anne K., and Richard Matlack, eds. *British Literature, 1770–1830*. Harcourt Brace Jovanovich, 1996.

Meynell, Alice C. *The Second Person Singular*. Freeport, N.Y.: Books for Libraries Press, 1922 (rpt. 1968).

Mitford, Mary Russell. *The Dramatic Works of Mary Russell Mitford*, 1:243–49. 2 vols. London: Hurst and Blackett, 1854.

———. Vol. 1 of *Recollections of a Literary Life: or, Books, Places, and People*. 3 vols. London: Richard Bentley, 1852.

Mobley, Johnnie Patricia. *NTC's Dictionary of Theatre and Drama Terms*. Lincolnwood, Ill.: National Textbook Co., 1992.

Moody, Jane. " 'Fine words, legitimate!': Towards a Theatrical History of Romanticism." *Texas Studies in Literature and Language* 38.3/4 (1996): 223–44.

Moore, Tom. "Review of *The Private Theatre of Kilkenny, with Introductory Observations on other Private Theatres in Ireland, before it was opened*. By C. K. Bushe." *Edinburgh Review* 46 (1827): 368–90.

More, Hannah. "General Preface." *The Works of Hannah More*. New York: Harper and Brothers, 1835 (orig. 1830).

———. *Letters to Young Ladies*. Philadelphia: Young, Stewart, and M'Culloch, 1786.

Murray, Monica. "English Theater Costume and the Zeitgeist of the Eighteenth Century." *Studies in Voltaire and the Eighteenth Century* 265 (1989): 1340–43.

Myers, Sylvia Harcstarck. *The Bluestocking Circle: Women, Friendship, and the Life of the Mind in Eighteenth-Century England*. Oxford: Clarendon Press, 1990.

Nagler, A. M. *A Sourcebook in Theatrical History (Sources of Theatrical History)*. New York: Dover Publications, 1952.

Natalle, Elizabeth J. *Feminist Theatre: A Study in Persuasion*. Methuen, N.J., and London: The Scarecrow Press, 1985.

Nicoll, Allardyce. *A History of Late Eighteenth-Century Drama, 1750–1800*. Cambridge: Cambridge University Press, 1927.

———. Vol. 1 of *A History of Early Nineteenth-Century Drama*. 2 vols. Cambridge: Cambridge University Press, 1930.

Noble, Aloma. "Joanna Baillie as a Dramatic Artist." Ph.D. diss., University of Iowa, 1983.

Norton, M. "The Plays of Joanna Baillie." *Review of English Studies* 23 (1947): 131–43.

Opie, Amelia. *Adeline Mowbray; or The Mother and Daughter*. London, Boston, and Henley: Pandora, 1986 (orig. 1802).

Otten, Terry. *The Deserted Stage: The Search for Dramatic Form in Nineteenth-Century England*. Athens: Ohio University Press, 1972.

Page, Judith. *Wordsworth and the Cultivation of Women*. Berkeley and Los Angeles: University of California Press, 1994.

Parker, Andrew, and Eve Kosofsky Sedgwick. "Introduction: Performativity and Performance." In *Performativity and Performance*, ed. Andrew Parker and Eve Kosofsky Sedgwick, 1–18. New York and London: Routledge, 1995.

Parker, Reeve. "*Osorio*'s Dark Employments: Tricking Out Coleridgean Tragedy." *Studies in Romanticism* 33.1 (1994): 119–60.

———. "Reading Wordsworth's Power: Narrative and Usurpation in *The Borderers*." *ELH* 54.2 (1987): 299–331.

Parrinder, Patrick. *Authors and Authority: English and American Criticism 1750–1990*. Rev. ed. New York: Columbia University Press, 1991.

Pascoe, Judith. *Romantic Theatricality: Gender, Poetry, and Spectatorship*. Ithaca, N.Y.: Cornell University Press, forthcoming.

Peake, Richard Brinsley. *Amateurs and Actors: A Musical Farce in Two Acts*. London: John Cumberland, 1827 (orig. 1818).

Pearce, Charles E. *Madame Vestris and Her Times*. London, 1923.

Poovey, Mary. *The Proper Lady and the Woman Writer: Ideology as Style in the Works of Mary Wollstonecraft, Mary Shelley, and Jane Austen*. Chicago: University of Chicago Press, 1984.

Postlewait, Thomas. "Autobiography and Theatre History." In *Interpreting the Theatrical Past: Essays in the Historiography of Performance*, ed. Thomas Postlewait and Bruce A. McConachie, 248–72. Iowa City: University of Iowa Press, 1989.

Powell, James. *Private Theatricals: A Farce. In Two Acts*. 1787.

Purinton, Marjean D. *Romantic Ideology Unmasked: The Mentally Constructed Tyrannies in Dramas of William Wordsworth, Lord Byron, Percy Shelley, and Joanna Baillie*. Newark: University of Delaware Press, 1994.

Rabine, Leslie. "A Feminist Politics of Non-Identity." *Feminist Studies* 14.1 (1988): 11–31.

———. *The Romantic Heroine: Text, History, Ideology*. Ann Arbor: University of Michigan Press, 1985.

Radcliffe, Mary Anne. *The Female Advocate: or, An Attempt to Recover the Rights of Women from Male Usurpation*. London: Vernor and Hood, 1799.

Ranger, Paul. *'Terror and Pity reign in every Breast': Gothic Drama in the London Patent Theatres, 1750–1820*. London: The Society for Theatre Research, 1991.

Reiman, Donald H. "Introduction." In *Records of a Woman*. By Felicia Dorothea Hemans, v–xi. New York and London: Garland Publishing, 1978 (orig. 1828).

———. "Introduction." *A Series of Plays*, i:v–viii. By Joanna Baillie. 3 vols. New York and London: Garland Publishing, 1977.

Reinelt, Janelle G. "Introduction: Feminism(s)." In *Critical Theory and Performance*, ed. Janelle G. Reinelt and Joseph R. Roach, 225–30. Ann Arbor: University of Michigan Press, 1992.

Reinhardt, Nancy S. "New Directions for Feminist Criticism in Theatre and the Related Arts." In *The Feminist Perspective in the Academy: The Difference It Makes*, ed. Elizabeth Langland and Walter Gove, 25–51. Chicago and London: University of Chicago Press, 1981.

Relke, Diana M. A. "In Search of Mrs. Pilkington." In *Gender at Work: Four Women Writers of the Eighteenth Century*, ed. Anne Messenger, 114–49. Detroit State University Press, 1990.

Richards, Kenneth, and Peter Thomson, eds. *Essays on Nineteenth-Century British Theatre*. London: Methuen and Co., 1971.

Richards, Sandra. *The Rise of the English Actress*. New York: St. Martin's Press, 1993.

Richardson, Alan. *A Mental Theater: Poetic Drama and Consciousness in the Romantic Age*. University Park: Pennsylvania State University Press, 1988.

———. "*Proserpine* and *Midas*: Gender, Genre, and Mythic Revisionism in Mary Shelley's Dramas." In *The Other Mary Shelley: Beyond Frankenstein*, ed. Audrey A. Fisch, Anne K. Mellor, and Esther H. Schor, 124–39. New York and Oxford: Oxford University Press, 1993.

———. "Romanticism and the Colonization of the Feminine." In *Romanticism and Feminism*, ed. Anne K. Mellor, 13–25. Bloomington: Indiana University Press, 1988.

Roach, Joseph R. *The Player's Passion: Studies in the Science of Acting*. London and Toronto: Associated University Presses, 1985.

Rodin, Alvin E. *The Influence of Matthew Baillie's Morbid Anatomy*. Springfield, Ill.: Charles C. Thomas, 1973.

Rogers, Charles. Vol. 1 of *The Modern Scottish Minstrel: or, The Songs of Scotland of the Past Half Century*. 6 vols. Edinburgh: Adam and Charles Black, 1855.

Rogers, Katharine M. "Introduction." In *The Meridian Anthology of Restoration and Eighteenth-Century Plays by Women*, ed. Katharine M. Rogers, vii–xviii. New York: Penguin Books, 1994.

Rogers, Pat. "'Towering Beyond Her Sex': Stature and Sublimity in the Achievement of Sarah Siddons." In *Curtain Calls: British and American Women and the Theater, 1660–1820*, ed. Mary Anne Schofield and Cecilia Macheski, 48–67. Athens: Ohio University Press, 1991.

Rosenberg, Marvin. "Macbeth and Lady Macbeth in the Eighteenth and Nineteenth Centuries." In *Focus on Macbeth*, ed. John Russell Brown, 73–86. London and Boston: Routledge and Kegan Paul, 1982.

Rosenfeld, Sybil. "Jane Austen and Private Theatricals." *Essays and Studies* 15 (1962): 40–51.

———. *Temples of Thespis: Some Private Theatres and Theatricals in England and Wales, 1700–1820*. London: Society for Theatre Research, 1978.

Ross, Marlon B. *The Contours of Masculine Desire: Romanticism and the Rise of Women's Poetry*. New York: Oxford University Press, 1989.

Rousseau, Jean-Jacques. *La Nouvelle Héloïse*. Translated and abridged by Judith H. McDowell. University Park: Pennsylvania State University Press, 1968.

Rowton, Fredric, ed. *The Female Poets of Great Britain*. Philadelphia: Henry C. Baird, 1853. Facsimile reprint, ed. Marilyn L. Williamson. Detroit: Wayne State University Press, 1981.

Russell, Gillian. *The Theatres of War: Performance, Politics, and Society 1793–1815*. Oxford: Clarendon Press, 1995.

Rutter, Carol. *Clamorous Voices: Shakespeare's Women Today*. Ed. Faith Evans. New York: Routledge/Theatre Arts Books, 1989.

Sadler, Thomas. *A Sermon, Preached at Hampstead, on Sunday, March 9, 1851 on the Occasion of the Death of Mrs. Joanna Baillie*. London: Edward T. Whitfield, 1851.

Schnorrenberg, Barbara Brandon. "The Blue-Stocking Assembly: A Comment on Women's Lives in Eighteenth-Century England." In vol. 5 of *Views of Women's Lives in Western Tradition: Frontiers of the Past and Future*, ed. Frances Richardson Keller, 360–91. Lewiston, N.Y.: The Edwin Mellen Press, 1990.

Schofield, Mary Anne, and Cecilia Macheski, eds. *Curtain Calls: British and American Women and the Theater, 1660–1820*. Athens: Ohio University Press, 1991.

Scolnicov, Hanna. *Woman's Theatrical Space*. Cambridge: Cambridge University Press, 1994.

Sedgwick, Eve Kosofsky. *Between Men: English Literature and Male Homosocial Desire*. New York: Columbia University Press, 1985.

———. *Epistemology of the Closet*. Berkeley and Los Angeles: University of California Press, 1990.

Senelick, Laurence. "Introduction." In *Gender in Performance: The Presentation of Difference in the Performing Arts*, ed. Laurence Senelick, ix–xx. Hanover and London: University Press of New England, 1992.

Sennett, Richard. *The Fall of Public Man*. New York: Alfred A. Knopf, 1977.

Shee, Martin Archer. "Preface." *Alasco*. London: Sherwood, Jones, and Co., 1824.

Siddons, Henry. *Practical Illustrations of Rhetorical Gesture and Action*. London: Richard Phillips, 1807.

Siddons, Sarah. "Remarks on the Character of Lady Macbeth." In *Life of Mrs. Siddons*, by Thomas Campbell, 123–35. New York: Harper and Brothers, 1834.

———. *The Reminiscences of Sarah Kemble Siddons, 1773–1785*. Ed. William Van Lennep. Cambridge: Widener Library, 1942.

Simpson, David. *Romanticism, Nationalism, and the Revolt against Theory*. Chicago and London: University of Chicago Press, 1993.

Sinfield, Alan. "Closet Dramas: Homosexual Representation and Class in Postwar British Theater." *Genders* 9 (1990): 112–31.

Slagle, Judith Bailey. *The Collected Letters of Joanna Baillie*. In process.

Smith, Charlotte. *What Is She?* London: T. N. Longman and O. Rees, 1799.

Smith, Dane Farnsworth, and M. L. Lawhon. *Plays about the Theatre in England 1737–1800, or The Self-Conscious Stage from Foote to Sheridan*. London: Associated University Presses, 1979.

Smith, George Barnett. "Joanna Baillie." *The Dictionary of National Biography*, 1:885–89. 22 vols. Oxford: Oxford University Press, 1921.

Smith, John Talbot. *The Parish Theatre: A Brief Account of Its Rise, Its Present Condition, and Its Prospects*. Longmans, Green, and Co., 1917.

Smith, Sidonie, and Julia Watson. "Introduction." In *De/Colonizing the Subject: The Politics of Gender in Women's Autobiography*, ed. Sidonie Smith and Julia Watson, xiii–xxxi. Minneapolis: University of Minnesota Press, 1992.

Snyder, William C. "Mother Nature's Other Natures: Landscape in Women's Writing, 1770–1830." *Women's Studies* 21 (1991): 143–62.

Sommers, Christina Hoff. *Who Stole Feminism? How Women Have Betrayed Women*. New York: Simon and Schuster, 1994.

Sotheby, William, Esq. "To Joanna Baillie." In *Literary Souvenir; and Cabinet of Poetry and Romance*, ed. Alaric A. Watts. London: Longman, Rees, Orme, Brown, Green and John Andrews, 1827.

Spain, Daphne. *Gendered Spaces*. Chapel Hill and London: University of North Carolina Press, 1992.

Spender, Dale. "Foreword." In *Feminist Theories: Three Centuries of Key Women Thinkers*, ed. Dale Spender, 1–7. New York: Pantheon Books, 1983.

———. *Mothers of the Novel: 100 Good Women Writers before Jane Austen*. London and New York: Pandora, 1986.

———. *Women of Ideas and What Men Have Done to Them*. London: Pandora, 1988 (orig. 1982).

Stamp, Dudley Sir, ed. *Longmans Dictionary of Geography*. London: Longmans, Green and Co., 1966.

Stanton, Judith Phillips. "Statistical Profile of Women Writing in English from 1660 to 1800." In *Eighteenth-Century Women and the Arts*, ed. Frederick M. Keener and Susan E. Lorsch, 247–54. New York: Greenwood Press, 1988.

———. " 'This New-Found Path Attempting': Women Dramatists in England, 1660–1800." In *Curtain Calls: British and American Women and the Theater, 1660–1820*, ed. Mary Anne Schofield and Cecilia Macheski, 325–54. Athens: Ohio University Press, 1991.

Steadman, Susan M. *Dramatic Re-Visions: An Annotated Bibliography of Feminism and Theatre, 1972–1988*. Chicago and London: American Library Association, 1991.

Stephens, John Russell. *The Profession of the Playwright: British Theatre 1800–1900*. Cambridge: Cambridge University Press, 1992.

Stewart, Alan. "The Early Modern Closet Discovered." *Representations* 50 (1995): 76–100.

Straub, Kristina. "Actors and Homophobia." In *Cultural Readings of Restoration and Eighteenth-Century Theatre*, ed. J. Douglas Canfield and Deborah C. Payne, 258–80. Athens: University of Georgia Press, 1995.

———. *Sexual Suspects: Eighteenth-Century Players and Sexual Ideology*. Princeton, N.J.: Princeton University Press, 1992.

———. "Women, Gender, and Criticism." In *Literary Criticism and Theory: The Greeks to the Present*, ed. Robert Con Davis and Laurie Finke, 855–76. New York and London: Longman, 1989.

Sturgess, Keith. *Jacobean Private Theatre*. London and New York: Routledge and Kegan Paul, 1987.

Styles, John. *An Essay on the Character and Influence of the Stage on Morals and Happiness*. 2d ed. London: Williams and Smith, 1807 (orig. 1806).

Sumbel, Leah Wells. *Memoirs of the Life of Mrs. Sumbel, late Wells.* 3 vols. London: C. Chapple, 1811.

Swann, Karen. "Harassing the Muse." In *Romanticism and Feminism*, ed. Anne K. Mellor, 81–92. Bloomington: Indiana University Press, 1988.

Tobin, Terence. *Plays by Scots.* Iowa City: University of Iowa Press, 1974.

Todd, Janet. "Introduction." In *A Dictionary of British and American Women Writers, 1660–1800*, ed. Janet Todd, 1–26. London: Methuen and Co., 1987.

Toepfer, Karl. *Theatre, Aristocracy, and Pornocracy: The Orgy Calculus.* New York: Performing Arts Journal, 1991.

Tomlins, Frederick Guest. *The Past and Present State of Dramatic Art and Literature: addressed to Authors, Managers, and the Admirers of the Old English Drama.* 2d ed. London: C. Mitchell, 1839.

Tristram, Philippa. *Living Space in Fact and Fiction.* London and New York: Routledge, 1989.

Tuan, Yi-Fu. "Space and Context." In *By Means of Performance: Intercultural Studies in Theatre and Ritual*, ed. Richard Schechner and Willa Appel, 236–44. Cambridge: Cambridge University Press, 1990.

Turner, Victor. *Ritual to Theatre: The Human Seriousness of Play.* New York: Performing Arts Journal Publications, 1982.

Tytler, Sarah, and J. L. Watson. Vol. 2 of *The Songstresses of Scotland.* 2 vols. London: Strahan and Co. Publishers, 1871.

Uphaus, Robert W., and Gretchen M. Foster. "Joanna Baillie." In *The 'Other' Eighteenth Century: English Women of Letters 1660–1800*, ed. Robert Uphaus and Gretchen Foster, 343. East Lansing, Mich.: Colleagues Press, 1991.

Wagenknecht, David, ed. Special Issue: *The Borderers*: A Forum. *Studies in Romanticism* 27.3 (1988).

Wagner, Peter. *Eros Revived: Erotica of the Enlightenment in England and America.* London: Secker and Warburg, 1988.

Waitzkin, Leo. *The Witch of Wytch Street.* Cambridge, Mass.: Harvard University Press, 1933.

Wallace, Eglantine. *The Whim.* London: W. Epps, 1795.

Wandor, Michelene. *Carry On, Understudies: Theatre and Sexual Politics.* London and New York: Routledge and Kegan Paul, 1986 (orig. 1981).

Wang, Shou-ren. *The Theatre of the Mind: A Study of Unacted Drama in Nineteenth-Century England.* New York: St. Martin's Press, 1990.

Wardrop, James, Esq. *The Life of Matthew Baillie, M.D.* London: A. and R. Spottiswoode, 1825.

Wasserman, Earl N. "The Sympathetic Imagination in Eighteenth-Century Theories of Acting." *Journal of English and German Philology* 46 (1947): 264–72.

Watkins, Daniel P. *A Materialist Critique of English Romantic Drama.* Gainesville: University of Florida Press, 1993.

Wekerle, Gerda R., Rebecca Peterson, and David Morley. "Introduction." In *New Space for Women*, ed. Gerda R. Wekerle, Rebecca Peterson, and David Morley, 1–34. Boulder, Colo.: Westview Press, 1980.

West, Jane. "Preface to the Plays." *Poems and Plays*, 1:v–xv. London: T. N. Longman and O. Rees, 1799.

Westfall, Suzanne R. *Patrons and Performance: Early Tudor Household Revels*. Oxford: Clarendon Press, 1990.

Whitaker, Thomas R. "Reading the Unreadable, Acting the Unactable." *Studies in Romanticism* 27.3 (1988): 355–67.

———. "Some Reflections on 'Text' and 'Performance.'" *The Yale Journal of Criticism* 3.1 (1989): 143–61.

Wilshire, Bruce. *Role Playing and Identity: The Limits of Theatre as Metaphor*. Bloomington: Indiana University Press, 1982.

Wilson, Carol Shiner, and Joel Haefner, eds. *Re-Visioning Romanticism: British Women Writers, 1776–1837*. Philadelphia: University of Pennsylvania Press, 1994.

Wilson, John. Vol. 2 of *Noctes Ambrosianae*. 5 vols. New York: W. J. Widdleton, 1863.

Wolfson, Susan J. "Explaining to Her Sisters: Mary Lamb's *Tales from Shakespear*." *Women's Re-Visions of Shakespeare: On the Responses of Dickinson, Woolf, H.D., George Eliot, and Others*, ed. Marianne Novy, 16–40. Urbana and Chicago: University of Illinois Press, 1990.

Wollstonecraft, Mary. *An Historical and Moral View of the French Revolution. Mary Wollstonecraft: Political Writings*. Ed. Janet Todd, 299–387. Toronto and Buffalo: University of Toronto Press, 1993.

———. *[Letters Written during] A Short Residence in Sweden, Norway and Denmark*. Ed. Richard Holmes. New York: Viking Penguin, 1987 (orig. 1796).

———. *A Vindication of the Rights of Men. Mary Wollstonecraft: Political Writings*. Ed. Janet Todd, 5–65. Toronto and Buffalo: University of Toronto Press, 1993.

———. *A Vindication of the Rights of Woman*. Ed. Ulrich H. Hardt. Troy, N.Y.: The Whitson Publishing Co., 1982.

Woolf, Virginia. *A Room of One's Own*. New York and London: Harcourt Brace Jovanovich, 1989 (orig. 1929).

Wordsworth, Jonathan. "Introduction." *Joanna Baillie: A Series of Plays*. Oxford and New York: Woodstock Books, 1990.

Wu, Duncan, ed. *Romanticism: An Anthology*. Oxford and Cambridge, Mass.: Blackwell Publishers, 1994.

Young, Mary Julia. *Memoirs of Mrs. Crouch. Including a Retrospect of the Stage, During the Years She Performed*. 2 vols. London: James Asperne, 1806.

Yudin, Mary. "Joanna Baillie's Introductory Discourse as a Precursor to Wordsworth's Preface to Lyrical Ballads." *Compar(a)ison: An International Journal of Comparative Literature* 1 (1994): 101–12.

Zall, P. M. "The Cool World of Samuel Taylor Coleridge: Elizabeth Inchbald; or, Sex & Sensibility." *The Wordsworth Circle* 12 (1981): 27–73.

Zarrilli, Phillip B. "General Introduction: Between Theory and Practice." In *Acting (Re)Considered: Theories and Practices*, ed. Phillip B. Zarilli, 1–4. London and New York: Routledge, 1995.

Index